Your French E

This comprehensive vocabulary and phrase
book is one of a new series of books
written specifically to help students
of all ages
on foreign exchanges.

Helen & Nigel Harrison

YOUR FRENCH
EXCHANGE

Yarker Publishing

First published in Great Britain in 1997 by
Yarker Publishing
Gordon House
276 Banbury Road
Summertown
Oxford
OX2 7ED

Printed in Great Britain by
Redwood Books

British Library Cataloguing-in-Publication Data
A catalogue record for this book is available from
the British Library

ISBN 1-901609-00-6

ACKNOWLEDGEMENTS

Grateful thanks to
Floriane Loiselet who translated the text
and to
Pascal Peron and Kamilla Hajduk
for their assistance in checking the text.

Acknowledgement also to
Waddingtons Games Limited &
McDonald's Restaurants Limited

***and especially to
the Bosco family in Louveciennes.***

CONTENTS

Contents

Contents

Contents

Contents

Contents

THE EXCHANGE
L'ECHANGE

ARRIVING   *L'ARRIVEE*

MEETING THE FAMILY   *RENCONTRER LA FAMILLE*

Hello!	*Bonjour!*
I'm...	*Je m'appelle...*
Are you Madame / Monsieur..?	*Etes-vous Madame / Monsieur...?*
Thank you for coming to meet me.	*Merci d'être venu me chercher.*
I recognized you from the photos you sent me.	*Je vous ai reconnus grace aux photos que vous m'avez envoyées.*
I'm very pleased to meet you.	*Je suis ravi(e) de vous rencontrer.*
This is a present for you from my family.	*Voici un cadeau pour vous de la part de ma famille.*
It's really good to see you again.	*Cela me fait très plaisir de vous revoir.*

THEY MAY SAY TO YOU   *CE QU'ILS PEUVENT VOUS DIRE*

Did you have a good journey?	*Avez-vous / as-tu fait bon voyage?*
What was the flight like?	*Le vol s'est bien passé?*
What was the crossing like?	*La traversée s'est bien passée?*
Would you like to go to the toilet?	*Avez-vous / as-tu besoin d'aller aux toilettes?*
Would you like something to eat or drink?	*Voulez-vous / veux-tu manger ou boire quelque chose?*
Are you hungry / thirsty?	*Avez-vous / as-tu faim / soif?*
Are you tired?	*Vous êtes / tu es fatigué(e)?*

ARRIVING cont

L'ARRIVEE suite

THEY MAY SAY TO YOU cont.

CE QU'ILS PEUVENT VOUS DIRE suite

I'll show you round the house.	*Je vais vous / te montrer la maison.*
I'll show you your room.	*Je vais vous / te montrer votre / ta chambre.*
Do you want to unpack now or later?	*Voulez-vous / tu veux défaire vos / tes valises maintenant ou plus tard?*
Would you like to ring your family to say you have arrived safely?	*Voulez-vous / tu veux téléphoner à votre / ta famille pour leur dire que vous êtes / tu es bien arrivé(e)?*
Shall I dial the number for you?	*Voulez-vous / tu veux que je fasse le numéro?*

YOU MIGHT WANT TO SAY

CE QUE VOUS POURRIEZ AVOIR BESOIN DE DIRE

Yes, the journey was fine, thank you.	*Oui, le voyage s'est bien passé, merci.*
No, it was a dreadful journey.	*Non, le voyage a été pénible.*
We got held up.	*On a été retardé.*
The flight was very late leaving.	*L'avion est parti en retard.*
The flight was bumpy.	*Il y a eu des turbulences pendant le vol.*
The crossing was rough.	*La traversée a été mauvaise.*
I was seasick.	*J'ai eu le mal de mer.*

ARRIVING cont

L'ARRIVEE suite

YOU MIGHT WANT TO SAY cont.

CE QUE VOUS POURRIEZ AVOIR BESOIN DE DIRE suite

Could I ring my parents, please?	*Je peux appeler mes parents, s'il vous plaît?*
I like your house / your room.	*J'aime beaucoup votre maison / votre chambre.*
Where is the loo / toilet?	*Où sont les toilettes?*
Could I have a wash, please?	*Est-ce que je peux me laver, s'il vous plaît?*
Could I have a drink of water, please?	*Est-ce que je peux avoir un verre d'eau, s'il vous plaît?*

UNPACKING

DEFAIRE SES VALISES

Shall I unpack my case now?	*Est-ce que je peux défaire mes valises maintenant?*
Where shall I put my clothes?	*Où est-ce que je peux poser mes vêtements?*
You can use this half of the wardrobe.	*Vous pouvez / tu peux utiliser cette moitié de l'armoire.*
These drawers are for you.	*Ces tiroirs sont pour vous / toi.*

SLEEPING ARRANGEMENTS

LES DISPOSITIONS POUR LA NUIT.

I hope you don't mind sharing a room with me?	*J'espère que cela ne vous / te dérange pas de partager une chambre avec moi?*
Do you prefer to have a room on your own or be with me?	*Vous préférez / tu préfères une chambre seul ou avec moi?*

ARRIVING cont

L'ARRIVEE suite

SLEEPING ARRANGEMENTS cont.

LES DISPOSITIONS POUR LA NUIT suite

This is your bed.	*Voici votre / ton lit.*
Do you prefer a duvet or blankets?	*Vous préférez / tu préfères une couette ou des couvertures?*
Would you like another pillow?	*Voulez-vous / veux-tu un autre oreiller?*
Would you like the window open?	*Vous voulez / tu veux dormir la fenêtre ouverte?*
Do you prefer the window shut?	*Vous préférez / tu préfères fermer la fenêtre?*

NEEDING SOMETHING

QUAND VOUS AVEZ BESOIN DE QUELQUE CHOSE

Do you need anything?	*Avez-vous / as-tu besoin de quelque chose?*
Do you want something?	*Vous voulez / tu veux quelque chose?*
Have you got..?	*Avez-vous / as-tu..?*
• any more hangers?	• *d'autres cintres? (m)*
• a towel?	• *une serviette de toilette?*
I forgot to bring …	*J'ai oublié d'apporter...*
• an alarm clock.	• *un réveil*
• a hairdryer	• *un sèche-cheveux*
• a comb	• *un peigne*
• my toothbrush	• *ma brosse a dents*
Could I borrow..?	*Je peux emprunter..?*

ARRIVING - DAILY ROUTINE cont	**L'ARRIVEE - LA VIE QUOTIDIENNE suite**
What time do you usually get up?	A quelle heure vous levez-vous / tu te lèves d'habitude?
Will you wake me when you get up?	Pouvez-vous / tu peux me réveiller quand vous vous lèverez / tu te lèveras?
What time shall I set my alarm for?	Je dois mettre mon réveil à quelle heure?
Would you like to lie in tomorrow?	Vous aimeriez / tu aimerais faire la grasse matinée demain?
I'm really tired. Could I sleep until I waken tomorrow?	Je suis très fatigué(e). Est-ce que je peux dormir jusqu'à ce que je me réveille demain?
We have to get up early tomorrow because we are going out.	Il faudra se lever tôt demain car nous sortons.
What time do you have breakfast?	A quelle heure prenez-vous / prends-tu votre / ton petit déjeuner?
What do you like for breakfast?	Qu'est-ce que vous prenez / tu prends pour le petit déjeuner?
I usually have toast and cereal.	D'habitude je prends du pain grillé et des céréales.
What time do you have dinner?	A quelle heure mangez-vous / tu manges?

NIGHT-TIME	**LES NUITS**
What time do you usually go to bed?	A quelle heure vous couchez-vous / te couches-tu d'habitude?
You look tired.	Vous avez / tu as l'air fatigué.
Would you like to go to bed?	Vous voulez / tu veux vous / te coucher?
I am really tired.	Je suis vraiment fatigué(e).
I would like to go to bed now.	J'aimerais aller me coucher maintenant.
Can I stay up a little longer, please?	Puis-je rester encore un peu, s'il vous plaît?
Can I read in bed for a bit, please?	Je peux rester lire au lit un moment s'il vous plaît?

DAILY ROUTINE cont.

LIGHTS ON OR OFF?

LA VIE QUOTIDIENNE suite

LUMIERES ETEINTES OU ALLUMEES?

Could you leave the light on, please?	*Pouvez-vous / tu peux laisser la lumière allumée s'il vous plaît / s'il te plaît?*
Do you like a light on at night?	*Vous aimez / tu aimes avoir une lumière allumée la nuit?*
I prefer to sleep in the dark.	*Je préfère dormir dans le noir.*
I get nervous without a light.	*Sans lumière, je deviens inquiet(e).*
I am frightened of the dark.	*J'ai peur du noir.*
Would you like this nightlight left on all night?	*Vous voulez / tu veux laisser la veilleuse allumée toute la nuit?*

TOO HOT OR TOO COLD?

TROP CHAUD OU TROP FROID?

Are you warm enough?	*Vous avez / tu as assez chaud?*
Would you like an extra blanket?	*Voulez-vous / tu veux une autre couverture?*
Yes please / No thank you.	*Oui, s'il vous plaît / Non merci.*
Are you too hot?	*Vous n'avez pas / tu n'as pas trop chaud?*
Would you like a thinner duvet?	*Voulez-vous / tu veux une couette plus fine?*
Would you like a hot water bottle?	*Vous voulez / tu veux une bouilloire?*
Could I have a hot water bottle, please?	*Je peux avoir une bouilloire, s'il vous plaît?*
Would you like me to put the electric blanket on before you go to bed?	*Voulez-vous / tu veux que j'installe une couverture chauffante sur votre lit avant que vous alliez vous / que tu ailles te coucher?*
Don't forget to turn the electric blanket off before you get into bed.	*N'oubliez pas / n'oublie pas de débrancher la couverture chauffante avant d'aller au lit.*

DAILY ROUTINE cont.

PROBLEMS AT NIGHT

LA VIE QUOTIDIENNE suite

LES PROBLEMES PENDANT LA NUIT

Call me if you want anything in the night.	*Appelez-moi / appelle-moi si vous avez / si tu as besoin de quelque chose cette nuit.*
I had a nightmare.	*J'ai fait un cauchemar.*
I had a dream.	*J'ai fait un rêve.*
I can't get to sleep.	*Je n'arrive pas à dormir.*
I was scared.	*J'ai eu peur.*
I heard a noise.	*J'ai entendu un bruit.*
I don't want to be on my own.	*Je ne veux pas être seul(e).*
I am missing home.	*Ma maison me manque.*
Could I have a drink of water, please?	*Je peux avoir un verre d'eau, s'il vous plaît?*

DECIDING WHERE TO GO FOR A DAY OUT

DECIDER OÙ PASSER LA JOURNEE

What would you like to do today?	*Qu'aimeriez-vous / qu'aimerais-tu faire aujourd'hui?*
We thought we would go out somewhere.	*On a pensé qu'on pourrait sortir quelque part.*
Would you like to do some sightseeing?	*Aimeriez-vous / aimerais-tu faire du tourisme?*
Would you like to go to…?	*Vous aimeriez / tu aimerais aller à.?*
Have you ever been there before?	*Etes-vous / tu es déjà allé là?*
Would you like to visit…?	*Vous aimeriez / tu aimerais visiter…?*
It will be a long day.	*Ça sera une longue journée.*

DAILY ROUTINE cont.

LA VIE QUOTIDIENNE suite

DECIDING WHERE TO GO FOR A DAY OUT cont.

DECIDER OÙ PASSER LA JOURNEE suite

How long will it take?	*Ça prendra combien de temps?*
What time would we have to get up ?	*A quelle heure faudrait-il se lever?*
What time will we need to leave?	*A quelle heure devrons-nous partir?*
What time would we get back?	*A quelle heure serons-nous de retour?*
Do you feel up to doing that?	*Avez-vous / tu as envie de faire ça?*
We thought we would go out for a meal.	*On a pensé qu'on pourrait aller au restaurant.*
Would you like to go shopping?	*Vous aimeriez / tu veux faire du shopping?*
Is there anything you need to buy?	*Vous avez / tu as besoin d'acheter quelque chose?*

WHAT TO TAKE WITH YOU

CE QU'IL FAUT PRENDRE AVEC VOUS

Bring your camera, if you have one.	*Apportez votre / apporte ton appareil photo, si vous en avez un / si tu en as un.*
What should I wear?	*Qu'est-ce que je dois mettre?*
Wear old clothes / smart clothes.	*Mettez / mets des vieux vêtements / des vêtements élégants.*
Wear walking shoes.	*Mettez / mets des chaussures de marche.*
Wear comfortable shoes.	*Mettez / mets des chaussures confortables.*
Should I wear boots?	*Est-ce que je dois mettre des bottes?*
Bring a mack or a coat.	*Emmenez un imper ou un manteau.*
Bring your money.	*Emmenez de l'argent.*

SPEAKING PROBLEMS

LES PROBLEMES DE LANGUE

CAN YOU SPEAK SLOWER, PLEASE?

POUVEZ-VOUS PARLER PLUS LENTEMENT, S'IL VOUS PLAIT?

I don't understand what you said.	*Je ne comprends pas ce que vous avez dit.*
Can you repeat that, please?	*Pouvez-vous répéter, s'il vous plaît?*
Pardon?	*Pardon?*
Can you talk really slowly, please?	*Pouvez-vous parler vraiment lentement, s'il vous plaît?*

HOW DO YOU SPELL THAT?

COMMENT CELA S'EPELLE?

Can you write that down for me, please?	*Pouvez-vous l'écrire, s'il vous plaît?*
How do you pronounce this word?	*Comment prononcez-vous ce mot?*

LACK OF VOCABULARY

LA MANQUE DE VOCABULAIRE

I do not know the word in French.	*Je ne connais pas ce mot en français.*
I've forgotten the French word.	*J'ai oublié le mot français.*
What's that called in French?	*Comment cela s'appelle en français?*
Have you a dictionary?	*Avez-vous / as-tu un dictionnaire?*
I need to look a word up in the dictionary.	*J'ai besoin de chercher un mot dans le dictionnaire.*
What does that mean?	*Qu'est-ce que cela veut dire?*
I can only say a few words.	*Je peux seulement dire quelques mots.*
You are really fluent.	*Vous parlez / tu parles vraiment couramment.*
I am beginning to understand more.	*Je commence à mieux comprendre.*
I am nervous of speaking.	*J'ai peur de parler.*

SPEAKING PROBLEMS cont.

LES PROBLEMES DE LANGUE suite

ASKING TO BE CORRECTED

DEMANDER A ETRE CORRIGE

Will you correct my mistakes, please?	*Pouvez-vous / peux-tu corriger mes fautes, s'il vous plaît?*
Was that right?	*C'était bon?*
What was wrong?	*Qu'est-ce qui n'allait pas?*
Was my pronunciation wrong?	*Est-ce que ma prononciation était mauvaise?*

NOT GETTING ENOUGH PRACTICE AT SPEAKING FRENCH

QUAND ON N'A PAS UNE PRATIQUE SUFFISANTE DE LA LANGUE FRANÇAISE

Can we speak in English for an hour and then French for an hour?	*On peut parler anglais pendant une heure et ensuite français pendant une heure?*
Shall we play this game in French?	*Et si on jouait à ce jeu en français?*
We could play it in English next time.	*On pourrait le jouer en anglais la prochaine fois.*
Can you teach me how to play a French card game in French?	*Pouvez-vous / peux-tu m'apprendre un jeu de carte français, en français?*
I know I am rather slow but I would like to practise my French a bit more.	*Je sais que je suis plutôt lent(e) mais j'aimerais pratiquer mon français un peu plus.*
I know it's annoying for you when I try to speak French but I won't get any better unless I try.	*Je sais que c'est ennuyeux pour vous / toi quand j'essaie de parler français, mais je ne ferai jamais de progrès si je n'essaie pas.*

| GENERAL PROBLEMS | *PROBLEMES GENERAUX* |

HOMESICKNESS   *LE MAL DU PAYS*

You are very kind but I am feeling homesick.	*Vous êtes très gentils mais j'ai mal du pays.*
I am missing home.	*Ma maison me manque.*
I am missing my parents - could I possibly ring them up?	*Mes parents me manquent - est-il possible de leur téléphoner?*
If I ring them, they will ring me straight back.	*Si je leur téléphone, ils me rappelleront tout de suite.*
I am sorry to cry. I am happy really. It's just a bit of a strain speaking French.	*Pardon si je pleure. Ça va très bien. C'est juste épuisant de parler français.*
I will be O.K. in a minute.	*Cela ira mieux dans une minute.*

WANTING TO BE ALONE   *L'ENVIE D'ÊTRE SEUL(E)*

Do you mind if I go to my room to write some letters?	*Ça ne vous ennuie pas si je vais dans ma chambre pour écrire des lettres?*
I would really like to write to my family to tell them what I have been doing.	*J'aimerais vraiment écrire à ma famille pour leur dire ce que j'ai fait.*
I am in the middle of a good book at the moment and would like to read for a bit, if that's O.K.?	*Je suis au beau milieu d'un bon livre et aimerais lire encore un peu si cela ne vous dérange pas.*
Could I go to sleep for half an hour? I am feeling tired.	*Je peux aller dormir pendant une demi-heure? Je me sens fatigué(e).*

GENERAL PROBLEMS cont.

PROBLEMES GENERAUX suite

TIREDNESS

LA FATIGUE

I feel rather tired and would prefer to have a quiet day, if you don't mind.	*Je me sens assez fatigué(e) et préfèrerais me reposer aujourd'hui si cela ne vous dérange pas / ne te dérange pas.*
Could we just stay at home and watch a video or something?	*Pourrait-on simplement rester à la maison et regarder une cassette vidéo ou quelque chose de ce genre?*

FINDING THE FOOD STRANGE

QUAND LA NOURRITURE N'EST PAS A NOTRE GOUT

Could I try just a tiny bit, please?	*Je peux / puis-je goûter juste un petit morceau, s'il vous plaît?*
I am not very hungry at the moment.	*Je n'ai pas très faim pour l'instant.*
I don't usually eat very much.	*Je n'ai pas l'habitude de manger beaucoup.*
Could I possibly have my meat cooked a bit longer, please?	*Je pourrais avoir ma viande cuite un peu plus longtemps, s'il vous plaît?*
Do you have any... that I could eat? (See "Food" - p 167-187)	*Avez-vous des....que je pourrais manger?*

LEAVING   *LE DEPART*

SAYING YOUR THANKS   *LES REMERCIEMENTS*

Thank you.	***Merci.***
Thank you for having me to stay.	*Merci de m'avoir reçu(e).*
I've had a lovely time.	*J'ai passé un très bon moment.*
You have been very kind.	*Vous avez être très gentils.*
Thank you for taking me to see so much.	*Merci de m'avoir emmené voir tant de choses.*
I particularly enjoyed going to..	*J'ai surtout aimé aller à...*
You really helped me to improve my French.	*Vous m'avez vraiment aidé à faire des progrès en français.*

FUTURE PLANS   *LES PROJETS*

I will phone you when I get home.	***Je vous téléphone dès que j'arrive.***
Write to me.	*Ecrivez-moi.*
I hope I'll see you next year.	*J'espère vous voir l'année prochaine.*
Would you like to come to stay in England?	*Vous aimeriez venir en Angleterre?*

THE HOME
LA MAISON

HOUSES AND FLATS
MAISONS ET APPARTEMENTS

TYPES OF HOUSES
SORTE DE MAISONS

a flat	*un appartement*
a terraced house	*une maison attenant aux maisons voisines*
a semi-detached house	*une maison jumelée*
a detached house	*un pavillon*
a cottage	*un cottage*
old	*vieux (m) / vieille (f)*
eighteenth / nineteenth century	*dix-huitième / dix-neuvième siècle*
modern	*moderne*
ultra-modern	*ultramoderne*
homely	*confortable*
smart	*élégant(e)*
stylish	*chic*
charming	*charmant(e)*

THE OUTSIDE OF THE HOUSE
A L'EXTERIEUR DE LA MAISON

the gate	*le portail*
the entrance	*l'entrée*
the drive	*l'allée*
the path	*la petite allée*
the front / back door	*la porte d'entrée / de derrière*
the front / back garden	*le jardin de devant / de derrière*
the chimney	*la cheminée*
the roof	*le toit*
the windows	*les fenêtres*

INSIDE THE HOUSE / *A L'INTERIEUR DE LA MAISON*

| the basement | *le sous-sol* |
| a cellar | *une cave* |

the ground floor	*le rez-de-chaussée*
the porch	*le porche*
the lobby	*le vestibule*
the hall	*l'entrée*
the living room	*le salon*
the dining room	*la salle à manger*
the study	*l'étude*
the kitchen	*la cuisine*
the utility room	*la buanderie*
the downstairs loo	*les toilettes d'en bas*
the cloakroom	*le vestiaire*

the stairs	*les escaliers*
the staircase	*l'escalier*
downstairs	*en bas*
upstairs	*en haut*
to go downstairs / upstairs	*descendre / monter les escaliers*

the lift	*l'ascenseur*
to press the button	*appuyer sur le bouton*
Which floor do you want?	*Quel étage voulez-vous?*
The first / second / third / fourth floor, please.	*Le premier / second / troisième / quatrième étage, s'il vous plaît.*
The fifth / sixth / seventh / eighth floor, please.	*Le cinquième / sixième / septième / huitième étage, s'il vous plaît.*

INSIDE THE HOUSE — *A L'INTERIEUR DE LA MAISON*

the first floor	*le premier étage*
the main bedroom	*la chambre principal*
the spare bedroom	*la chambre d'amis*
my parents' room	*la chambre de mes parents*
my room	*ma chambre*
your room	*votre / ta chambre*
the toilet	*les toilettes*
the bathroom / the shower	*la salle de bain / la douche*

the attic	*le grenier*
the playroom	*la salle de jeux*
the junk room	*le débarras*
the games room	*la salle des jeux*

INDIVIDUAL ROOMS — *LES PIECES*

THE LIVING ROOM — *LE SALON*

For comprehensive details on using the equipment see Sections on "T.V., Video & Radio" (145-151), "Music" (153-158), "Contacting people by phone" (335-339) & "Reading" (159-166).

FURNITURE	*LE MOBILIER*
an armchair	*un fauteuil*
to sit in	*s'asseoir*
to relax	*se reposer*
to get up from	*se lever de*
to plump up the cushion	*tapoter le coussin*
a sofa	*un canapé*
to put your feet up	*relever ses pieds*

THE LIVING ROOM cont.　　　*LE SALON suite*

a rocking chair	***un rocking-chair***
to rock	*se balancer*
a book case	***une bibliothèque***
a shelf	*une étagère*
to read (See "Reading" 159-166)	*lire*
a table	***une table***
an occasional table	*un guéridon*
a flower vase	*un vase à fleurs*
a card table	***une table de jeu***
to play cards	*jouer aux cartes*
(See "Games - Cards" 96-113)	

CLOCKS　　　*LES HORLOGES*

a grandfather clock	*une horloge de parquet*
to wind up	*remonter*
to strike the hour	*sonner*
a cuckoo clock	*un coucou*
a digital clock	*une horloge digitale*
What time is it?	*Quelle heure est-il?*
Is the clock fast / slow?	*La pendule avance / retarde?*
It's ten minutes fast / slow.	*Elle avance / retarde de dix minutes.*

LIGHTING　　　*L'ECLAIRAGE*

lamps	***les lampes***
to turn on / off	*allumer / éteindre*
a standard lamp	*un pied de lampe*
a lampshade	*un abat-jour*
a central light	*une lumière centrale*
wall lights	*les lumières murales*
a dimmer switch	*un variateur de lumière*
to dim the lights	*baisser les lumières*

THE LIVING ROOM cont.   *LE SALON suite*

LIGHTING cont.   *L'ECLAIRAGE suite*

a candlestick	***un chandelier***
a candle	*une bougie*
to light	*allumer*
a match	*une allumette*
by candlelight	*aux chandelles*
to blow out	*souffler*

EQUIPMENT   *LE MATERIAL*

(See "T.V., Video & Radio" 145-151)

the radio	***la radio***
to turn on / off	*allumer / éteindre*
to listen to	*écouter*
the television	***la télévision***
to turn on / off	*allumer / éteindre*
to watch	*regarder*
the video player	***le magnétoscope***
to record a programme	*enregistrer une émission*
to hire a video	*louer une cassette vidéo*
to watch a video	*regarder une cassette vidéo*
the hi-fi (See "Music" 153-158)	***la chaîne hi-fi***
the record player	*le tourne-disque*
a record	*un disque*
the cassette player	*le magnétophone*
a cassette	*une cassette*
the C.D. player / a C.D.	*le lecteur - C.D. / un C.D.*
to listen to	*écouter*
to turn up / to turn down	*monter / baisser*

THE LIVING ROOM cont.   *LE SALON suite*

EQUIPMENT cont.   *LE MATERIAL suite*

(For detailed expressions to do with telephones - see 335-339)

THE TELEPHONE	*LE TELEPHONE*
to ring (someone)	*appeler*
to ring (the sound)	*sonner*
to answer	*répondre*
to pick up	*décrocher*
to use	*utiliser*
an extension	*un poste*
an answer phone	*un répondeur*
a message	*un message*
to listen	*écouter*
to play back	*réécouter*

FURNISHING AND DECORATION   *LE MOBILIER ET LA DECORATION*

a rug	*un petit tapis*
a carpet	*un tapis*
a fitted carpet	*une moquette*
the wallpaper	*le papier peint*
the colour of the paint	*la couleur de la peinture*
the curtains	*les rideaux*
the blinds	*les stores*

THE LIVING ROOM cont.   *LE SALON suite*

THE HEATING   *LE CHAUFFAGE*

Central heating	*Le chauffage central*
to turn the heating on / off	*mettre le chauffage en marche / éteindre le chauffage*
to turn the thermostat up / down	*relever / baisser le thermostat*
Is the heating on?	*Le chauffage est-il en marche?*
to feel the radiator	*toucher le radiateur*
Do you mind if we turn the heating on / off / up / down?	*Cela ne vous / t'ennuie pas si on met le chauffage en marche / on éteint / monte / baisse le chauffage?*
a fireplace	*un cheminée*
to light the fire	*allumer le feu*
a match	*une allumette*
to strike	*craquer*
a real fire	*un véritable feu*
to get it going well	*bien l'entretenir*
kindling	*petit bois*
firelighters	*des allume-feux*
old newspapers	*des vieux journaux*
logs	*des bûches*
coal	*du charbon*
a pair of tongs	*des pincettes*
a poker	*un tisonnier*
to sit by the fire	*s'asseoir près du feu*
to toast crumpets	*faire griller des petits pains*
a toasting fork	*une fourche à griller*
to burn	*brûler*
an electric fire	*un radiateur électrique*
a gas fire	*un appareil de chauffage à gaz*
to turn on / off	*allumer / fermer*

33

THE DINING ROOM *LA SALLE A MANGER*

THE DINING TABLE *LA TABLE*

| the chairs | *les chaises* |

LAYING THE TABLE *METTRE LA TABLE*

Would you like me to lay the table for you? *Voulez-vous que je mette la table?*

How many people shall I lay for? *Je mets la table pour combien de personnes?*

Where do you keep..? *Où gardez-vous…?*
- the table mats *les sets de table*
- a tablecloth *une nappe*
- napkins *des serviettes*

What cutlery do we need? *Quels couverts nous avons besoin?*
- knives *couteaux (m)*
- forks *fourchettes (f)*
- soup spoons *cuillères à soupe (f)*
- fish knives and forks *couteaux et fourchettes à poisson*
- dessert spoons and forks *cuillères et fourchettes à dessert*
- teaspoons *cuillères a café*
- serving spoons *cuillères à service*

What crockery shall I put out? *Quelle vaisselle je dois mettre?*
- dinner plates *les assiettes à dîner*
- side plates *les assiettes à pain*
- dishes *les plats*
- serving plates *les plats*

THE DINING ROOM cont.

LAYING THE TABLE cont.

LA SALLE A MANGER suite.

METTRE LA TABLE suite

What glasses do we need?	*Quels verres avons-nous besoin?*
• water glasses	• *les verres à eau (m)*
• a jug of water	• *un pot d'eau*
• red wine glasses	• *les verres à vin rouge*
• white wine glasses	• *les verres à vin blanc*
• champagne glasses	• *les flûtes à champagne*

Do you want..?	*Voulez-vous / veux-tu..?*
salt and pepper	*du sel et du poivre*
mustard	*moutarde (f)*
butter	*beurre (m)*
preserves	*confiture (f)*
marmalade	*marmelade (f)*
cereals	*céréales (f)*
fruit juice	*jus de fruit (m)*
sugar	*sucre (m)*
milk	*lait (m)*
cream	*crème (f)*

Do you want candles?	*Voulez-vous / tu veux des bougies?*
a candelabra	*un candélabre*
a candle	*une bougie*
to light	*allumer*
a match	*une allumette*
to blow out	*souffler*

CLEARING THE TABLE.	*DESSERVIR LA TABLE.*
Would you like me to clear the table?	*Voulez-vous que je débarrasse la table?*
Where shall I put..?	*Où dois-je mettre…?*
Where do you keep..?	*Où mettez-vous…?*

THE DINING TABLE cont.   *LA TABLE suite*

SEATING ARRANGEMENTS	*LA DISPOSITION DE LA TABLE*
Would you like to sit there?	*Voulez-vous vous / tu veux t' asseoir là?*
Sit next to me.	*Asseyez-vous / assieds-toi à côté de moi.*
Sit opposite me.	*Asseyez-vous / assieds-toi en face de moi.*
Sit anywhere.	*Asseyez-vous / assieds-toi où vous voulez / tu veux.*

THE STUDY   *L'ETUDE*

For comprehensive details on using the equipment see "Computers" 131-138, "Computer Games" 139-144 and "Contacting people by phone" 335-339.

a desk	***un bureau***
a drawer	*un tiroir*
the desk top	*le dessus de bureau*
a desk lamp	*une lampe de bureau*
an anglepoise lamp	*une lampe d'architecte*
a calculator	*une calculatrice*
a diary	*un agenda*
an address book	*un carnet d'adresses*
a blotter	*un buvard*
a pen holder	*un plumier*
a paperweight	*un presse-papiers*
a telephone (See 335-339)	*un téléphone*
a chair	***une chaise***
to sit down	*s'asseoir*
to get up	*se lever*

THE STUDY   *L'ETUDE*

a bookcase	***une bibliothèque***
a bookshelf	*un étagère*
a book	*un livre*
to read (See 159-166)	*lire*
a typewriter (See 133-137)	*une machine à écrire*
a computer (See 131-138)	*un ordinateur*

THE KITCHEN   *LA CUISINE*

THE COOKER   *LA CUISINIERE*

gas	***le gaz***
to turn on / off	*allumer /fermer*
to turn up / down	*augmenter / baisser*
to light	*allumer*
a match	*une allumette*
automatic	*automatique*
electricity	***l'électricité***
halogen	*l'halogène*
a ceramic hob	*une plaque en céramique*
an Aga)	*fourneaux à bois / à charbon*
a Rayburn)	*traditionnels*
a microwave	***un micro-onde***
to microwave	*cuisiner au micro-onde*
to heat up	*réchauffer*
to defrost	*décongeler*
to set the timer for five minutes	*mettre le minuteur sur cinq minutes*

THE KITCHEN cont.   *LA CUISINE suite*

THE COOKER cont.   *LA CUISINIERE suite*

THE OVEN	*LE FOUR*
the oven door	*la porte du four*
to open	*ouvrir*
to shut	*fermer*
temperature	*température*
to adjust	*régler*
high / medium / low	*élevée / moyenne / faible*
degrees	*degrés*
Fahrenheit	*Fahrenheit*
Centigrade	*Centigrade*
Gas Mark Four	*Thermostat quatre*
a shelf	*une plaque*
top / middle / bottom	*en haut / au milieu / en bas*
a glass door	*une porte vitrée*
an oven light	*une lumière du four*
cooking time	*le temps de cuisson*
an auto-timer	*un programmateur*
a minute timer	*un minuteur*
to set	*régler*

THE HOB	*LES PLAQUES CHAUFFANTES*
a ring	*une plaque*
front / back	*devant / derrière*
left / right	*gauche / droite*

THE KITCHEN cont.　　　*LA CUISINE suite*

OVEN UTENSILS	*LES USTENSILES*
a casserole	*une cocotte*
a roasting dish	*un plat à rôtir*
an oven tin	*un moule*
a round tin	*un moule rond*
an oblong tin	*un moule à gratin*
a cake tin	*un moule à gâteaux*
a bun tray	*un plateau*
a loaf tin	*un moule à cake*
a deep tin	*un moule profond*
an oven glove	*un gant isolant*

COOKING VERBS (abc)	*VERBES CULINAIRES*
to bake	*faire cuire au four*
to be nearly ready	*être bientôt prêt*
to boil	*bouillir*
to casserole	*mijoter*
to check	*vérifier*
to cook	*cuire*
to cover	*couvrir*
to heat gently / quickly	*chauffer à feu doux / à feu fort*
to put on	*ajouter*
to roast	*rôtir*
to see if it's done	*voir si c'est prêt*
to simmer	*laisser frémir*
to take off	*enlever*

EQUIPMENT	*L'EQUIPEMENT*
a saucepan / a lid	***une casserole / un couvercle***
large / medium / small	*grande / moyenne / petite*
to cover partially	*couvrir en partie*
to cover / to uncover	*couvrir / découvrir*

THE KITCHEN - EQUIPMENT cont.	*LA CUISINE - L'EQUIPEMENT suite*
a frying pan	*une poêle à frire*
a fish slice	*une pelle à poisson*
a wooden spoon	*une cuillère en bois*
to stir	*mélanger*
a wok	*un wok*
to stir fry	*faire sauter à feu vif*

THE SINK	*L'EVIER*
the bowl	*la cuvette*
the draining board	*l'égouttoir*
the taps	***les robinets***
hot / cold	*chaud / froid*
a mixer tap	*un mélangeur*
to turn on / off	*ouvrir / fermer*
too hot	*trop chaud*
not hot enough	*pas assez chaud*
to fill the sink with water	*remplir l'évier d'eau*
washing up liquid	***le liquide-vaisselle***
to squirt	*verser*
bubbles	*les bulles*
grease / greasy	*graisse / gras*
clean	*propre*
dirty	*sale*
to rinse off	*rincer*
sink equipment	***l'équipement ménager***
a brush / a sponge	*un brosse / une éponge*
a wire wool pad	*une éponge métallique*
a dishcloth	*un torchon*
to brush	*balayer*
to rub	*frotter*
to scour	*récurer*
to wash	*laver*

Your French Exchange

THE KITCHEN cont.

DRYING DISHES

LA CUISINE suite

FAIRE SECHER LA VAISELLE

to drain	*égoutter*
a rack	*un égouttoir*
a cutlery basket	*un range-couverts*
to leave to dry	*laisser sécher*
to dry	*sécher*
a tea towel	*une serviette*
to put away	*ranger*
to stack	*empiler*

THE FRIDGE

LE REFRIGERATEUR

to refrigerate	*réfrigérer*
the fridge door	*la porte du réfrigérateur*
a bottle rack	*un casier à bouteille*
an egg rack	*un compartiment à oeufs*
a salad drawer	*un bac à légumes*
an ice compartment	*le freezer*
an ice cube tray	*un bac à glaçons*
ice cubes	*glaçons*
a shelf	*une clayette*

THE FREEZER

LE CONGELATEUR

to freeze	*congeler*
to defrost	*décongeler*
to thaw out	*dégeler*
to melt	*fondre*
the fast freeze button	*le bouton de congélation accélérée*
maximum / minimum	*maximum / minimum*

THE KITCHEN cont.   *LA CUISINE suite*

THE DISHWASHER   *LE LAVE-VAISSELLE*

to load / unload	*remplir / vider*
to stack	*remplir*
to turn on / off	*mettre en marche / arrêter*
a drawer	*un panier de rangement*
a cutlery basket	*un range-couverts*
to need	*avoir besoin*
dishwasher powder / salt / rinse-aid	*la poudre de lavage / le sel de lavage / la poudre de rinçage*

DISHWASHER PROGRAMMES   *LES PROGRAMMES DU LAVE-VAISSELLE*

a normal wash	*lavage normal (m)*
a quick wash	*lavage rapide*
a delicates programme	*lavage délicat*
a long wash	*lavage intensif*
rinse and hold	*rincer et attendre*

KITCHEN WASTE   *LES ORDURES MENAGERES*

the waste bin	*le panier á ordures*
to empty	*vider*
to be full	*être plein(e)*
a dustbin	*la poubelle*
a waste disposal unit	*un broyeur d'ordures*

THE KITCHEN cont.

LA CUISINE cont.

KITCHEN CUPBOARDS

LES PLACARDS DE CUISINE

a wall unit	*un bloc mural*
a base unit	*l'élément bas*
a carousel	*un plateau tournant*
The work surfaces	***Les surfaces de travail***
kitchen paper	*le sopalin ®*
a knife rack	*le casier à couteaux*
a herb rack	*une étagère à épices*
a hand towel	*un essuie-main*
A crockery cupboard	***Un placard à vaisselle***
a dinner plate	*une assiette à dîner*
a side plate	*une assiette à pain*
a cup	*une tasse*
a saucer	*une soucoupe*
a soup bowl	*un bol*
a dish	*un récipient*
an egg cup	*un coquetier*
a serving dish	*un plat*
a milk jug	*un pot à lait*
a sugar bowl	*une sucrière*
a butter dish	*un beurrier*
A glass cupboard	***Un placard à verre***
a tumbler	*un verre à sirop*
a wine glass	*un verre à vin*
a glass jug	*une carafe*

KITCHEN CUPBOARDS cont.
LES PLACARDS DE CUISINE suite

A cutlery drawer	***Un tiroir à couverts***
a knife / a fork	*un couteau / une fourchette*
a spoon	*une cuillère*
a teaspoon	*une cuillère à café*
a dessertspoon	*une cuillère à dessert*
a tablespoon	*une cuillère à soupe*
a serving spoon	*une cuillère à service*
a soup ladle	*une louche*
a measuring spoon	*une cuillère à mesure*

A kitchen tool drawer	***Un tiroir pour outils de cuisine***
a can opener	*un ouvre-boîte*
a bottle opener	*un ouvre-bouteille*
a potato peeler	*un éplucheur*
a sharp knife	*un couteau affûté*
a bread knife	*un couteau à pain*
a potato masher	*un presse-purée*
a lemon zester	*une râpe à citron*
a fish slice	*une pelle à poisson*
kitchen tongs	*des pincettes*
a whisk	*un fouet*
a balloon whisk	*un batteur*
a spatula	*une spatule*
a garlic press	*un pressoir*
a skewer	*une brochette*

OTHER KITCHEN EQUIPMENT
AUTRES APPAREILS MENAGERS

The kettle	***La bouilloire***
an electric kettle	*une bouilloire électrique*
an automatic kettle	*une bouilloire automatique*
to turn on / off	*mettre en marche / éteindre*
to boil	*bouillir*
to pour	*verser*

OTHER KITCHEN EQUIPMENT cont.

AUTRES APPAREILS MENAGERS suite

The bread bin	***La huche à pain***
the bread board	*la planche à pain*
the bread knife	*le couteau à pain*
to cut	*couper*
to butter	*beurrer*
to soften	*ramollir*
too hard	*trop dur*
a butter dish	*un beurrier*
a butter knife	*un couteau à beurre*
to melt	*fondre*
a loaf of bread	*une miche de pain*
a slice of bread	*une tranche de pain*
crumbs	*des miettes*

The toaster	***Le grille-pain***
to make toast	*griller du pain*
to set the toaster	*régler le grille-pain*

A pastry board	***Une planche à pâtisserie***
a rolling pin	*un rouleau à pâtisserie*
cutters	*des coupoirs*

A coffee grinder	***Un moulin à café***
coffee beans	*des grains de café*
to grind	*moudre*
a coffee maker	*une cafetière*
filter paper	*un filtre à café*
a plunger	*un piston*

KITCHEN EQUIPMENT cont.   *KITCHEN EQUIPMENT suite*

Scales	*Les balances (f)*
to weigh	*peser*
to measure	*mesurer*
to balance	*équilibrer*
weights	*les poids (m)*

A food processor	*Un robot électrique*
a goblet	*une coupe*
a lid	*un couvercle*
to liquidize	*passer au mixeur*
fast / slow	*rapide / lent*
to purée	*réduire en purée*
to chop	*hacher*
to mix	*mixer*
to blend	*mélanger*

Smaller equipment	*Appareils plus petits (m)*
an electric hand whisk	*un fouet électrique*
a salt mill	*un moulin à sel*
a pepper mill	*un moulin à poivre*
a lemon squeezer	*un presse-citron*
a sieve	*un tamis*
a colander	*une passoire*
a steamer	*un couscoussier*
a salad spinner	*un panier à salade*
a measuring jug	*un pot gradué / un verre doseur*
a pestle and mortar	*un pilon et mortier*

THE UTILITY ROOM   *LA BUANDERIE*

WASHING, DRYING &   *LAVER, SECHER,*
IRONING CLOTHES   *REPASSER LES VÊTEMENTS*

Dirty clothes	*Les vêtements sales (m)*
soiled	*sali*
a stain	*une tache*
stain remover	*un détachant*
to treat quickly	*traiter rapidement*
to pre-soak	*pré-tremper*
to bleach	*blanchir*
to scrub	*frotter*
clean clothes	*vêtements propres (m)*

The washing machine	*La machine à laver*
to open the door	*ouvrir la porte*
to put the clothes in	*mettre les vêtements dans*
to put the powder in	*mettre la poudre dans*
biological powder	*poudre biologique (f)*
non-biological powder	*poudre non-biologique*
washing liquid	*la lessive (liquide)*
pre-wash spray	*un jet de prélavage*
to add conditioner	*ajouter un adoucissant*

To choose a cycle	*choisir le cycle*
to press a button	*appuyer sur le bouton*
to turn a dial	*régler le cadran*
Type of wash (abc)	*Types de lavage*
boil	*bouillir*
coloured	*couleur*
cool	*froid*
hot	*chaud*
rinse	*rinçage*
white	*blanc*
woollens	*lainage*

WASHING, DRYING & IRONING CLOTHES cont.	*LAVER, SECHER, REPASSER LES VÊTEMENTS (m) suite*

Type of spin	*Types d'essorage*
short	*court*
long	*long*

DRYING CLOTHES — *FAIRE SECHER LES VETEMENTS*

Outside	*A l'extérieur*
a washing line	*une corde à linge*
a prop	*une perche*
to peg	*étendre à l'aide de pinces à linge*
a peg	*une pince à linge*
a peg bag	*un sac de pinces à linge*
a linen basket	*un panier à linge*
to dry	*sécher*
to put out	*mettre dehors*
to take in	*rentrer*
It's raining.	*Il pleut.*

Inside	*A l'intérieur*
an airer	*un aérateur*
a clothes horse	*un chevalet*
by the fire	*près du feu*
on a radiator	*sur un radiateur*

In the tumble drier	*Dans le sèche-linge*
to put the clothes in	*mettre les vêtements dans*
to take them out	*les sortir*
to set them timer	*régler le minuteur*
hot / cool	*chaud / froid*
to add a conditioning sheet	*ajouter un feuille adoucissante*
to prevent static	*empêcher l'électricité statique*
to clean the grill	*nettoyer le filtre*
to remove the fluff	*enlever la peluche*

IRONING CLOTHES	*REPASSER LES VETEMENTS (m)*

The ironing board	*La planche à repasser*
to put up	*dresser*
to take down	*replier*
the iron	*le fer à repasser*
to iron	*repasser*
to do the ironing	*faire le repassage*

A steam iron	*Un fer à vapeur*
to fill with water	*remplir d'eau*
to run out of water	*manquer d'eau*
to squirt	*gicler*
to steam	*fumer*

The temperature of the iron	*La température du fer*
a cool / warm / hot iron	*un fer froid / tiède / chaud*
too cold / too hot	*trop froid / trop chaud*
to scorch	*roussir*
a burn	*une brûlure*

The ironing	*Le repassage*
creased	*froissé*
crumpled	*chiffonné*
to fold	*plier*
to smooth out	*défroisser*
to turn the clothes the right way out	*mettre les vêtements du bon côté / à l'endroit*
inside out	*à l'envers*
to air	*aérer*

DOING THE CLEANING

FAIRE LE MENAGE

Vacuuming	*Passer l'aspirateur*
a vacuum cleaner	*un aspirateur*
to undo the flex	*dérouler le fil*
to plug in	*brancher*
a power point	*une prise de courant*
to switch on	*mettre en marche*
a carpet	*un tapis / une moquette*
a solid floor	*un sol dur*
an upright cleaner	*un aspirateur à balai*
a cylinder cleaner	*un aspirateur à chariot / traîneau*
to empty the dustbag	*vider le sac de poussière*

Cleaning tools for the vacuum	*Les outils de nettoyage pour l'aspirateur*
a thin nozzle	*un bec fin*
a soft / hard brush	*une brosse souple / dure*
a wide brush	*une brosse large*
the hose	*le tuyau*
to suck up	*aspirer*
poor / good suction	*une mauvaise / bonne aspiration*

Brushing	*Balayer*
a broom	*un balai*
a soft brush	*une brosse souple*
a hard brush	*une brosse dure*
a dustpan	*une pelle à poussière*
to sweep up	*balayer*
a pile	*un tas*
to collect	*ramasser*
to throw away	*jeter*
dust	*poussière*
dirt	*saleté*

DOING THE CLEANING cont.   *FAIRE LE MENAGE suite*

Washing surfaces	*Nettoyer les surfaces*
a bucket / water	*un seau / de l'eau*
cleaning agent	*un agent nettoyant / un détergent*
disinfectant	*un désinfectant*
to disinfect	*désinfecter*
a spray	*une bombe aérosol*
to spray	*vaporiser*
a sponge	*une éponge*
to soak	*tremper*
to squeeze	*presser*
to wring out	*essorer*
to wipe	*essuyer*
to rub	*frotter*
a mop	*un serpillière*
a scrubbing brush	*une brosse dure*
to scrub	*récurer*

Polishing	*Astiquer*
a duster	*un chiffon à poussière*
to dust	*épousseter*
the dust	*la poussière*
a cobweb	*une toile d'araignée*
to polish	*astiquer*
polish	*le cirage (for shoes) / la cire (for furniture)*
spray polish	*une bombe pour l'entretien des meubles / la cire en bombe*
a tin of polish	*une boîte de cire / cirage*
furniture polish	*cire pour les meubles*
floor polish	*cire à parquet*
beeswax	*cire d'abeille*
to apply lightly	*appliquer légèrement*
to make something shine	*faire briller*
to buff up	*polir*
to clean the silver / the brass	*nettoyer l'argenterie / les cuivres*

DOING THE CLEANING cont.   *FAIRE LE MENAGE suite*

CLEANING THE BATHROOM   *NETTOYER LA SALLE DE BAIN*

Cleaning the loo	*Nettoyer les toilettes*
a lavatory brush	*une balayette / une brosse*
lavatory cleaner	*produit d'entretien des toilettes*
to squirt	*gicler*
to wipe	*essuyer*
to flush the toilet	*tirer la chasse d'eau*
to put out more loo rolls	*mettre plus de rouleaux de papier toilette*
Cleaning...	*Nettoyer...*
the basin	*la cuvette*
the bath	*la baignoire*
the mirrors	*les miroirs*
the shelves	*les étagères*

REMOVING RUBBISH   *SORTIR LES POUBELLES*

To empty ...	*Vider...*
the ashtrays	*les cendriers (m)*
the waste bins	*les poubelles (f)*
to put the dustbins out	*sortir les poubelles*
to take the bottles to a bottle bank	*mettre les bouteilles au recyclage*
to recycle	*recycler*

OFFERING TO HELP

PROPOSER SON AIDE

Can I help you with the...?	*Puis-je vous aider avec le/la/les..?*
cooking - See 173-183	*la cuisine*
Shall we get ourselves a snack?	*On se fait un casse-croûte?*
Shall I cook my favourite recipe?	*Je fais ma recette favorite?*
Shall I make a cake?	*Je fais un gâteau?*
Shall I make some biscuits?	*Je fais des biscuits?*
cleaning - See 50-52	*le ménage*
Can I help you with the cleaning?	*Je peux vous aider avec le ménage?*
ironing - See 49	*le repassage*
Would you like me to do the ironing?	*Voulez-vous que je repasse?*
washing up - See 40-41	*la vaisselle*
dusting - See 51	*les poussières.*
Shall I dust the living room?	*Est-ce que je fais les poussières dans le salon?*
shopping - See 20	*les courses*
Is there anything you want from the shops?	*Avez-vous besoin d'acheter quelque chose?*
Do you want to give me a list?	*Voulez-vous me donner une liste?*

WOULD YOU LIKE ME TO...?   *VOULEZ-VOUS QUE JE...?*

post your letters - see 332-334	*poste vos lettres*
dry the dishes - see 41	*essuie la vaisselle*
lay / clear the table - see 34-35	*mette / débarrasse la table*
load / unload	*remplisse / vide le lave-vaisselle*
the dishwasher - see 42	
make some toast - see 45	*fasse du pain grillé*
make the beds - see 55	*fasse les lits*
put the kettle on - see 44	*mette la bouilloire à chauffer -*
tidy up	*range*
vacuum - see 50	*passe l'aspirateur*
do the laundry - see 47-49	*lave le linge*
walk the dog - see 234	*sorte le chien*
mow the lawn - see 70	*tonde la pelouse*

THE BEDROOM   *LA CHAMBRE*

Types of bed	***Les types de lit***
a single bed	*un lit simple*
a double bed	*un lit double*
bunk beds	*des lits superposés*
to climb the ladder	*grimper l'échelle*
to get down	*descendre*
to choose	*choisir*
the top / bottom bunk	*le lit d'en haut / d'en bas*
a camp bed	*un lit de camp*
an inflatable mattress	*un matelas gonflable*

THE BEDROOM cont.　　　*LA CHAMBRE suite*

The bed linen	*Les draps de lit et taies d'oreillers*
to make the beds	*faire les lits*
to throw over	*étendre*
to put on	*couvrir*
to straighten	*tirer*
to tuck	*border*
to turn down	*retourner*
to change the bed	*changer le lit*
A sheet	*Un drap*
the bottom / the top sheet	*le drap du dessous / du dessus*
a single / double sheet	*un drap simple / double*
an undersheet	*un protège matelas*
A pillow / a pillow case	*Un oreiller / une taie d'oreiller*
to plump up	*tapoter*
Bed covers	*Les dessus de lit*
a duvet	*une couette*
a duvet cover	*une housse de couette*
a blanket	*une couverture*
How many blankets do you like?	*Combien de couvertures voulez-vous?*

BEDROOM FURNITURE　　*LE MOBILIER DE LA CHAMBRE*

The bedside table	*La table de chevet*
a bedside lamp	*une lampe de chevet*
to turn on / off	*allumer / éteindre*
to need a new bulb	*avoir besoin d'une nouvelle ampoule*

THE BEDROOM cont.   *LA CHAMBRE suite*

An alarm clock	*Un réveil*
to set the alarm	*régler le réveil*
to go off	*se mettre en marche / à sonner*
to switch off the alarm	*éteindre le réveil*
What time shall I set the alarm?	*A quelle heure dois-je régler le réveil?*
What time do you want to get up tomorrow?	*A quelle heure voulez-vous vous / veux-tu te lever demain?*
Will you wake me, please?	*Pouvez-vous / peux-tu me réveiller, s'il vous plaît / s'il te plaît?*
to wind the clock	*remonter le réveil*
to sleep through the alarm	*ne pas entendre la sonnerie du réveil*

The wardrobe	*L'armoire*
a double / single wardrobe	*une armoire double / simple*
a hanger	*un cintre*
a skirt hanger / a coat hanger	*un cintre à jupe / un cintre à manteau*
a rail	*une tringle*
to hang up	*pendre*
full hanging / half hanging	*une penderie / une armoire-penderie*

A chest of drawers	*Une commode*
the top / middle / bottom drawer	*le tiroir du haut / du milieu / bas*
to open / to shut	*ouvrir / fermer*

A dressing table / a stool / to sit	*Une coiffeuse / un tabouret / s'asseoir*
a mirror	*un miroir*
to look at one's reflection in	*regarder son reflet dans*
to look good / to look terrible	*être beau / être affreux*

THE BEDROOM cont.   *LA CHAMBRE suite*

Doing one's hair	*Se coiffer*
a hair brush	*une brosse à cheveux*
to do one's hair	*se coiffer*
to brush one's hair	*se brosser*
a comb	*un peigne*
to comb one's hair	*peigner ses cheveux*

THE WINDOW   *LA FENETRE*

to open / shut the window	*ouvrir / fermer la fenêtre*
to air the room	*aérer la chambre*
to draw the curtains	*fermer / tirer les rideaux*
to open the curtains	*ouvrir les rideaux*
to lower the blind	*baisser le store*
to raise the blind	*lever le store*

THE BATHROOM   *LA SALLE DE BAIN*

Having a bath	*Prendre un bain*
to get undressed	*se déshabiller*
to have a bath	*prendre un bain*
to put the plug in	*mettre le bouchon*
to run the bath	*faire couler un bain*
to turn on the taps	*tourner les robinets*
hot / cold / a mixer tap	*chaud / froid / un mélangeur*
to add bubble bath	*ajouter du bain moussant*
bath oil / bath salts	*huile de bain (f) / sels de bain (m)*
essential oil	*huile essentielle*
to get in the bath	*rentrer dans la baignoire*
to use a shower cap	*utiliser un bonnet de bain*
to sit down	*s'asseoir*
to lie down	*s'allonger*
to immerse oneself	*s'immerger*

HAVING A BATH cont.   *PRENDRE UN BAIN suite*

Washing oneself	*Se laver*
soap	*savon (m)*
a flannel	*un gant de toilette*
a loofah	*un loofa*
a pumice stone	*une pierre ponce*
a back brush	*une brosse à dos*
to have a long soak	*prendre un bon bain chaud*

Staying in the bath too long	*Rester dans le bain trop longtemps*
to hurry up	*se dépêcher*
How long are you going to be?	*Vous allez / tu vas être long(ue)?*
I would like to use the bathroom soon.	*J'aimerais utiliser la salle de bain bientôt.*

Getting out	*Sortir*
to stand up	*se lever*
to get out	*sortir*
to pull out the plug	*déboucher*
to wash out the bath	*rincer la baignoire*
a bath mat	*un tapis de bain*

Drying oneself	*Se sécher*
to dry oneself	*se sécher*
a towel	*une serviette*
a towel rail	*un porte-serviettes*
a heated towel rail	*un porte-serviettes chauffant*
a bath towel / a hand towel	*une serviette de bain / un essuie-mains*
dry / wet	*sec / mouillé*
clean / dirty	*propre / sale*

USING THE BATHROOM cont.

UTILISER LA SALLE DE BAIN suite

Talcum powder and deodorant	*Le talc et le déodorant*
a powder puff	*un poudrier*
to put on	*mettre*
anti-perspirant	*déodorant (m)*
a spray	*un vaporisateur*
a roll-on	*un rouleau*
a gel	*un gel*

Getting dressed	*L'habillement*
to get dressed	*s'habiller*
a bathrobe	*un peignoir*
a dressing gown	*une robe de chambre*

Using the basin	*Utiliser le lavabo*
to wash one's hands	*se laver les mains*
to wash one's face	*se laver la figure*
to open one's toiletry bag	*ouvrir son sac / sa trousse de toilette*
to look in the mirror	*regarder dans la glace*

Cleaning one's teeth	*Se laver les dents*
to clean one's teeth	*se laver les dents*
a tube of toothpaste	*un tube de dentifrice*
to squeeze	*presser*
a toothbrush	*une brosse à dents*
soft / medium / hard	*souple / moyenne / dure*
natural bristle / nylon	*poil naturel / Nylon*
to brush	*brosser*
to rinse out the mouth	*se rincer la bouche*
to gargle	*se gargariser*
to use mouthwash	*utiliser une eau dentifrice / un bain de bouche*

USING THE BATHROOM cont.	UTILISER LA SALLE DE BAIN suite
Shaving	***Se raser***
to shave	*se raser*
an electric razor	*un rasoir électrique*
to plug in	*brancher*
to turn on / off	*mettre en marche / arrêter*
a razor / a razor blade	*un rasoir / une lame de rasoir*
shaving soap / cream / brush	*mousse / crème à raser / blaireau*
to lather	*mousser*
to nick	*entailler*
to bleed / to stop bleeding	*saigner / arrêter de saigner*
to rinse off	*rincer*
to use aftershave	*utiliser un after-shave / un après rasage*
to splash on	*éclabousser / étaler*
to trim one's beard	*tailler sa barbe*

Having a shower	***Prendre une douche***
to take a shower	*prendre une douche*
to shut the curtain	*fermer les rideaux*
to shut the shower door	*fermer la porte de la douche*
to turn on the shower	*ouvrir la douche*
to adjust the temperature	*régler la température*
to wash oneself	*se laver*

Washing one's hair	***Se laver les cheveux***
to wash one's hair	*se laver les cheveux*
shampoo	*shampooing (m)*
for dry / normal / greasy hair	*pour cheveux secs / normaux / gras*
dandruff shampoo	*shampooing antipelliculaire (m)*
to apply	*appliquer*
to rub in	*frotter*
to lather	*mousser*
to rinse	*rincer*
conditioner	*après-shampooing (m)*

USING THE BATHROOM cont.

UTILISER LA SALLE DE BAIN suite

Drying one's hair	*Le séchage des cheveux*
to dry one's hair	*se sécher les cheveux*
to rub with a towel	*frotter avec une serviette*
to put one's hair in a turban	*mettre ses cheveux en turban*
to use a hairdryer	*utiliser un sèche-cheveux*
to borrow a hairdryer	*emprunter un sèche-cheveux*
to put on mousse / spray	*appliquer une mousse / un spray // mettre de la mousse*
firm / medium / light control	*fixation forte / moyenne / souple*
to blow dry	*faire un brushing*
to straighten	*lisser*
to curl	*boucler*

Using the loo	*L'utilisation des toilettes*
the toilet	*les toilettes*
to need the loo	*avoir besoin d'aller aux toilettes*
to go to the loo	*aller aux toilettes*
to put the seat up / down	*relever / abaisser le siège*
loo roll	*un rouleau de papier toilette*
We have run out of loo roll.	*Il n'y a plus de papier toilette*
Is there any more loo roll, please?	*Il reste du papier toilette, s'il vous plaît?*
to flush the loo	*tirer la châsse-d'eau*
the bidet	*le bidet*

Other objects on the bathroom shelf	*Autres objets dans la salle de bain*
cotton wool	*du coton*
tissues	*des Kleenex ® / mouchoirs (m)*
cotton wool buds	*des coton-tiges (f)*

USING THE BATHROOM cont.

UTILISER LA SALLE DE BAIN suite

FOR WOMEN

POUR LES FEMMES

Perfume	*Le parfum*
to put on	*mettre*
toilet water	*eau de toilette (f)*
a spray / an atomiser	*un vaporisateur / un atomiseur*
a bottle	*une bouteille*

Personal hygiene	*L'hygiène intime*
sanitary towels	*des serviettes périodiques (f)*
tampons	*des tampons (m)*
depilatory cream	*une crème dépilatoire*

Make-up / cosmetics	*Maquillage (m)/ cosmétiques (m)*
a make-up bag	*un nécessaire à maquillage*
to put on make-up	*se maquiller*

Make-up for the face	*Le maquillage pour le visage*
foundation	*fond de teint (m)*
blusher	*blush / fard à joue (m)*
concealer	*un anti-cerne*
powder	*poudre (f)*
to dot / spread evenly / smooth	*parsemer / répandre uniformément / doux*

For the lips	*Pour les lèvres*
a tube of lipstick	*un tube de rouge à lèvre*
a lip brush	*un pinceau à lèvre*
lip outliner	*un crayon à lèvre*
lip gloss	*un brillant à lèvre*
a lip salve	*un baume à lèvre*
a pencil	*un crayon*
to outline	*faire le contour (des lèvres)*
to fill in	*compléter*

MAKE-UP cont.   *LE MAQUILLAGE suite*

For the eyes	*Pour les yeux (m)*
eyeliner	*eye-liner (m)*
eyeshadow	*fard à paupière (m)*
mascara	*mascara (m)*

For the eyebrows	*Pour les sourcils (m)*
a pair of tweezers	*une pince à épiler*
to pluck	*épiler*
to shape / to brush	*modeler / brosser*

Taking make-up off	*Enlever le maquillage*
to apply	*appliquer*
make-up remover	*un démaquillant*
cotton wool	*du coton*
to wipe	*essuyer*
to remove	*enlever*
eye make-up remover pads	*du Démake-up ®*
to cleanse	*nettoyer*
cleansing lotion	*lotion nettoyante*
to tone	*adoucir*
to nourish	*nourrir*
cream	*crème (f)*
a night / day cream	*crème du nuit / de jour*

THE GARDEN
LE JARDIN

TYPES OF GARDEN	*LES TYPES DE JARDIN*
a cottage garden	*un jardin à l'anglaise*
a herb garden	*un coin à herbes aromatiques*
a kitchen garden	*un (jardin) potager*
a knot garden	*Jardins apparus au 17e siècle caractérisés par des lits de fleurs élevés et représentant des figures géométriques élaborées*
an orchard	*un verger*
a wild flower garden	*un jardin en friche / de fleur des champs*
a public garden / a park	*un jardin public / un parc*

DESCRIBING GARDENS	*DECRIRE LES JARDINS*
large / small	*grand / petit*
formal / wild	*entretenu / sauvage*
pretty	*joli*
untidy	*négligé*
overgrown	*envahi par l'herbe*

COMMON GARDEN CONTENTS	*CONTENU D'UN JARDIN ORDINAIRE*
A flower bed	***Un parterre de fleurs***
a flower	*une fleure*
a bud	*un bourgeon*
a plant	*une plante*
a weed	*une mauvaise herbe*

A lawn	***Une pelouse***
a border	*une plate-bande*
a path	*un chemin / une allée*
a seat	*un banc*

GARDENS cont.

LES JARDINS suite

Trees	Les arbres
a tree	un arbre
a trunk	un tronc
a branch	une branche
a twig	une brindille
a leaf	une feuille
a bush	un buisson

OTHER GARDEN FEATURES

AUTRES CARACTERISTIQUES

a greenhouse	une serre
a conservatory	une véranda
a pond	un bassin
a fountain	une fontaine
a wall	un mur
a fence	une barrière
a hedge	un haie

COMMON FLOWERS (abc)

LES FLEURS ORDINAIRES

carnation	oeillet (m)	narcissus	narcisse (m)
daffodil	jonquille (f)	rose	rose (f)
geranium	géranium (m)	snowdrop	perce-neige (m)
lavender	lavande (f)	tulip	tulipe (f)
lily of the valley	muguet (m)		

COMMON WILD PLANTS (abc)

LES FLEURS SAUVAGES

bluebell	jacinthe des bois (f)	dandelion	pissenlit (m)
buttercup	bouton d'or (m)	dock leaf	patience (f)
cowslip	coucou (m)	nettle	ortie (f)
daisy	marguerite (f)		

GARDENS cont.

LES JARDINS suite

COMMON TREES AND BUSHES (abc)

ARBRES ET ARBUSTES ORDINAIRES

ash	*frêne (m)*	hawthorn	*aubépine (m)*
beech	*hêtre (m)*	holly	*houx (m)*
birch	*bouleau (m)*	oak	*chêne (m)*
chestnut	*marronnier (m)*	privet	*troène (m)*
elm	*orme (m)*	sycamore	*sycomore (m)*
fir	*sapin (m)*	yew	*if (m)*

COMMON ANIMALS (abc)

ANIMAUX ORDINAIRES

a bat	*une chauve-souris*	a molehill	*une taupinière*
a hedgehog	*un hérisson*	a rabbit	*un lapin*
a mole	*une taupe*	a squirrel	*un écureuil*

COMMON INSECTS (abc)

INSECTES ORDINAIRES

an ant	*une fourmis*	a fly	*une mouche*
a bee	*une abeille*	a moth	*une mite*
a butterfly	*un papillon*	a spider	*une araignée*
a caterpillar	*une chenille*	a wasp	*une guêpe*

COMMON BIRDS (abc)

OISEAUX ORDINAIRES

a blackbird	*un merle*	a robin	*un rouge-gorge*
a blue tit	*un oiseau-bleu*	a rook	*un corneille*
a crow	*un corbeau*	a starling	*un étourneau*
a dove	*une colombe*	a thrush	*une grive*
a magpie	*une pie*	a bird table	*une mangeoire*
an owl	*un hibou*	a bird's nest	*un nid d'oiseau*
a pigeon	*un pigeon*	an egg	*un œuf*

GARDENS cont.   *LES JARDINS suite*

GARDEN FURNITURE   *LE MOBILIER DE JARDIN*

a garden seat	*un siège de jardin*
a sunbed	*un lit-pliant / une chaise longue*
a deckchair	*un transat*
a hammock	*un hamac*
a statue	*une statue*
an urn	*un urne*
a bird table	*une mangeoire*

GARDEN ENTERTAINMENT   *LES JEUX DE JARDIN*

HAVING A BONFIRE   *FAIRE UN FEU DE JOIE*

to gather wood	*ramasser du bois*
to find kindling	*trouver du petit-bois*
to light	*allumer*
smoke	*fumée (f)*
flames	*flammes (f)*
sparks	*étincelles (f)*
to cook jacket potatoes	*faire cuire des pommes de terre (f)*
the direction of the wind	*le direction du vent*
to change	*changer*
to get out of control	*ne plus maîtriser*
to put out	*éteindre*
a bucket of water	*un seau d'eau*
a hose	*un tuyau d'arrosage*

GARDEN ENTERTAINMENT - HAVING FIREWORKS	LES JEUX DE JARDIN - FAIRE DES FEUX D'ARTIFICE
to stand well clear	s'éloigner
to watch from over there	regarder de loin / là-bas
to light	allumer
a fuse	un fusible / un détonateur
a match	une allumette
to go out	s'éteindre
to leave it alone	l'éloigner
to have another	en faire un autre
a fireworks display	une démonstration de feux d'artifice
Guy Fawkes' night	la nuit Guy Fawkes (mais cette nuit n'est pas célébrée en France. Au dix-septième siècle Guy Fawkes fut l'instigateur d'un complot visant à faire exploser le Palais de Westminster).
The fifth of November	Le cinq novembre
a box of fireworks	une boîte de feux d'artifice
a sparkler	un cierge magique
a catherine wheel	un soleil
a rocket	une fusée
a Roman candle	une chandelle romaine

BARBECUES	BARBECUES
See "Food" 184-5, 313	

GARDEN GAMES	LES JEUX DE JARDIN
Playing mini golf	**Jouer au mini-golf**
a golf club	un club de golf
a golf ball	une balle de golf
a hole	un trou
to pot the ball in one	mettre la balle dans le trou en un
clock golf	le jeu de l'horloge
to strike	frapper

GARDEN ENTERTAINMENT   *LES JEUX DE JARDIN*

Playing croquet	*Jouer au croquet*
a croquet mallet	*un maillet de croquet*
a hoop	*un arceau*
the central stick	*la crosse centrale*
to go straight through	*aller directement*
to hit the hoop	*toucher l'arceau*
to knock someone out of the way	*faire un carreau*

Playing bowls	*Jouer aux boules*
to throw	*lancer*
to roll	*rouler*
to hit	*frapper*
to miss	*manquer*
to be the nearest	*être le plus près*
to be hit out of the way	*être sorti / être mis à carreau*

Trampolining	*Faire du trampoline*
a trampoline	*un trampoline*
to bounce	*sauter*

GARDENING   *JARDINAGE*

The equipment	*Le matériel*
the garden shed	*la remise*
a wheelbarrow	*une brouette*
a spade / a fork	*une pelle / une fourche*
a trowel	*un déplantoir*
a hoe / a rake	*une houe / un râteau*
a pair of clippers	*une tondeuse*
a hedge trimmer	*un sécateur*
a broom	*un balai*
a dustbin	*une poubelle*

GARDENING cont.   *JARDINAGE suite*

Mowing the lawn	*Tondre la pelouse*
a lawn mower	*une tondeuse à gazon*
an electric mower	*une tondeuse électrique*
a hand mower / a motor mower	*une tondeuse à main / à moteur*
to cut the grass	*couper l'herbe*
to push / to pull	*pousser / tirer*
to alter the setting	*changer le paysage*
to turn the corner	*faire les coins (m)*
straight lines	*lignes droites (f)*
to empty the box	*vider la caisse*
grass cuttings	*les coupes d'herbe (f)*
The grass needs cutting.	*L'herbe a besoin d'être coupée.*

Doing the weeding	*S'occuper des mauvaises herbes*
a weed	*une mauvaise herbe*
to pull out	*arracher*
to uproot	*déraciner*

Watering the garden	*Arroser le jardin*
The garden needs watering.	*Le jardin a besoin d'être arrosé.*
a watering can	*un arrosoir*
to fill	*remplir*
to spray	*vaporiser*
a hose pipe	*un tuyau d'arrosage*
a sprinkler	*une diffuseur*
an automatic sprinkler	*un diffuseur automatique*
to turn on / off	*mettre en marche / arrêter*

PETS
ANIMAUX DOMESTIQUES

A budgerigar	***Une perruche***
a cage	*une cage*
a perch	*une perche*
a swing / to swing	*une balançoire / se balancer*
a mirror / to admire himself	*un miroir / s'admirer*
a bell / to ring	*une cloche / sonner*

A cat	***Un chat***
a kitten	*un chaton*
a cat basket	*un panier*

A dog	***Un chien***
a puppy	*un chiot*
a dog kennel	*une niche*
to take the dog for a walk - See 234	*Sortir le chien*
to go to dog training classes	*aller à des cours d'élevage de chiens*

A dove	***Un colombe***
a dove cote	*un colombier*

A goldfish	***Un poisson rouge***
a goldfish bowl	*un aquarium*
water	*eau (f)*
to swim around	*nager en rond*
weeds	*des herbes aquatiques (f)*
pebbles	*des galets (m)*
to clean out the tank	*nettoyer le réservoir*

PETS cont.

LES ANIMAUX
DOMESTIQUES suite

Other pets	*Autres animaux*
a guinea pig	*un cochon d'Inde*
a hamster	*un hamster*
a mouse	*une souris*
a parrot - to talk	*un perroquet - parler*

Useful expressions	*Expressions utiles*
Does it bite?	*Est-ce qu'il mord?*
Don't put your finger in the cage.	*Ne mettez pas vos / ne mets pas tes doigts dans la cage.*
I have to take it to the Vets.	*Je dois l'emmener chez le vétérinaire.*

GAMES
LES JEUX

COMMON EXPRESSIONS	*EXPRESSIONS USUELLES*
Would you like to play?	***Voudriez-vous / voudrais-tu jouer?***
What would you like to play?	*A quoi aimeriez-vous / aimerais-tu jouer?*
Do you like playing..?	*Vous aimez / tu aimes jouer à..?*
Shall we have a game of..?	*Et si on jouait à...?*

How many can play?	***Combien de personnes peuvent jouer?***
It's a game for two people.	*C'est un jeu pour deux personnes.*
You need four people to play.	*Il faut quatre personnes pour jouer.*
We haven't got enough people.	*Nous ne sommes pas assez. / Ont n'est pas assez.*
We have too many people.	*Nous sommes trop. / Ont n'est trop.*

You play in teams.	***On joue en équipe.***
How many are in each team?	*Il y a combien de personnes dans chaque équipe?*
Will you be in my team?	*Vous serez / tu seras dans mon équipe?*
I'll be in the other team.	*Je serai dans l'autre équipe.*

What do you need to be able to play?	***Que faut-il pour jouer?***
You need paper and a pencil.	*Il faut du papier et un crayon.*
This pencil is blunt.	*Le crayon n'est pas taillé.*
My lead has broken.	*Ma mine a cassé.*
Have you another pencil?	*Avez-vous / tu as un autre crayon?*
Could I have more paper, please?	*Je peux avoir une autre feuille, s'il vous plaît?*

STARTING GAMES cont. *COMMENCER UN JEU suite*

Where shall we play?	*Où jouons-nous?*
Shall we play in..?	*Et si on jouait dans...?*
..my / your room	*..ma / ta / votre chambre?*
..the living room?	*..le salon?*
..on this table?	*..sur cette table?*
..on the floor?	*..par terre?*

How long does a game take?	*Un jeu dure combien de temps?*
This game doesn't take long.	*Ce jeu ne dure pas longtemps.*
This game takes too long.	*Ce jeu dure trop longtemps.*
It takes at least an hour.	*Il dure au moins une heure.*
This is a quick game.	*C'est un jeu rapide.*

How do you play it?	*Comment on y joue?*
You have to..	*Vous devez / Il faut....*
The object of the game is to..	*Le but du jeu est de ....*
You start here.	*On commence ici.*
You go this way round the board.	*On tourne dans ce sens-là.*

Choose a token	*Choisissez / choisis un jeton.*
Which token would you like?	*Quel jeton voulez-vous / veux-tu?*
Which colour would you like to be?	*Quelle couleur voulez-vous / veux-tu être?*

What happens if you land here?	*Qu'est-ce qui se passe si on arrive ici?*
You get another turn.	*On gagne un autre tour.*
You lose a turn.	*On perd un tour.*
You go back three spaces.	*On recule de trois cases.*
You go forward two spaces.	*On avance de deux cases.*
You have to go back to the beginning.	*On recommence depuis le début.*

GAMES cont.

JEUX suite

Where is the finish?	Où est l'arrivée?
You finish here.	On arrive ici.
The first person to finish wins.	La première personne arrivée a gagné.

Pick up a card.	Piochez/ pioche une carte.
What does the card say?	Que dit la carte?
I can't read what's on the card.	Je ne peux pas lire ce qu'il y a sur la carte.
What does that mean?	Qu'est-ce que cela veut dire?
Show me what I have to do now	Montrez-moi / montre-moi ce que je dois faire maintenant.
You can keep the card till later.	Vous pouvez / tu peux garder la carte pour plus tard.

Money	L'argent
Who's going to be banker?	Qui est le banquier?
Can I be banker?	Puis-je être le banquier?
Will you be banker?	Voulez-vous / veux-tu être le banquier?
How much money do you start with?	On commence avec combien d'argent?
You have twenty thousand pounds to start with.	On commence avec vingt mille livres.
Each time you go round you get given..	A chaque tour on reçoit...

GAMES cont.

JEUX suite

Buying and selling	*Acheter et vendre*
You can buy a..	*On peut acheter un(e)..*
Do you want to buy it?	*Voulez-vous / tu veux l'acheter?*
I'd like to buy..	*J'aimerais acheter...*
I haven't got enough money.	*Je n'ai pas assez d'argent.*
How much money do I have to pay?	*Combien dois-je payer?*
You have to pay..	*Il faut payer..*
Have you change for a fifty pound note?	*Avez-vous / tu as la monnaie sur un billet de cinquante livres?*
You didn't give me my change.	*Vous ne m'avez / tu ne m'as pas donné ma monnaie.*
You have to give me / all the other players..	*Il faut me donner / il faut donner à tous les autres joueurs..*
You have to pay a fine.	*Il faut payer une amende.*
You pay ten times what's on the dice.	*On paie dix fois la somme des dés.*

The rules	*Le règlement*
Can I read the rules, please?	*Puis-je lire le règlement, s'il vous plaît?*
It's against the rules.	*C'est contraire au règlement.*
That's cheating.	*C'est de la triche.*
You can't do that.	*On ne peut pas faire cela.*

Who starts?	*Qui commence?*
The highest starts.	*Le plus grand nombre commence.*
The lowest starts.	*Le plus petit nombre commence.*
You need a six to start.	*Il faut faire / avoir un six pour commencer.*
You need a double to start.	*Il faut faire / avoir un double pour commencer.*
Shall we toss a coin to see who starts?	*On fait pile ou face pour voir qui commence?*
Heads or tails? It's heads.	*Pile ou face? C'est face.*

GAMES cont.   *JEUX suite*

Throw the dice.	***Jeter les dés.***
How many dice do you use?	*On joue avec combien de dés?*
You use two dice.	*On joue avec deux dés.*
You only use one.	*On joue avec un dé seulement.*
Have you got a shaker?	*Avez-vous / as-tu un shaker?*
The dice rolled off the table.	*Les dés sont tombés de la table.*
The dice fell on the floor.	*Les dés sont tombés par terre.*
Shake again.	*Mélangez / mélange encore.*

What did you throw?	***Qu'est-ce que vous avez / tu as jeté?***
I threw a..	*J'ai jeté un...*
..one / two / three	*..un / deux / trois*
..four / five / six	*..quatre / cinq / six*
You have to throw a six.	*Il faut jeter un six.*
You have to throw a double.	*Il faut jeter un double.*
Throw again.	*Jetez / jette encore.*

Do you like this game?	***Aimez-vous / aimes-tu ce jeu?***
This game is..	*Ce jeu est....*
..too difficult / too easy.	*..trop difficile / trop facile*
..rather boring / excellent.	*..assez ennuyeux / super*

How do you win?	***Comment on gagne?***
The winner is the first person to finish.	*Le gagnant est la première personne qui finit.*
The winner is the person with the most..	*Le gagnant est celui qui a le plus...*
..money.	*..d'argent.*
..points.	*..de points.*
Shall we see who's won?	*On regarde qui a gagné?*
Count up your money.	*Comptez votre / ton argent.*
How much money have you got?	*Combien d'argent avez-vous / as-tu?*
Add up your points.	*Faites le total de vos / tes points.*
How many points have you got?	*Combien de points avez-vous / as-tu?*

GAMES cont.   *JEUX suite*

Who's won?	*Qui a gagné?*
I've won / You've won.	*J'ai gagné. Vous avez / tu as gagné.*
He's won / She's won.	*Il a gagné / Elle a gagné.*
We've won / They've won.	*Nous avons gagné / Ils ont gagné.*
Our team won.	*Notre équipe a gagné.*
Their team won.	*Leur équipe a gagné.*
Well played!	*Bien joué!*
Bad luck!	*Pas de chance!*

Shall we stop now?	*On arrête maintenant?*
Shall we have one more game?	*On rejoue?*
Is there time for another game?	*On a le temps de rejouer?*
Shall we play the best of three?	*On fait la belle?*
Shall we play something else?	*On joue à autre chose?*
It's time to stop.	*Il est temps d'arrêter.*
We'd better put it away.	*On ferait mieux de le mettre de côté.*

MONOPOLY

MONOPOLY

The Board

Le Plateau de Jeu

to pass Go	*passer la case "Départ"*
I just passed Go.	*Je viens de passer la case "Départ".*
Collect two hundred pounds salary as you pass Go.	*Recevez un salaire de vingt mille francs si vous passez par la case "Départ".*
Can I have my salary, please?	*Puis-je avoir mon salaire, s'il vous plaît?*

In Jail	***En Prison***
Just Visiting	*Simple visite*
I am just visiting.	*Je suis un simple visiteur.*
In Jail.	*En prison.*
I am in jail.	*Je suis en prison.*
I've been sent to jail.	*J'ai été envoyé en prison.*
I have/haven't a card to get out of jail free.	*J'ai / je n'ai pas de carte "Sortez de prison".*
I threw doubles three times in succession so I have to go to jail.	*J'ai jeté un double trois fois de suite donc je vais en prison.*
You need to throw a double to get out.	*Il faut faire un double pour sortir.*
Will you sell me your get out of jail free card?	*Pouvez-vous / tu peux me vendre votre / ta carte "Sortez de prison"?*
How much do you want for your get out of jail free card?	*Combien voulez-vous / tu veux pour votre / ta carte "Sortez de prison"?*
I will pay the fifty pound fine now.	*Je paie l'amende de cinq mille francs maintenant.*
I have to pay the fifty pound fine now.	*Je dois payer l'amende de cinq mille francs maintenant.*
I've missed three turns so I can come out this go.	*J'ai sauté trois tours donc je peux sortir au prochain.*

MONOPOLY cont.

MONOPOLY suite

Income Tax	***Impôts sur le Revenu***
Pay two hundred pounds.	*Payez vingt mille francs.*
You pay all taxes to the Bank.	*Payez tous les impôts à la Banque.*
Super Tax	***Taxe de Luxe***
Pay one hundred pounds.	*Payez dix mille francs.*

Other squares	***Les autres cases***
Free Parking	*Parc gratuit*
Go to Jail	*Allez en prison*

The Properties	***Les Propriétés***
a street	*une rue*
a road	*une avenue*
a square	*une place*

The Stations	***Les Gares***
Rent	*le loyer*
If two / three / four stations are owned..	*Si deux / trois / quatre gares sont possédées..*

The Utilities	***Les Entreprises de Service Public***
The Waterworks	*La compagnie de distribution des eaux*
The Electricity Company	*La compagne de distribution d'électricité*
If one utility is owned, rent is four times amount shown on one die.	*Si une entreprise est achetée, le loyer est égal à quatre fois la somme d'un dé.*
If both utilities are owned, rent is ten times amount shown on one die.	*Si les deux entreprises sont achetées, le loyer est de dix fois la somme d'un dé.*

MONOPOLY cont.

MONOPOLY suite

THE CARDS

LES CARTES

Property Cards	*Les Propriétés*
a site	*un terrain*
a Title Deed	*un Titre de propriété*
rent - site only	*Terrain à louer seulement*
rent with one / two / three / four houses	*loué avec une / deux / trois / quatre maisons*
rent with a hotel	*loué avec un hôtel*
If a player owns all the sites of any colour group, the rent is doubled on unimproved sites in that group.	*Si un joueur possède tous les terrains d'un groupe de couleur, le loyer est doublé pour tout terrain non-bâti de ce groupe.*
Cost of houses - one hundred pounds each.	*Coût des maisons - dix mille francs chacune.*
Cost of hotels - one hundred pounds plus four houses.	*Coût des hôtels- dix mille francs plus quatre maisons.*
Mortgage value of site.	*Valeur hypothécaire du terrain.*

Chance cards	*Les cartes Chance*
Pick up a Chance card.	*Piochez une carte chance.*
Take the top card.	*Piochez la carte du dessus.*
Put the used card at the bottom of the pile.	*Mettez la carte choisie sous le paquet.*
What does it say?	*Que dit-elle?*
It says...	*Elle dit...*
Advance to Go	*Avancez jusqu'à la case "Départ".*
Advance to Mayfair.	*Rendez vous à la Rue de la Paix*
Advance to Pall Mall - If you pass Go collect two hundred pounds.	*Avancez au Boulevard de la Villette - Si vous passez par la case "Départ" recevez vingt mille francs.*
Bank pays you a dividend of fifty pounds.	*La Banque vous verse un dividende de cinq mille francs.*

MONOPOLY cont

MONOPOLY suite

Chance cards cont

Drunk in charge - Fine twenty pounds.

Get out of Jail free - This card may be kept until needed or sold.

Go back three spaces.

Go to Jail. Move directly to Jail. Do not pass Go. Do not collect two hundred pounds.

Make general repairs on your houses - for each house pay twenty five pounds.

Speeding fine - fifteen pounds.

Take a trip to Marylebone Station and if you pass Go collect two hundred pounds.

You are assessed for street repairs - forty pounds per house, one hundred and fifteen pounds per hotel.

Your building loan matures - Receive one hundred and fifty pounds.

You have won a crossword competition - Collect one hundred pounds.

Les cartes Chance suite

Amende pour ivresse - Deux mille francs.

Vous êtes libéré de prison. Cette carte peut être conservée jusqu'à ce qu'elle soit utilisée ou vendue

Reculez de trois cases.

Allez en prison. Rendez vous directement à la prison. Ne franchissez pas la case "Départ". Ne touchez pas vingt mille francs.

Faites des réparations dans toutes vos maisons. Versez pour chaque maison deux mille cinq cent francs.

Amende pour excès de vitesse - mille cinq cent francs.

Allez à la gare de Lyon - si vous passez par la case "Départ" - recevez vingt mille francs.

Vous êtes imposé pour les réparations de voirie à raison de: quatre mille francs par maison et onze mille cinq cent francs par hôtel.

Votre immeuble et votre prêt rapportent. Vous devez touchez quinze mille francs.

Vous avez gagné le prix de mots croisés. Recevez dix mille francs.

MONOPOLY cont. | *MONOPOLY suite*

Community Chest Cards. What does it say?	*Les cartes de la Caisse de Communauté. Que dit-elle?*
It says.. (abc)	*Elle dit…(abc)*
Advance to Go.	*Allez à la case "Départ".*
Annuity matures - Collect one hundred pounds.	*Recevez votre revenu annuel - dix mille francs.*
Bank error in your favour - Collect two hundred pounds.	*Erreur de la Banque en votre faveur - Recevez vingt mille francs.*
Doctor's fee - Pay fifty pounds.	*Payez la note du Médecin - cinq mille francs.*
From sale of stock - You get fifty pounds.	*La vente de votre stock vous rapporte cinq mille francs.*
Get out of Jail free - This card may be kept until needed or sold.	*Vous êtes libéré de prison. Cette carte peut être conservée jusqu'à ce qu'elle soit utilisée ou vendue.*
Go back to Old Kent Road.	*Retournez à Belleville.*
Go to Jail. Move directly to Jail. Do not pass Go. Do not collect two hundred pounds.	*Allez en prison. Avancez tout droit en prison. Ne passez pas par la case "Départ". Ne recevez pas vingt mille francs.*
Income Tax Refund - Collect twenty pounds.	*Les Contributions vous remboursent la somme de deux mille francs.*
It is your Birthday - Collect ten pounds from each player.	*C'est votre anniversaire: chaque joueur doit vous donner mille francs.*
Pay a ten pound Fine or take a "Chance".	*Payez une amende de mille francs ou bien tirez une carte "Chance".*
Pay Hospital one hundred pounds.	*Payez à l'Hôpital dix mille francs.*
Pay your Insurance Premium - fifty pounds.	*Payez votre Police d'Assurance s'élevant à cinq mille francs.*
Receive interest on seven per cent Preference Shares - twenty five pounds.	*Recevez votre intérêt sur l'emprunt à sept pour cent: deux mille cinq cent francs.*
You have won Second Prize in a Beauty Contest - Collect ten pounds.	*Vous avez gagné le deuxième Prix de Beauté - Recevez mille francs.*
You inherit one hundred pounds.	*Vous héritez dix mille francs.*

MONOPOLY cont. The Play	MONOPOLY suite Le Jeu

Choosing the pieces	*Choisir les pions*
Which piece do you want to be?	*Quel pion voulez-vous? Tu veux quel pion?*
What colour do you want to be?	*Quelle couleur voulez-vous? Tu veux quelle couleur?*

Starting a game	*Commencer une partie*
Shake two dice to start.	*Jetez deux dés pour commencer.*
The player with the highest total starts.	*Le joueur ayant le plus grand total commence.*
I start.	*Je commence.*
You start.	*Tu commences.*
He / she starts.	*Il / elle commence.*

Whose turn is it now?	*C'est à qui le tour maintenant?*
It's my / your / his / her go.	*C'est à moi / à toi /à vous / à lui / à elle.*
We are playing clockwise / anticlockwise.	*On joue dans le sens des aiguilles d'une montre / dans le sens contraires des aiguilles d'une montre.*
It's not your turn.	*Ce n'est pas votre / ton tour.*
You went out of turn.	*Tu as sauté ton tour.*
You'd better miss your next go.	*Tu ferais mieux de sauter ton prochain tour.*

Throwing the dice	*Jeter les dés.*
to throw a double	*jeter un double*
I threw a double so I throw again.	*J'ai jeté un double donc je rejoue.*
I threw three doubles so I have to go to jail.	*J'ai jeté trois doubles donc je dois aller en prison.*
to throw three sixes	*jeter trois six*

MONOPOLY cont.   *MONOPOLY suite*

Moving the tokens	*Avancer les pions*
I shook a three so I move three places.	*J'ai jeté un trois donc j'avance de trois cases.*
We can both be on that space at the same time.	*On peut être tous les deux dans cette case au même moment.*
I have to advance to Go.	*Je dois aller à la case "Départ".*
I have to go directly to jail.	*Je dois aller directement en prison.*

Landing on squares	*Arrêt sur les cases*
I hope you land on my property.	*J'espère que vous allez / tu vas tomber sur ma propriété.*
Oh no! I just landed on your property.	*Oh non! Je tombe sur votre / ta propriété.*
Does anyone own the property I just landed on?	*Est-ce que quelqu'un possède la propriété sur laquelle je viens de tomber?*
It's mine, so you owe me..	*C'est à moi, donc vous me devez / tu me dois...*
How much do I have to pay you?	*Combien je vous / te dois?*
You have to pay me twenty two pounds rent - site only.	*Vous me devez / tu me dois deux cents francs de loyer - terrain nu.*
I have three houses, so that's nine hundred pounds you owe me.	*J'ai trois maisons donc vous me devez / tu me dois neuf mille francs.*
You have landed on my hotel.	*Vous vous êtes / tu t'es arrêté sur mon hôtel.*

Buying property	*Acheter des propriétés*
Do you want to buy that?	*Vous voulez / tu veux acheter cela?*
Yes, I'll buy it, please.	*Oui, je l'achète, s'il vous / te plaît.*
No, I don't think I'll buy it.	*Non, je pense que je ne l'achèterai pas.*
No, I haven't enough money.	*Non, je n'ai pas assez d'argent.*
Have you any change?	*Vous avez / tu as de la monnaie?*

MONOPOLY cont.

MONOPOLY suite

Selling property	Vendre des propriétés
Would you like to sell me..?	Veux-tu me vendre...?
I want to sell these houses back to the bank.	Je voudrais revendre mes maisons à la Banque.
You only get half price if you sell property back to the Bank.	Tu ne peux pas revendre tes propriétés à la Banque que pour la moitié du prix.

Putting houses on	Mettre des maisons
Houses are green.	Les maisons sont vertes.
I want to put a house on here.	Je veux mettre une maison ici.
I have two houses, so you have to pay me..	J'ai deux maisons donc tu dois me payer...
Could I buy a house, please?	Je peux acheter une maison, s'il vous plaît?
I would like four houses, please.	Je voudrais quatre maisons, s'il vous plaît.
You have to put houses evenly over your properties.	Il faut construire uniformément sur ses propriétés.
The Bank has run out of houses, so you'll have to wait.	Le Banque n'a plus de maisons à vendre, donc il faut attendre.
The Bank now has houses again - would you like to bid for them?	La Banque a de nouveau des maisons. Tu veux enchérir?

Putting a hotel on	Mettre un hôtel
Hotels are red.	Les hôtels sont rouges.
I want to buy a hotel now.	Je veux acheter un hôtel maintenant.
You can't put a hotel on until you have four houses on each site.	Tu ne peux pas construire un hôtel tant que tu n'as pas quatre maisons sur chaque terrain.
You give the Bank the four houses and pay the difference for a hotel.	Tu donnes à la Banque les quatre maisons et paies la différence pour un hôtel.
Here are the houses in exchange.	Voici les maisons en échange.
I have to pay.....extra.	Je dois payer....supplémentaires.

MONOPOLY cont.

MONOPOLY suite

The Banker	*Le Banquier*
Do you want to buy it?	*Veux-tu l'acheter?*
It costs..	*Cela coûte...*
You owe the Bank..	*Tu dois à la Banque..*
Does anyone want to bid for this property?	*Quelqu'un veut faire une enchère pour cette propriété?*
You are the highest bidder.	*Tu es le plus offrant.*
I haven't got the right change.	*Je n'ai pas la monnaie exacte.*
Can someone change this note, please?	*Quelqu'un peut-il me faire de la monnaie sur ce billet?*
The Bank has run out of money.	*La Banque n'a plus d'argent.*
The Bank will have to give you an I.O.U. (an I owe you).	*La Banque doit te donner une reconnaissance de dettes.*

Mortgaging property	*Les propriétés hypothéquées*
I would like to mortgage this, please.	*Je voudrais hypothéquer cela, s'il vous plaît.*
The mortgage value is printed on each Title Deed.	*La valeur hypothécaire est marquée sur chaque Titre de Propriété.*
Turn the card face down to show it's mortgaged.	*Retourner la carte face contre table pour montrer qu'elle est hypothéquée.*
There is no rent to pay because the property is mortgaged.	*Il n'y a pas loyer à payer car la propriété est hypothéquée.*
You have to pay ten per cent when you lift the mortgage.	*Il faut payer dix pour cent pour lever l'hypothèque.*
You can't mortgage houses or hotels.	*On ne peut pas hypothéquer des maisons ou des hôtels.*
You can't build on mortgaged property.	*On ne peut pas construire sur des propriétés hypothéquées.*
You have to pay off the mortgage first.	*Il faut rembourser l'hypothèque, d'abord.*

MONOPOLY cont.

MONOPOLY suite

Being bankrupt	*Etre en faillite*
I'm afraid I can't pay you.	*Je crains de ne pas pouvoir te payer.*
I haven't any money.	*Je n'ai pas d'argent.*
I shall have to return my houses/hotels to the Bank.	*Je vais devoir redonner mes maisons / hôtels à la Banque.*
You only get half their value if you return them.	*On ne reçoit que la moitié de leur valeur quand on les revend.*
Will you take part cash and part property?	*Tu acceptes la moitié en liquide et la moitié en propriété?*

Seeing who has won	*Voir qui a gagné*
Shall we stop now and see who has won?	*Et si on arrêtait maintenant pour voir qui a gagné?*
Shall we leave the game here and carry on playing later?	*On laisse le jeu ici et on continuera de jouer plus tard?*
Add up all your money.	*Comptez tout votre argent.*
Add up the value of your property.	*Comptez la valeur de votre propriété.*
How much do you own?	*Combien possédez-vous / possèdes-tu?*
I own..	*Je possède....*
You have won.	*Vous avez / tu as gagné.*
I think I've won.	*Je crois que j'ai gagné.*

CLUEDO

CLUEDO

THE OBJECT OF THE GAME

LE BUT DE JEU

To solve by elimination and deduction the murder of Dr. Black, the owner of Tudor Close, whose body has been found at the foot of the stairs leading to the cellar at a spot marked "X". The winner is the first player to guess correctly:-	*Résoudre par élimination et par déduction l'énigme du crime du Docteur Lenoir, le propriétaire de la villa, dont le corps a été retrouvé au pied des escaliers menant à la cave, à l'endroit marqué d'une croix. Le vainqueur est le premier joueur qui parvient à identifier dans une même accusation:*
• Who the murderer was.	• *Le meurtrier*
• Which weapon was used.	• *L'arme du crime*
• The room in which the crime was committed.	• *La pièce dans laquelle a été commis le meurtre*

The spot marked "X"	***L'endroit marqué d'une croix***
the stairs leading to the cellars	*l'escalier menant à la cave*
the envelope marked "Murder Cards"	*l'étui confidentiel*

The three "Murder Cards"	***Les cartes***
the murderer	*l'assassin*
the weapon	*l'arme*
the room in which the crime was committed	*la pièce dans laquelle le meurtre a été commis*

CLUEDO cont

CLUEDO suite

Selecting the three "Murder Cards"	*Le choix des trois cartes*
Shuffle the nine room cards well.	*Battez les neuf cartes "Pièce".*
Shuffle the six weapon cards separately.	*Battez les six cartes "Arme" séparément.*
Shuffle the six person cards too.	*Battez les six cartes "Suspect" aussi.*
Cut the piles of cards.	*Coupez les piles.*
Place the top card of each pile unseen into the Murder Envelope.	*Placez la première carte de chaque pile dans l'étui confidentiel sans que personne ne la voit.*
There should be a room card, a weapon card and a person card.	*Il doit y avoir une carte "Pièce", une carte "Arme" et une carte "Suspect".*

The people and their pieces	*Les personnages et leurs pions*
Colonel Mustard - Yellow	*Colonel Moutarde - Jaune*
Professor Plum - Purple	*Professeur Violet - Violet*
The Reverend Green - Green	*Docteur Olive - Vert*
Mrs. Peacock - Blue	*Madame Pervenche - Bleu*
Miss Scarlett - Red	*Mademoiselle Rose - Rouge*
Mrs. White - White	*Madame Leblanc - Blanc*

The Board	*Le Plateau*
the ground floor plan of Tudor Close	*le rez-de-chaussée de la villa*
start	*Départ*
a square	*une case*
a door	*une porte*

CLUEDO cont

CLUEDO suite

The rooms	*Les pièces*
the lounge	*le petit salon*
the dining room	*la salle à manger*
the kitchen	*la cuisine*
the ballroom	*le grand salon*
the conservatory	*la véranda*
the billiard room	*la salle de billard*
the library	*la bibliothèque*
the study	*le bureau*
the hall	*le hall*

The secret passages	*Les passages secrets*
from the study to the kitchen and vice versa	*du bureau à la cuisine et vice-versa*
from the lounge to the conservatory and vice versa	*du petit salon à la véranda et vice-versa*
You can use a secret passage instead of throwing the dice.	*On peut utiliser un passage secret au lieu de jeter les dés.*
Using a secret passage counts as one move.	*L'utilisation d'un passage secret compte pour un tour.*

The Weapons	*Les Armes*
The Candlestick	*le Chandelier*
The Dagger	*le Poignard*
The Lead Piping	*la Matraque*
The Revolver	*le Revolver*
The Rope	*la Corde*
The Spanner	*la Clef Anglaise*
the tokens	*les pions*

CLUEDO cont

CLUEDO suite

"Detective Notes" cards	*le Carnet de Détective*
Suspected Persons	*les Suspects (m or f)*
Probable Implements	*les Armes (f)*
Suspected Scene of Murder	*les Pièces*
Have you got some pencils?	*Avez-vous des crayons?*
Could I have a pencil, please?	*Je peux avoir un crayon, s'il vous plaît?*
to tick off	*cocher*
to cross off	*barrer*
to make a note of	*noter*
to record	*enregistrer*
to eliminate from your enquiries	*éliminer par enquêtes*
Using "Detective Notes" cards	*L'utilisation du Carnet de Détective*
to query	*enquêter*
to get confused	*s'embrouiller*
to forget	*oublier*
You asked me that before.	*Tu m'as déjà demandé cela.*

Playing	*Le Jeu*
Place the pieces on their starting squares.	*Placez les pions sur leur case "Départ".*
Put the weapons in different rooms.	*Placez chaque arme dans une pièce différante.*
Draw the three Murder Cards (see above).	*Tirez les trois cartes "Suspect".*
Put the Murder Cards in the Murder Envelope.	*Placez les cartes dans l'étui confidentiel.*
Put the Murder Envelope on the spot marked "X".	*Placez l'étui confidentiel à l'endroit marqué d'une croix.*
Shuffle all the cards together.	*Battez toutes les cartes ensemble.*

PLAYING CLUEDO cont   *LE JEU DE CLUEDO suite*

Deal out the cards one at a time clockwise round the table.	*Distribuez les cartes une à une dans le sens des aiguilles d'une montre.*
Sometimes some players have more cards than others. It is easier for them.	*Certains joueurs peuvent recevoir plus de cartes que d'autres et être avantagés.*
Each player decides to be one of the murder suspects and uses their token.	*Chaque joueur choisit d'être un suspect et utilise le pion correspondant.*
Miss Scarlett always moves first.	*Mademoiselle Rose commence toujours.*
Play in a clockwise direction.	*Jouez dans le sens des aiguilles d'une montre.*
Shake the dice and move your token accordingly.	*Lancez les dés et déplacez le pion du nombre de cases indiqué par les dés.*
You may not move diagonally.	*One ne peut pas se déplacer en diagonale.*
You have to enter and leave rooms through the doors or secret passages.	*Il faut entrer et sortir des pièces par la porte ou le passage secret.*

Making a suggestion	***Formuler des hypothèses***
When you enter a room, you can make a "suggestion" by calling into that room any other person (who has to go immediately into the room) and any weapon (which is then placed in the room). You cannot use any other room in your suggestion, only the room you are in.	*Lorsqu'un joueur entre dans une pièce, il peut formuler une hypothèse. Il fait alors venir dans la pièce le suspect (qui doit se rendre tout de suite dans la pièce) et l'arme de son choix (qui est alors placée dans la pièce). Un joueur ne peut formuler une hypothèse que s'il se trouve dans la pièce mentionnée dans cette hypothèse.*

CLUEDO cont

CLUEDO suite

A sample suggestion	*Un exemple d'hypothèse*
"I suggest that the murder was committed in the Lounge by the Reverend Green with the Spanner."	*"Je soupçonne le Docteur Olive d'avoir commis le crime dans le petit salon avec la clef anglaise".*

After the suggestion	*Après l'hypothèse*
The player who is making the suggestion, does so to the player on his / her left.	*Le joueur qui formule l'hypothèse s'adresse au joueur situé à sa gauche.*
This player has to examine his / her cards and if he has one (or more) of the suggested cards he must show one (and one only) of them secretly to the other person. (He should not admit to having more than one of the requested cards.)	*Le joueur examine ses cartes. S'il possède l'une (ou plus) des trois cartes de l'hypothèse, il la montre à l'autre joueur sans que les autres puissent la voir. (Il ne doit pas avouer qu'il en possède des autres.)*
If this player has none of the cards, the person to his left is then asked the same question.	*S'il n'a aucune des cartes, le joueur situé à sa gauche examine ses cartes et procède de la même façon.*
As soon as someone has shown one of the suggested cards, that turn is ended and play passes to the next player to the left.	*Dès que quelqu'un a montré une des cartes de l'hypothèse, le tour est fini et le jeu se poursuit avec le joueur situé à gauche.*
Each person tries by a process of elimination to discover the three Murder Cards.	*Chaque joueur tente de découvrir par élimination les trois cartes de l'étui.*

CLUEDO cont

CLUEDO suite

Making an accusation

When a player think he knows what the three Murder Cards are, he can, provided it is his turn (even if he has just made a suggestion), make an Accusation by writing down what he thinks the three cards in the Murder Envelope are and checking with the contents of the Murder Envelope, taking care that no-one else sees the cards.

L'accusation

Si un joueur croit connaître les trois cartes de l'énigme, il peut, si c'est son tour, porter une accusation précise en écrivant le contenu de son accusation sur sa feuille. Puis il compare en secret son accusation avec le contenu de l'étui.

If the accusation is incorrect ..

If the player is not correct, he cannot make any more accusations in the game. He should replace the three cards in the Murder Envelope so that the other players can continue the game. He still has to answer other players' suggestions.

Si l'accusation est fausse..

Si son accusation est fausse, il ne peut plus enquêter. Il replace les cartes dans l'étui pour que les autres joueurs continuent. Il doit cependant toujours répondre aux hypothèses des autres joueurs.

N.B. If a player says he does not hold any of the suggested cards when he in fact **does** hold one, this player has no further turns in the game.

N.B. Si un joueur n'a pas montré une carte d'hypothèse alors qu'il en possède effectivement, il n'a plus le droit d'enquêter.

CARD GAMES

LES JEUX DE CARTE

GENERAL EXPRESSIONS

EXPRESSIONS GENERALES

Would you like to play cards?	*Voulez-vous / tu veux jouer aux cartes?*
What games do you know?	*Quel jeu connaissez-vous / connais-tu?*
What would you like to play?	*Vous aimeriez / tu aimerais jouer?*
Can you play..?	*Vous savez / tu sais jouer à..?*
Shall we play..?	*Et si on jouait à...?*
I'd like to play..	*J'aimerais jouer à....*
I've forgotten how to play.	*J'ai oublié comment jouer.*
Can you remind me how to play?	*Pouvez-vous / peux-tu me rappeler comment jouer?*
Can you teach me how to play?	*Pouvez-vous / peux-tu m'apprendre à jouer?*

A pack of cards	*Un jeu de cartes*
Have you got a pack of cards?	*Avez-vous / as-tu un jeu de cartes?*
I brought a pack of cards with me.	*J'ai apporté un jeu de cartes avec moi.*
I'll go and get them.	*Je vais les chercher.*

Is it a full pack?	*C'est un jeu complet?*
Shall we check the pack?	*On vérifie le jeu?*
Are there any missing?	*Il en manque?*
There is one missing.	*Il en manque une.*
Have you got another pack?	*Avez-vous / as-tu un autre jeu?*

The different suits	*Les différentes suites (f)*
clubs	*trèfles (m)*
diamonds	*carreaux (m)*
hearts	*cœurs (m)*
spades	*piques (f)*

CARD GAMES cont

LES JEUX DE CARTE suite

The number cards	*Les numéros des cartes*
ace	*as (m)*
ace high / ace low	*as / un*
the ace of hearts	*l'as de cœur*
two	*deux*
the two of diamonds	*le deux de carreaux*
three / four / five / six	*trois / quatre / cinq / six*
seven / eight / nine / ten	*sept / huit / neuf / dix*

The face cards	*Les têtes*
Jack	*le Valet*
Queen	*la Reine*
King	*le Roi*
Joker	*le Joker*

PLAYING CARD GAMES

JOUER AUX CARTES

Shuffling	*Battre*
Shuffle the cards.	*Battez / mélangez les cartes.*
I'll shuffle / you shuffle.	*Je mélange / vous mélangez / tu mélanges.*
Give the cards a good shuffle.	*Mélangez / mélange bien.*
The cards aren't shuffled properly.	*Les cartes ne sont pas bien mélangées.*

Cutting	*La coupe*
to cut	*couper*
You cut to me.	*Coupez / coupe pour moi.*
I'll cut to you.	*Je coupe pour toi.*

CARD GAMES cont.   *LES JEUX DE CARTES suite*

Dealing	*Distribuer / donner*
It's your deal.	*C'est votre / ta donne.*
You deal the cards face up / face down.	*Tu distribues à jeu ouvert / face contre table.*
You dealt two cards then.	*Tu as distribué deux cartes là.*
You missed one out.	*Tu as oublié une carte*
I'm the dealer this time.	*Je distribue cette fois.*
I've forgotten where I'm up to.	*J'ai oublié où j'en suis.*
Count your cards.	*Comptez vos / compte tes cartes.*
I am one short.	*Il m'en manque une.*
I have one extra.	*J'en ai une de trop.*
We'd better re-deal.	*On ferait mieux de redistribuer.*

Assessing your hand	*Evaluer sa main*
I haven't sorted my hand yet.	*Je n'ai pas encore arrangé mon jeu.*
Let me just arrange my cards.	*Laisse moi juste ranger mes cartes.*
I've got a good hand this time.	*J'ai un bon jeu cette fois.*
I've got a poor hand again.	*J'ai encore une mauvaise main.*

Leading	*Jouer*
You lead.	*A vous / toi de jouer.*
It's my / his / her / our / your / their lead.	*C'est à moi / lui / elle / nous / vous / eux de jouer*
She led the three of diamonds.	*Elle a joué le trois de carreaux.*
What did you lead?	*Qu'avez-vous / qu' as-tu joué?*

Playing one's hand	*Jouer*
He played an ace.	*Il a joué un as.*
What did he play?	*Qu'a-t-il joué?*
I don't know what to play.	*Je ne sais pas quoi jouer.*

CARD GAMES cont.

LES JEUX DE CARTES suite

Following suit	***Avoir les suites de couleur***
You must follow suit if you can.	*Vous devez / tu dois avoir une couleur.*
I can't follow suit.	*Je n'ai pas de couleur.*
A strong suit	*une couleur longue / forte (bridge)*
a weak suit	*une couleur courte / faible (bridge)*

Trumping	***Prendre avec l'atout***
What are trumps?	*Que sont les atouts?*
Spades are trumps.	*Atout pique.*
The three of trumps.	*Le trois d'atout.*
I haven't got any trumps.	*Je n'ai pas atout.*
He was holding all the trumps.	*Il avait tous les atouts.*

Throwing away cards	***Rejeter les cartes***
to discard	*se défausser*
the stock pile	*la pioche*
I need to throw one away.	*Je dois en rejeter une.*
I don't know which to throw away.	*Je ne sais pas laquelle rejeter.*

Picking up cards	***Piocher des cartes***
Have you picked up yet?	*Vous avez / tu as pioché?*
Pick one up off the pile.	*Piochez / pioche une carte.*
What did you pick up?	*Qu'avez-vous / qu'as-tu pioché?*

Putting cards down	***Poser les cartes***
to put a card face down	*poser une carte face contre table*
to put a card face up	*poser une carte*
What did she put down?	*Qu'a-t-elle posé?*

CARD GAMES cont.
LES JEUX DE CARTES suite

Missing a turn	*Passer un tour*
I missed my turn.	*J'ai passé mon tour.*
You missed your turn.	*Vous avez / tu as passé votre / ton tour.*
You have to miss a turn.	*Vous devez / tu dois passer un tour.*

Passing	*Passer*
I can't play anything.	*Je ne peux rien jouer.*
I shall have to pass.	*Je vais devoir passer.*
I pass.	*Je passe.*
She passed.	*Elle a passé.*

Winning tricks	*Faire les levées*
How many tricks have you won?	*Combien de levées avez-vous / as-tu fait?*
Well done!	*Bravo! / Bien jouer!*
I just won that trick.	*Je viens de faire cette levée.*
I don't think I'm going to win many.	*Je ne pense pas faire beaucoup de levées.*
We only need to win another one.	*Il ne reste plus qu'une levée à faire.*
We need to win seven tricks.	*Il faut faire sept levées.*

Losing tricks	*Perdre des levées*
How many tricks can we afford to lose?	*Combien de levées peut-on se permettre de perdre?*
How many tricks have we lost?	*Combien de levées avons-nous perdues?*
Sorry!	*Désolé!*

CARD GAMES cont.   *LES JEUX DE CARTES suite*

Cheating	*Tricher*
Did you cheat?	*Vous avez / tu as triché?*
I never cheat.	*Je ne triche jamais.*
You shouldn't cheat.	*Vous ne devriez pas / tu ne devrais pas tricher.*
Don't look at my cards.	*Ne regardez pas / ne regarde pas mes cartes.*
I can see your cards.	*Je peux voir vos / tes cartes.*

Memorising cards	*Mémoriser les cartes*
to remember	*se souvenir*
to forget	*oublier*
to count	*compter*
I can't remember if the Ace has gone.	*Je ne me souviens plus si l'As est parti.*
I have forgotten how many..	*J'ai oublié combien de...*
How many trumps have gone?	*Combien d'atouts sont partis?*
Try to remember the tricks.	*Essayez de vous / essaie de te souvenir des levées.*
Count the aces / the trumps.	*Comptez vos / compte tes As / atouts.*
Have all the hearts gone?	*Tous les cours sont partis?*

WHIST

LE WHIST

You need:	***Il faut:***
A fifty two card pack	*Un jeu de cinquante-deux cartes*
Four people (two pairs of partners)	*Quatre personnes (deux paires)*

The Object of the Game	***Le But du Jeu***
To win as many of the thirteen available tricks as possible.	*Gagner le maximum de levées sur les treize à faire.*

HOW TO PLAY

COMMENT JOUER

- The dealer deals out all the cards one by one and face down to each player in turn so that each has thirteen cards.
- He should start by dealing to the person on his left so that the last card is dealt to himself.
- This last card is dealt face up and determines what trumps are.
- The player to the dealer's left starts the play with any card.
- The other players have to follow suit if they can but can trump the trick if they cannot.
- If more than one trump is played, the higher trump wins the trick.

- *Le donneur distribue toutes les cartes une par une, face contre table, afin que chaque joueur ait treize cartes.*
- *Il commence par le joueur situé à sa gauche afin de terminer par lui.*
- *La dernière carte est retournée et détermine l'atout.*
- *Le joueur à gauche du donneur commence à jouer n'importe quelle carte.*
- *Les autres joueurs doivent suivre la couleur mais. s'ils n'ont pas la couleur, peuvent couper à l'atout.*
- *Si plus d'un seul atout est joué, c'est l'atout le plus grand qui remporte la levée.*

HOW TO PLAY WHIST cont

COMMENT JOUER LE WHIST suite

- If no trumps are played, the highest card of the suit wins with ace counting high.

- The person who wins the trick leads the first card in the next round.

- *Si aucun atout n'est joué, la carte la plus haute de la suite remporte la levée avec les as comptant le maximum.*

- *La personne qui a fait la levée jette la première carte du tour suivant.*

Scoring
- Each trick over six won by either pair of players counts as one point.

- A game is won when seven points have been won.

Les points
- *Chaque levée faite par l'un ou l'autre des partenaires, à partir de la sixième donne un point.*

- *Le jeu est gagné par la paire qui a totalisé sept points.*

RUMMY

LE RAMI

You need:
A fifty two card pack
Any number of players from two to six.

Il faut:
Un jeu de cinquante-deux cartes
De deux à six joueurs.

The Object of the Game Rummy
To get rid of all your cards by laying them down on the table in front of you.

Le but du jeu
Se débarrasser de toutes ses cartes en les étalant sur la table.

RUMMY cont.

LE RAMI suite

Players try to collect and arrange cards in the following ways: • Three of a kind or four of a kind - e.g. three Aces or four Sixes • A sequence of three or more cards of the same suit - e.g. Two, Three, Four, Five of Spades.	*Les joueurs tentent de piocher et d'arranger les cartes de la manière suivante:* • *Un brelan ou un carré - ex: trois As ou quatre six* • *Une suite de trois cartes ou plus de la même couleur - ex: le Deux, le Trois, le Quatre et le Cinq de Pique*

HOW TO PLAY RUMMY

COMMENT JOUER AU RAMI

Cut for dealer who deals to each player: • ten cards each if there are two players • seven cards each if there are three or four players • six cards each if there are five or six players	*Coupez pour le donneur qui distribue:* • *dix cartes chacun s'il y a deux joueurs* • *sept cartes chacun s'il y a trois ou quatre joueurs* • *six cartes chacun s'il y a cinq ou six joueurs*
Place remaining cards face down on the table to form a stock pile.	*Placez le reste des cartes face contre table pour faire une pioche.*
Turn up the top card of the stock pile and lay it face up beside the stock pile to form a waste pile.	*Retournez la carte au-dessus de la pile et placez-la à côté de la pioche, toujours retournée, pour former la pile de rejet.*
The player on the dealer's left starts the game.	*Le joueur situé à la gauche du distributeur commence le jeu.*
Players look at their hands for the beginnings of any of the above groups or sequences of cards.	*Les joueurs regardent leur main / jeu pour guetter le début d'un brelan, un carré ou une suite.*

HOW TO PLAY RUMMY cont.

COMMENT JOUER AU RAMI suite

If you are lucky enough to have any group or sequence you can lay it on the table in front of you.	*Si vous avez la chance d'avoir l'une ou l'autre de ces combinaisons, vous pouvez les étaler sur la table.*
If not, you can either pick up the turned-up waste card or take one from the stock pile.	*Sinon, vous pouvez soit prendre la carte retournée de la pile de rebut ou en prendre une de la pioche.*
You have to throw one card away - either the one you have just picked up or one from your existing hand.	*Il faut jeter une carte - soit celle que vous venez de piocher, soit une carte de votre main / jeu.*
Players can also add cards to any other player's cards already laid on the table.	*Les joueurs peuvent aussi ajouter des cartes à celles posées sur la table par d'autres joueurs.*
You win when you are the first person to get rid of all your cards.	*Le vainqueur est la première personne qui s'est débarrassé de toutes ses cartes.*

SCORING

LES POINTS

When someone has won the game, all other players add up the points they still hold in their hand as follows:-	*Quand quelqu'un a gagné, les autres joueurs comptent les points qu'il leur reste de la manière suivante:*
• Aces count low as one.	• *Les As comptent un point.*
• Number cards count their number value.	• *Les cartes numérotées rapportent leur valeur en points.*
• Jacks, Queens and Kings count ten each.	• *Les Valets, Reines et Rois rapportent dix points chacun.*

RUMMY - SCORING cont.

RAMI - LES POINTS suite

The winner is awarded the total number of points held by all other players.	*Le gagnant remporte la somme totale des points retenus par les autres joueurs.*
If the winner was able to put all his cards straight down on the table on his first go then he is said to have "gone rummy" and gets awarded double the other players' total points.	*Si le gagnant a posé toutes ses cartes en un seul tour, on dit alors qu'il a "fait un Rami" et il remporte le double de la somme des points des autres joueurs.*
The overall winner can be the first one to reach five hundred points or some other pre-determined score.	*Le gagnant est le premier qui atteint cinq cent points ou un autre total fixé.*

PONTOON

LE VINGT-ET-UN

You need:	***Il faut:***
A fifty two card pack	*Un jeu de cinquante-deux cartes*
Dead matchsticks or counters for laying bets.	*Des bâtons d'allumette ou des jetons pour miser.*
Someone to be banker / dealer.	*Un banquier / un donneur.*

Scoring	***Les Points***
• Kings, Queens & Jacks count as ten each.	• *Les Rois, Reines et Valets valent dix points chacun.*
• Aces count 'low' as one or 'high' as eleven - whichever is convenient at the time.	• *Les As valent soit un point, soit onze point, suivant la situation.*
• All the number cards have their ordinary value.	• *Les cartes numérotées ont leur propre valeur.*

PONTOON cont.

LE VINGT-ET-UN suite

How to Play

- Choose someone to be dealer who in the game of Pontoon is called the banker.
- Players can take turns to be banker.
- The banker plays against the other players.
- Any reasonable number of people can play.
- All suits are ignored.
- The banker shuffles the cards (which are not shuffled again until a new banker takes over).

Comment Jouer

- *Choisissez un donneur qui sera, dans ce jeu, appelé le banquier.*
- *Les joueurs peuvent être banquiers chacun à leur tour.*
- *Le banquier joue contre les autres joueurs.*
- *Il faut un nombre raisonnable de joueurs.*
- *Les couleurs sont ignorées.*
- *Le banquier bat les cartes (qui ne devront pas être rebattues jusqu'à ce qu'un autre banquier le remplace.*

THE RULES OF PONTOON

LES REGLES DU VINGT-ET-UN

- The banker deals one card face down to each player, including himself.
- The other players look at their own card, keeping it secret, but the banker cannot look at his own card yet.
- Each player then makes a bet with counters or matchsticks, putting a lot on if they think their card is good and only one counter if not. Each has to bet something.

- *Le banquier donne une carte face contre table à chacun, lui inclus.*
- *Les autre joueurs regardent leur carte discrètement, mais le banquier ne peut pas encore regarder la sienne.*
- *Ensuite chaque joueur mise avec un allumette ou un jeton; la mise est importante si ils pensent que leur carte est bonne, sinon, elle est minime. Tout le monde doit miser.*

RULES FOR PONTOON CONT.

LES REGLES DU VINGT-ET-UN suite

- The banker then deals a second card to each player.
- The aim of the game is to score twenty one exactly, or as close to twenty one as possible.
- Players add up their score.

- The banker then asks each player in turn if they want to "stick" (i.e. not take any more cards) or if they want to "twist" (i.e. be dealt another card but this time face up).
- Players can twist up to three times (making a maximum total of five cards).

- If the total score in a player's hand exceeds twenty one then that player is "bust" and puts his cards down on the table.
- When all players have decided either to stick or are bust, the banker turns his cards over for everyone to see and proceeds to stick or twist like everyone else.
- The banker takes all the counters bet by players who either went bust or scored lower than himself or the same as himself.

- *Ensuite le banquier donne une seconde carte à chacun.*
- *Le but du jeu est de marquer vingt-et-un point exactement, ou d'approcher le plus possible cette somme.*
- *Les joueurs font le total de leurs points.*
- *Le banquier demande alors à chaque joueur s'il conserve sa mise ou s'il a besoin d'une autre carte, qui sera cette fois ouverte.*

- *Les joueurs peuvent demander jusqu'à trois cartes (pour un nombre maximum de cinq cartes).*

- *Si le total des points dans une main excède vingt-et-un, alors le joueur est éliminé et étale ses cartes sur la table.*
- *Quand tous les joueurs ont décidé de garder la mise ou sont éliminés, le banquier retourne sa carte et procède comme pour les autres joueurs.*
- *Le banquier prend la mise des joueurs qui ont été éliminés ou qui ont marqué un total de points inférieur ou égal au sien.*

RULES FOR PONTOON cont.

LES REGLES DU VINGT-ET-UN suite

- He has to pay players who scored higher than he did himself the same number of counters as they bet.
- If the banker scores twenty one made with an Ace together with any King, Queen or Jack he calls "Pontoon" and receives double stakes from each player, **unless** one of the players has a five card trick (which beats Pontoon) or a "Royal Pontoon" which consists of three sevens and beats everything.
- A player with a Royal Pontoon receives treble stakes. If the banker has a Royal Pontoon it only counts as an ordinary Pontoon.

- *Il doit payer les joueurs qui ont marqué plus de points que lui le nombre de jetons qu'ils ont misé.*
- *Si le banquier marque vingt-et-un points avec un As et soit un Roi, une Reine, ou un Valet, il dit: "Vingt-et-un" et reçoit le double de la mise de chaque joueur, **à moins** que l'un des joueurs ait une levée de cinq cartes (qui bat le vingt-et-un) ou un "Vingt-et-un Royal" qui consiste en trois sept et qui bat tous les autres.*
- *Un joueur avec un "Vingt-et-un Royal" reçoit le triple de la mise. Si le banquier a un Vingt-et-un Royal, cela ne compte que comme un Vingt-et-un.*

BRIDGE

LE BRIDGE

Counting the points in your hand:
ALLOW:

Le total des points dans une main:
IL FAUT COMPTER:

• four points for an Ace	• *quatre points pour un As*
• three points for a King	• *trois points pour un Roi*
• two points for a Queen	• *deux points pour un Reine*
• one point for a Jack	• *un point pour un Valet*

PLUS
PLUS

Either:

Soit:

• one point for each trump over four trumps	• *un point pour chaque atout à partir de quatre atouts*
• one point for each card over three in each side suit	• *un point pour chaque carte à partir de trois dans chaque suite qui n'est pas à l'atout*

Or:

Ou alors:

• one point for each suit with two cards in it	• *un point pour chaque suite a deux cartes*
• two points for each singleton	• *deux points pour chaque singleton*
• three points for each void suit	• *trois points pour chaque chicane*

Who is bidding?	***Qui fait les enchères?***
Who's turn is it to bid first?	*C'est à qui de faire la première enchère?*
It's my / your / his / her / our / their bid.	*C'est à moi / toi / lui / elle / nous / vous / eux.*
Are you ready to bid?	*Etes-vous / es-tu prêt à faire un enchère?*
Are you going to bid?	*Allez-vous / vas-tu faire un enchère?*
to open the bidding	*ouvrir une enchère*

BRIDGE cont.

LE BRIDGE suite

What are you bidding?	*Quelle est votre / ton enchère?*
No bid.	*Je passe.*
One club/diamond/heart/spade.	*Un trèfle / carreau / cœur / pique.*
One no-trump.	*Un sans-atout.*
Two clubs/diamonds/hearts/spades	*Deux trèfles / carreaux / cœurs / piques.*
An opening bid of two of a suit.	*Une entame du deux de la couleur.*
He / she did not bid.	*Il / elle a passé.*
I did not bid.	*J'ai passé.*
My partner did not bid.	*Mon partenaire a passé.*

The type of bid	*Les types des enchères*
A forcing bid.	*Un forcing de manche.*
A weak bid.	*Une enchère faible.*
A strong bid.	*Une enchère forte.*
A raising bid.	*Une surenchère.*
A no-trump bid.	*Une enchère à sans-atout.*
A pre-emptive bid.	*Une demande de barrage.*
A re-bid.	*Ré-enchérir.*

The responses	*Les réponses*
Pass / No bid.	*Je passe / Je passe.*
to re-bid	*ré-enchérir*
to raise the bidding..	*surenchérir*
..in your partner's suit	*..dans la couleur de votre / ton partenaire*
..in your own suit.	*..dans votre / ta propre couleur*
A single raise.	*Une surenchère simple.*
A double raise.	*Un jump.*
to jump	*jumper*
to keep on bidding	*continuer les enchères*
to continue bidding	*continuer les enchères*
a biddable suit	*une couleur d'enchère*
a rebiddable suit	*une couleur de surenchère*
to force to game	*faire un forcing*

BRIDGE cont.   *LE BRIDGE suite*

Scoring	*Les points*
Who is going to keep the score?	*Qui tient le marque?*
I'll score.	*Je vais marquer.*
Will you score?	*Vous allez / tu vas marquer?*
What's the score at the moment?	*Quel est le score à présent?*

Necessary numbers	*Nombres nécessaires*
ten / twenty / thirty / forty / fifty	*dix / vingt / trente / quarante / cinquante*
sixty / seventy / eighty / ninety	*soixante / soixante-dix /quatre-vingts / quatre-vingts dix*
one hundred	*cent*
one hundred and ten / twenty etc.	*cent dix / cent vingt.....*
two hundred / three hundred etc	*deux cent / trois cent .....*
one thousand	*mille*
one thousand, five hundred and fifty	*mille cinq cent cinquante*

The tricks	*Les levées*
the first trick	*la première levée*
subsequent tricks	*les levées suivantes*
an undertrick	*une levée manquante*
an overtrick	*une levée de mieux*

Doubling	*Doubler*
doubled	*doublé*
undoubled	*sous-doublé*
redoubled	*sur-doublé*

Vulnerable	*Vulnérable*
not vulnerable	*pas vulnérable*

Above the line	*Au-dessus de la marque*
below the line	*au-dessous de la marque*

BRIDGE cont.   *LE BRIDGE suite*

Slams	Chelems
a small slam	un petit chelem
a grand slam	un grand chelem

Honours	Les Honneurs
four trump honours	honneurs à quatre atouts
five trump honours	honneurs à cinq atouts
four aces in one hand	quatre as dans une main

Rubbers	Les Robres
a two / three game rubber	un robre à deux / trois manches
an unfinished rubber	un robre non-terminé

Games	Les Manches
for one game	pour une manche
for part score in unfinished game	pour un résultat partiel dans une manche non-terminé

CHESS   *LES ECHECS (m)*

The Chessboard	L'échiquier (m)
portable	portable
electronic	électronique
a black square	une case noire
the white squares	les cases blanches
the right / left corner	le coin droit / le coin gauche
opposite	en face
diagonal	en diagonale

CHESS cont.   *LES ECHECS suite*

The pieces	*Les Pions (m)*
The King	*Le Roi*
The Queen	*La Reine*
The Bishop	*Le Fou*
The Knight	*Le Chevalier*
The Rook	*La Tour*
The Pawns	*Les Pions (m)*

Common words (abc)	*Les mots usuels*
backwards	*en arrière*
behind	*derrière*
black	*noir*
to capture	*prendre / saisir*
to castle	*roquer*
"check"	*"Echec"*
to check	*mettre en échec*
checkmate	*Echec et Mat*
a draw	*un ex-aequo*
defensive	*défense*
forward	*en avant*
in front of	*devant*
lined up	*aligné*
mate	*mat*
a move	*un tour*
my / your move	*mon / votre / ton tour*
to move	*bouger / se déplacer*
occupied	*occupé*
opposite	*en face*
powerful	*puissant*
protected	*protégé*
to remove	*déplacer*
safe	*en sécurité / sauf*

CHESS cont.   *LES ECHECS suite*

COMMON WORDS (abc) cont.   *LES MOTS USUELS suite.*

to take	*prendre*
shielded	*protégé (à l'aide d'un bouclier)*
taken	*pris*
threatened	*menacé*
unoccupied	*inoccupé*
unprotected	*non-protegé*
white	*blanc*

DRAUGHTS   *LES DAMES*

The Pieces	*Les Pions*
black	*noir*
white	*blanc*
red	*rouge*

Rules for Draughts	*Les Règles pour les Dames*
• A game for two players	• *Une jeu pour deux joueurs*
• Each player has twelve pieces.	• *Chaque joueur a douze pions*
• One player has all white pieces.	• *Un joueur a tous les pions blancs.*
• The other player has all black pieces.	• *L'autre joueur a tous les pions noirs.*
• Both players move only on the black squares.	• *Les deux joueurs se déplacent sur les cases noires seulement*
• Black always starts.	• *Les noirs commencent toujours. (In France white always starts.)*

RULES FOR DRAUGHTS cont.

LES REGLES POUR LES DAMES suite

- The pieces move forwards diagonally one square at a time.
- A player can take his opponent's pieces by jumping over them provided there is an empty square to land on.
- A player can capture more than one of his opponent's pieces at once.
- When a piece reaches the opposite side of the board it is made into a king / queen (by placing a second piece on top of the first).
- A king / queen can move backwards as well as forwards one square at a time.
- The winner is the one who takes all his/her opponent's pieces or who immobilizes his/her opponent's pieces.

- *Les pions avancent en diagonale, d'une case seulement.*
- *Un joueur peut prendre les pions de son adversaire en sautant par dessus, à condition d'atterrir sur une case vide.*
- *Un joueur peut prendre plus d'un seul pion à la fois à son adversaire.*
- *Quand un pion atteint l'autre côté de l'échiquier, il devient roi / une reine (en plaçant un deuxième pion sur le premier).*
- *Un roi / une reine peut avancer ou reculer d'une case.*
- *Le vainqueur est celui qui prend tous les pions de son adversaire ou immobilise tous les pions de son adversaire.*

DOMINOES

LES DOMINOS

The Pieces	*Les Pièces / les Carrés*
a blank	*un blanc*
a double blank	*un double blanc*
a spot / a pip	*un point*
one / two / three spots	*un / deux / trois points*
four / five / six spots	*quatre / cinq / six points*
a piece with a six and a five	*un carré à six et cinq*
a double six	*un double six*
face up / face down	*face découverte / face cachée*
One end is a..	*Un bout est un....*
The other end is a..	*L'autre bout est un...*

Playing dominoes	*Jouer aux dominos*
• Shall we play dominoes?	• *On joue aux dominos?*
• Have you got a set of dominoes?	• *Avez-vous / as-tu un jeu de dominos?*
• Is it a full set of twenty eight?	• *C'est un jeu complet de vingt-huit?*
• Turn the pieces face downwards.	• *Retournez / retourne les carrés.*
• Mix the pieces up.	• *Mélangez / mélange les carrés.*
• Any number of people can play.	• *Le nombre de joueurs est illimité.*
• Draw a piece to see who starts.	• *Tirez un carré pour voir qui commence.*
• The player who draws the highest domino is the first to play.	• *Le joueur qui tire le carré le plus grand commence.*
• Each player then takes it in turn to select one domino until all the dominoes are used up.	• *Les joueurs choisissent chacun leur tour un domino jusqu'à ce qu'il n'en reste plus.*

PLAYING DOMINOES cont.　　*JOUER AUX DOMINOS suite*

- Each player sets his dominoes on edge so that his opponent cannot see his dominoes.

- The first player places a domino face up on the table.

- The second player then has to add one of his dominoes to form a match - i.e. if the first domino played was one with three spots at one end and four spots at the other, the second player must put down a domino with either three or four spots on one side.

- The dominoes are laid short end to short end unless a double is played. Doubles are placed crosswise at right angles to the line of dominoes.

- If a player has no domino that matches either end of the line he has to miss his go.

- The game ends when one player manages to play all his dominoes.

- *Chaque joueur dispose ses dominos de telle façon que ses adversaires ne puissent pas les voir.*

- *Le premier joueur place son domino face contre table.*

- *Le second joueur doit ajouter un domino assorti - c.-à-d. - si le premier domino posé a un côté à trois points et un autre à quatre points, le second joueur doit poser un domino composé soit d'un trois, soit d'un quatre.*

- *Les dominos sont placés en long les uns à la suite des autres, à l'exception des doubles qui se placent verticalement.*

- *Si un joueur n'a pas de domino correspondant à chacun des bouts, il doit passer son tour.*

- *Le jeu est fini quand un joueur a placé tous ses dominos.*

PLAYING DOMINOES cont.   *JOUER AUX DOMINOS suite*

- If at any stage no player can play a domino, everyone counts up the number of spots on their remaining dominoes and the winner is the player with the fewest spots.
- If there is a draw between two players with the same number of spots, the winner is the person with the fewest dominoes.

- *Si aucun des joueurs ne peut plus jouer, chacun compte le nombre de points sur leurs dominos restants et le vainqueur est celui qui a le plus petit nombre de points.*
- *Si deux joueurs sont ex-aequo avec le même nombre de points, le vainqueur est celui qui a le moins de dominos.*

JIGSAW PUZZLES   *LES PUZZLES*

Types of jigsaws	*Les Types de Puzzle*
a one hundred piece puzzle	*un puzzle à cent pièces*
a five hundred piece puzzle	*un puzzle à cinq cent pièces*
a one thousand piece puzzle	*un puzzle à mille pièces*
an easy one	*un facile*
a difficult one	*un difficile*
a pretty one	*un joli*

JIGSAW PUZZLES cont.   *LES PUZZLES suite*

Choosing and starting a jigsaw	***Choisir et commencer un puzzle***
Would you like to do a jigsaw?	*Vous voulez / tu veux faire un puzzle?*
Shall we do a jigsaw together?	*On fait un puzzle ensemble?*
Which one would you like to do?	*Lequel voudriez-vous / voudrais-tu faire?*
Where shall we do it?	*On le fait où?*
Have you got a tray to do it on?	*Avez-vous / as-tu un plateau pour le faire?*
Can we use this table?	*On peut utiliser cette table?*
Turn over all the pieces.	*Retournez / retourne toutes les pièces.*
face up / face down	*face ouverte / face cachée*
Shall we sort out all the edge pieces first?	*On commence par les pièces des bords?*
Have we got the four corner pieces?	*On a les pièces des quatre coins?*
Here is..	*Voici....*
..one corner piece	*..une pièce d'un coin*
Here is another corner piece.	*Voici une pièce d'un autre coin.*
Here's the last corner piece.	*Voici la pièce du dernier coin.*
Shall we sort the pieces out into colour groups?	*On trie les pièces par couleur?*
There is one piece missing.	*Il manque une pièce.*

Finding particular pieces	***Trouver certaines pièces***
Have you seen the piece that goes here?	*Avez-vous / as-tu vu la pièce qui va ici?*
It has two tabs and one indent.	*Elle a deux pattes et un creux.*
It has one straight edge.	*Elle a un côté droit.*
Have you seen a sky piece?	*Avez-vous / as-tu une pièce du ciel?*
Have you seen a piece with yellow flowers on?	*Avez-vous / as-tu une pièce avec des fleurs jaunes?*

JIGSAW PUZZLES cont.   *LES PUZZLES suite*

FINDING PARTICULAR   *TROUVER CERTAINES*
PIECES cont.   *PIECES suite*

I'm looking for a mainly green piece with a bit of red on it.	*Je cherche une pièce centrale verte avec un peu de rouge dessus.*
Try this one.	*Essayez / essaie celle-ci.*
This might fit.	*Celle-ci va peut-être aller.*
It fits.	*Elle va.*
It doesn't fit.	*Elle ne va pas.*

Useful verbs (abc)	*Verbes utiles*
to break it up	*briser*
to carry on	*continuer*
to collect together	*coller*
to find	*trouver*
to finish	*finir*
to get it out	*le / la sortir*
to leave it	*le / la laisser*
to look at the picture	*regarder l'image*
to look for	*chercher*
to put it away	*mettre de côté*
to put a piece on one side	*mettre une pièce d'un côté*
to search for	*rechercher*
to sort	*trier*
to start	*commencer*
to stop	*arrêter*
to try	*essayer*
to turn over	*retourner*

SHORTER GAMES

SNAP

DES JEUX PLUS COURTS

LA BATAILLE

You need: A pack of fifty two cards for two to five players. Two packs of cards for more than five players.	*Il faut:* *Un jeu de cinquante-deux cartes pour deux à cinq joueurs.* *Deux jeux de cartes pour plus de cinq joueurs.*

The Object of the Game To win all the cards.	*Le But du Jeu* *Gagner toutes les cartes.*

How to Play	*Comment Jouer*

- Deal out all the cards face down equally between all players.

- Players must not look at their cards but should keep them in a pile face down in front of them.

- The first player turns over the top card of his pile and places this face up in the middle of the table.

- The next player does the same.

- If any of the players notice that the second card is of the same rank as the one underneath they can shout "Snap!".

- *Distribuez un nombre égal de cartes à chaque joueur, face contre table.*

- *Les joueurs ne doivent pas regarder leurs cartes et doivent les disposer en pile face contre table devant eux.*

- *Le premier joueur retourne la première carte de la pile et la place au milieu de la table, face ouverte.*

- *Le joueur suivant fait la même chose.*

- *Si l'un des joueurs remarque que la seconde carte est identique à celle du dessous, il peut dire "Bataille!"*

SNAP - HOW TO PLAY cont.

LA BATAILLE - COMMENT JOUER suite

- The first person to shout "Snap!" picks up the central pile of cards and adds them, face down, to the bottom of his pile. He then turns over his top card and the game proceeds as before.

- If you lose all your cards you are out of the game.

- *La première personne qui a crié "Bataille!" ramasse la pile centrale et la place au-dessous de sa pile, face contre table. Il retourne ensuite la première carte et le jeu se poursuit.*

- *Si on perd toutes ses cartes, on est éliminé de la partie.*

BEETLE

LE SCARABEE

You need:
Paper and pencils.
A dice and a shaker.
Any number of people can play.

Il faut:
Du papier et un crayon.
Un dés et un shaker.
Le nombre de joueurs est illimité.

How to Play
- The object of the game is to draw a complete beetle.
- The players take it in turns to throw one dice.
- Each person has to throw a six to start because a six means that you can draw the beetle's body.
- Throwing a five means that you can add a head to the body.

Comment Jouer
- *Le but du jeu est de dessiner un scarabée entier.*
- *Les joueurs jettent un dé chacun à leur tour.*
- *Chaque joueur doit faire un six pour commencer car le six permet de dessiner le corps du scarabée.*
- *Jeter un cinq permet d'ajouter une tête.*

BEETLE

LE SCARABEE

HOW TO PLAY cont.

COMMENT JOUER suite

- Throwing a four gives your beetle a leg (a complete beetle needs six legs).

- Throwing a three gives your beetle an eye (two eyes needed).

- Throwing a two gives your beetle an antenna (two needed).

- Throwing a one gives your beetle a tail.

- Eyes and antennae cannot be drawn without first getting a five for a head.

- The first person to complete their beetle wins the game.

- *Jeter un quatre permet d'ajouter un patte (un scarabée complet comporte six pattes).*

- *Jeter un trois permet de dessiner un œil (il faut deux yeux).*

- *Jeter un deux permet de dessiner une antenne (il en faut deux).*

- *Jeter un un permet de dessiner la queue du scarabée.*

- *Il est nécessaire d'obtenir un cinq pour la tête pour dessiner les yeux et les antennes.*

- *La première personne qui obtient un scarabée complet a gagné.*

I SPY

LE JEU DES OBJETS

How to Play	***Comment Jouer***
• Any number can play.	• *Le nombre de joueur est illimité.*
• The first person says:	• *La première personne dit:*
"I spy with my little eye something beginning with…."	***"J'aperçois avec mes petits yeux quelque chose commençant par.."***
• He/she then adds the first letter of an object they can see.	• *Il / elle ajoute ensuite la première lettre d'un objet qu'il / elle voit.*

• The other people have to guess what the word is by asking:
      "Is it a…..?"
	• *Les autres personnes doivent deviner l'objet en demandant:*
	      "Est-ce que c'est un(e)..?

• and then adding a word beginning with the chosen letter.	• *et en énonçant un mot commençant par la lettre choisie.*
• The person who guesses the object correctly takes over and becomes the next person to spy a new object.	• *La personne qui a deviné l'objet a gagné et c'est à elle d'apercevoir un nouvel objet.*

NOUGHTS AND CROSSES

LE JEU DU MORPION

You need:	*Il faut:*
Paper and two pencils.	*Du papier et deux crayons.*
Two people to play.	*Deux joueurs.*

Useful expressions	*Expressions utiles*
Draw a noughts and crosses frame.	*Dessinez un tableau à morpion.*
Are you going to be noughts?	*Vous serez / tu seras les ronds?*
I'll be noughts.	*Je serai les ronds.*
You can be crosses.	*Vous pouvez / tu peux être les croix.*
You start.	*Vous commencez / tu commences.*
It's my turn to start.	*C'est à moi de commencer.*
You have to get three noughts or three crosses in a row.	*Il faut arriver à avoir trois ronds ou trois croix dans une même rangée.*
The rows can be horizontal, vertical or diagonal.	*Les rangées peuvent être horizontales, verticales ou diagonales.*
I've won / You've won.	*J'ai / vous avez / tu as gagné.*
to win	*gagner*
to lose	*perdre*
Shall we play again?	*On rejoue?*
Shall we play the best of three?	*On fait la belle?*

OUTDOOR GAMES

LES JEUX D'EXTERIEUR

SKIPPING
to skip
a skipping rope

LE SAUT A LA CORDE
sauter
une corde à sauter

HOP SCOTCH
to hop
to turn around

LA MARELLE
sauter (à cloche-pied)
se retourner

HIDE AND SEEK
Cover your eyes.
Don't peep.
Count to a hundred.
Coming ready or not.
to hide / to look for / to find

CACHE-CACHE
Fermez / ferme les yeux
Ne regardez pas / ne regarde pas.
Comptez / compte jusqu'à cent.
J'ai fini.
se cacher / chercher / trouver

A TREASURE HUNT
Divide into teams.
Will you be on my team?

Do it in pairs.
Here is a clue.
Read the clue.
What does it say?
What does that mean, do you think?
to look for
to find
to be unable to find
to win
to get the prize

LA CHASSE AU TRESOR
Faites des équipes.
Vous serez / tu seras être dans mon équipe?
On le fait par équipe de deux.
Voici un indice.
Lisez / lis l'indice.
Que dit-il?
Cela veut dire quoi, vous pensez / tu penses?
chercher
trouver
être incapable de trouver
gagner
gagner le prix

OUTDOOR GAMES *LES JEUX D'EXTERIEUR*

ROLLER SKATING	*LE ROLLER-SKATE*
a pair of roller skates	*une paire de patins à roulette*
roller boots	*des roller-skates*
roller blades	*des lames de roller-skates*
Have you got any roller skates?	*Vous avez / tu as des patins à roulette?*
May I borrow your roller skates?	*Je peux emprunter vos / tes patins à roulette?*
to put on	*mettre*
to lace up	*lacer*
to adjust	*ajuster*
to balance	*équilibrer*
to hold on to something	*se retenir à quelque chose*
to fall over	*tomber*
to take off	*décoller*

FLYING A KITE	*SE DEPLOYER LES CERFS-VOLANT*
a kite	*un cerf-volant*
a string	*une corde*
to hold on to	*tenir*
to rise up	*s'élever*
to fall	*tomber*
to swoop	*descendre en piquée*
the wind	*le vent*
There isn't enough wind.	*Il n'y a pas assez de vent.*
It's too windy.	*Il y a trop de vent.*

OTHER ACTIVITES	*AUTRES ACTIVITES*
to do cartwheels	*faire la roue*
to do handstands	*faire le poirier*
to climb trees	*grimper aux arbres*

PUTTING A TENT UP	*INSTALLER UNE TENTE*
Have you got a tent?	*Avez-vous / as-tu une tente?*
Shall we try to put it up?	*On essaie de l'installer?*
Can you remember how to do it?	*Vous vous souvenez / tu te souviens comment faire?*
Would your mother / father help?	*Votre / ta mère / votre / ton père pourrait nous aider?*
to put up the tent pole	*mettre le mât*
to put the frame together	*installer l'armature*
to throw over the canvas	*mettre la toile de tente*
to hammer in the pegs	*planter les piquets*
to tighten the guy ropes	*tendre les cordes*
to put down a ground sheet	*mettre une bâche*
to do up the zip	*remonter la fermeture éclair*
to unzip the door flap	*ouvrir la fermeture éclair*
to spend a night in the tent	*passer une nuit dans la tente*
a torch	*une torche*
to switch on / switch off	*allumer / éteindre*
to get cold	*avoir froid*
to go inside	*rentrer dans*

GARDEN PLAY EQUIPMENT   *LES JEUX DE JARDIN*

SWINGING	*LA BALANÇOIRE*
a swing	*une balançoire*
to swing	*se balancer*
to give someone a push	*pousser quelqu'un*
Will you push me, please?	*Vous pouvez / tu peux me pousser, s'il te plaît?*
Do you want a push?	*Vous voulez / tu veux que je vous / te pousse?*
To stand up	*se mettre debout*
to sit down	*s'asseoir*
to go very high	*se balancer très haut*
to jump off	*sauter*

GARDEN PLAY EQUIPMENT cont.   *LES JEUX DE JARDIN suite*

A SEE-SAW	***UN JEU DE BASCULE***
to see-saw	*basculer*
to go up and down	*monter et descendre*
to balance	*rester en équilibre*
to bump	*cogner*

A SLIDE	***UN TOBOGGAN***
to climb the ladder	*grimper l'échelle*
to sit down	*s'asseoir*
to slide down	*glisser*
feet first / head first	*les pieds en avant / la tête en avant*
to have another go	*recommencer*

A CLIMBING FRAME	***UNE CAGE A POULES***
a ladder	*une échelle*
to climb	*grimper*
a monkey bar	*une barre horizontale*
to hang from	*se pendre de*
to hang upside down	*faire le cochon pendu*

COMPUTERS
LES ORDINATEURS

TYPES OF COMPUTER	*LES TYPES D'ORDINATEUR*
a personal computer	*un P.C.*
a desktop computer	*un ordinateur de bureau*
a laptop computer	*un ordinateur portable*
a network computer	*un réseau*

HARDWARE	*HARDWARE / LE MATERIEL*
the monitor	*le moniteur*
the screen	*l'écran*
the keyboard - see 133-136	*le clavier*

THE MOUSE	*LA SOURIS*
to click	*cliquer*
to double-click	*cliquer deux fois*
to right click / to left click	*cliquer sur le bouton (droit / gauche)*
a mouse mat	*un tapis de souris*
a joystick	*une manette de jeu / un joystick*

A TOWER	*UNE TOUR*
the CD-ROM drive	*l'unité de CD-ROM*
the floppy disk drive	*l'unité de disquette*
the tape drive	*l'unité de cassette*

A MODEM	*UN MODEM*
a fax	*un fax*
e mail	*courrier électronique / e mail*
an e mail address	*une adresse de courrier électronique / adresse e mail*
to send	*envoyer*
to receive	*recevoir*

COMPUTERS cont.   *LES ORDINATEURS suite*

THE SPEAKERS	*LES HAUT-PARLEURS*
multi-media	*multimédia*
to turn up / down	*augmenter/ diminuer*

THE PRINTER	*L'IMPRIMANTE*
a colour printer	*une imprimante-couleur*
a black and white printer	*une imprimante noir-et-blanc*
a print preview	*aperçu avant impression*
to zoom in / out	*agrandissement/ réduction*
to print out	*imprimer*
all pages	*toutes les pages*
odd / even pages	*page impaire/ paire*
the current page	*la page courante*
selected pages	*pages sélectionnées*
three copies	*trois copies (f)*

THE MEMORY	*LA MEMOIRE*
ROM	*ROM / MEM*
RAM	*RAM / MEV*
How much memory does your computer have?	*Combien de mémoire a votre/ton ordinateur?*
My computer doesn't have enough memory.	*Mon ordinateur n'a pas assez de mémoire.*

THE SOFTWARE	*LE LOGICIEL*
system software	*logiciel de base*
application software	*logiciel applicatif / Progiciel*
a floppy disk	*une disquette*
a CD-ROM	*un CD-ROM*
a programme	*un programme*

COMPUTERS - THE SOFTWARE cont.

LES ORDINATEURS - LE LOGICIEL suite

a computer game (See page 139-144)	*un jeu-vidéo / jeu sur ordinateur*
educational software	*logiciel éducatif/ didacticiel*
word processing software	*logiciel de traitement de texte*
database software	*logiciel de bases de données*
desktop publishing software	*logiciel de Publication Assistée par Ordinateur*
draw / paint software	*logiciel de dessin*
a typing course	*des cours de dactylographie*
an encyclopaedia	*une encyclopédie*
art gallery software	*logiciel d'imagerie*

THE KEYBOARD

LE CLAVIER

TYPING	***TAPER/ DACTYLOGRAPHIER***
to touchtype	*taper au toucher*
speed	*vitesse (f)*
to be slow	*être lent*
to be quick	*être rapide*
accuracy	*précision (f)*
to make mistakes	*faire des fautes (f)*
to be very accurate	*être précis*
to type with two fingers	*taper avec deux doigts (m)*

THE KEYS

LES TOUCHES (f)

The Alphabet	***L'Alphabet (m)***
capital letters	*lettres capitales (f)*
lower case letters	*lettres*
caps lock	*le verrouillage-majuscule*

THE KEYBOARD cont.   *LE CLAVIER suite*

Punctuation	*La Ponctuation*
a full stop	*un point*
a comma	*une virgule*
a semi-colon	*un point-virgule*
a colon	*deux points*
an exclamation mark	*un point d'exclamation*
a question mark	*un point d'interrogation*
inverted commas	*des guillemets*
an apostrophe	*une apostrophe*
brackets	*des parenthèses*

Numeric keys	*Touches numériques*
addition	*addition*
subtraction	*soustraction*
multiplication	*multiplication*
division	*division*
brackets	*parenthèses*
a decimal point	*une virgule décimale*
the equals sign	*un signe "égal"*
the ampersand	*l'esperluète*

The function keys	*Les touches de fonction*
the enter key	*la touche "entrée"*
the return key	*la touche "retour"*
the tab key	*la touche de tabulation / "tab"*
the shift key	*la touche majuscule / "shift"*
the caps lock key	*le verrouillage des majuscules*
the number lock key	*le verrouillage numérique*
control	*contrôle*
alt	*alt*
escape	*échappement*

THE KEYBOARD cont.   *LE CLAVIER suite*

The edit keys	Les touches d'édition
scroll up / down	faire défiler vers le haut/ vers le bas
scroll left / right	faire défiler à gauche/ à droite
delete	effacer
insert	insérer
home	haut de texte / gauche
end	fin de texte / droite
page up / down	page précédente/ suivante
print screen	écran d'imprimerie

WORD PROCESSING   *TRAITEMENT DE TEXTE*

Entering text	Entrer un texte
a cursor	un curseur
to type	taper
to enter	entrer
to insert	insérer
to overwrite	recouvrir

Editing	Editer
to edit	éditer
to cut	couper
to paste	afficher
to copy	copier
to delete	effacer
to spell-check	vérifier l'orthographe
to indent	indenter
word-wrap	retour à la ligne
to sort text alphabetically	classer alphabétiquement

WORD PROCESSING cont.

TRAITEMENT DE TEXTE suite

Formatting	***Formatage/ mise au format***
to format	*formater/ mettre au format*
the font	*la fonte/ la police*
font style / font size	*style de police/ taille de police*
colour	*couleur*
italics	*italique*
bold	*gras*
underlined	*souligné*
highlighted	*mis en relief*

The page set-up	***L'assemblage***
a page break	*arrêt de défilement des pages*
page layout view	*vue de la mise en page*
to set the margins	*régler les marges*
headers and footers	*les en-tête et les notes en bas de page*

Paragraphs	***Paragraphes***
single / double line spacing	*interligne simple/ double*
left / right indents	*marque de retrait gauche/ droite*
to align	*aligner*
the tabs	*les tabulations*

Justification	***Justification***
right / left justification	*cadrage droit/ gauche*
to justify both sides	*cadrer des deux côtés*
justification on / off	*cadrage "on"/ "off"*
to centre	*centrer*

The tools	***Les outils***
a tool bar	*une barre d'outils*
to word count	*compter les mots*
a dictionary	*un dictionnaire*
the spell-checker	*vérificateur d'orthographe*
a thesaurus	*un thésaurus*

WORD PROCESSING cont.

TRAITEMENT DE TEXTE suite

File management	*Gestion de fichier*
a file	*un fichier*
to open	*ouvrir*
to close	*fermer*
to save	*sauvegarder*
to name	*nommer*
to re-name	*renommer*

THE INTERNET

INTERNET

The Superhighway	*La Super-autoroute de l'information*
The World Wide Web	*Le World-Wide-Web*

Getting on to the Internet	*Se brancher sur Internet*
an access provider	*un modem*
an online service provider	*un prestataire de service on-line*
an e mail address	*une adresse électronique*
a joining fee	*un droit d'inscription*
to pay a subscription	*s'abonner*
a subscriber	*un abonné*
to register	*s'inscrire*

Browsing	*Naviguer*
to log in	*se connecter*
to use your password	*utiliser le mot de passe*
to browse	*fureter*
a web browser	*un butineur sur le Web*
to surf	*naviguer / surfer*
an interest group	*un groupe d'intérêt*
a newsgroup	*un groupe d'information*
an information source	*une source d'information*

THE INTERNET cont.   *INTERNET suite*

hypertext	*hypertexte*
to click on	*cliquer*
to return to the home page	*retourner à la page de départ*
to download information	*téléchanger une information*
to join a mailing list	*s'inscrire à une liste de diffusion*
to prepare a message	*préparer un message*
on-line	*en ligne*
off-line	*hors ligne*

Internet jargon	*le Jargon Internet*
Gopher	*Gopher*
Archie	*Archie*
netiquette	*nétiquette/ néthique*
to flame someone	*descendre quelqu'un en flamme*
virtual reality	*réalité virtuelle*
a Cyber café	*un Cyber café*
a Cyber pub	*un Cyber pub*
Cyberspace	*Cyberespace*
Sig (Signature file)	*Fichier de signature*
Usenet	*sous-réseau Internet*
Winsock	*interface logiciel réseau*

Smileys	*les Smileys*
a smiley / an emoticon	*un Smiley/ une touche d'affection*
☺ happy	*merci*
;-) winking	*clin d'oeil*
:-p tongue in cheek	*ironiquement*

COMPUTER GAMES
LES JEUX VIDEO

GENERAL EXPRESSIONS	*EXPRESSIONS GENERALES*
Would you like to play on the computer?	*Voulez-vous / veux-tu jouer avec l'ordinateur?*
Do you have any good computer games?	*Avez-vous / as-tu des bons jeux sur ordinateur?*
I have a Game Gear.	*J'ai un Game Gear.*
I have a Super Nintendo.	*J'ai un Super Nintendo.*
Does it run on batteries or mains?	*Est-ce qu'il marche sur piles ou sur le secteur?*
Have you a mains adaptor?	*Avez-vous / as-tu un adapteur?*
May I have a turn now?	*Je peux jouer maintenant?*
You've had a long go.	*Tu as eu un long tour.*
How many can play at once?	*On peut jouer à combien en même temps?*
This game is for one / two players only.	*Ce jeu est pour un seul/ deux joueurs seulement.*
I'd like to get it - was it expensive?	*J'aimerais bien l'avoir - c'est cher?*

STARTING A GAME	*COMMENCER UNE PARTIE*
Where is the on / off button?	*Où est le bouton commutateur?*
How do you load the game?	*Comment change-t-on le jeu?*
You type in the word…	*Vous tapez / tu tapes le mot...*
Then you press this..	*Ensuite vous appuyez / tu appuies ce...*
What's the password?	*Quel est le mot de passe?*
The password is..	*Le mot de passe est...*
What's the aim of the game?	*Quel est le but du jeu?*
Explain to me what happens.	*Expliquez / explique-moi ce qu'il se passe.*
Are there any secret passageways or hidden rooms?	*Est-ce qu'il y a des passages secrets ou des chambres secrètes?*

COMPUTER GAMES cont.   *LES JEUX VIDEO suite*

THE CONTROLS	*LES COMMANDES*
Do you use a joystick or a mouse or special keys?	*On utilise un manche ou une souris ou des touches spéciales?*
You right click / left click the joystick / the mouse.	*Vous cliquez / tu cliques le joystick / la manette de jeu / la souris vers la droite/ la gauche.*
You shoot with the joystick.	*Vous tirez / tu tires avec le joystick / la manette de jeu.*
Which keys do you use?	*Quelles touches utilise-t-on?*
What do the different keys do?	*Que font les différentes touches?*
These keys make you go up / down.	*Les touches vous / te font avancer/ reculer*
These keys make you go right / left.	*Les touches vous / te font aller vers la droite/ la gauche.*
What does the space bar do?	*Que fait la barre d'espacement?*
The space bar makes you jump.	*La barre d'espacement vous / te fait sauter.*
Can you pause this game?	*Est-ce qu'on peut interrompre ce jeu?*
You pause it like this..	*Vous l'interrompez / tu l'interromps comme ceci...*

The Volume	*le Volume*
How do you turn the volume up / down?	*Comment augmente/ baisse-t-on le volume?*
You increase / decrease the volume like this.	*On augmente/ baisse le volume comme ceci.*
It's a bit loud.	*C'est un peu fort.*
It's disturbing people.	*Ça dérange les gens.*
It's too quiet.	*C'est trop bas.*
I can't hear it properly.	*Je ne l'entends pas bien.*

COMPUTER GAMES cont.   *LES JEUX VIDEO suite*

SCORING   *LES POINTS*

Lives and bonus points	*Les vies et les bonus*
How many lives do you have to start with?	*Vous devez / tu dois commencer avec combien de vies?*
I've just lost a life.	*Je viens de perdre une vie.*
I've got three lives left.	*Il me reste trois vies.*
How do you get bonuses?	*Comment on obtient des bonus?*
You have to pick up these things to score extra.	*Il faut ramasser ces choses pour obtenir plus de points.*

Time limits	*Les temps-limite*
Is there a time limit?	*Est-ce qu'il y a un temps-limite?*
No, there's no need to hurry.	*Non, on n'a pas besoin de se presser.*
Yes, the time limit is five minutes.	*Oui, le temps-limite est de cinq minutes.*

Level of difficulty	*Niveau de difficulté*
Have you ever managed to finish this game?	*Vous avez / tu as déjà réussi à finir ce jeu?*
No, it's very difficult.	*Non, il est très difficile.*
Yes, but it takes a lot of practice.	*Oui, mais il demande de la pratique.*
What level have you got to?	*A quel niveau êtes-vous / es-tu arrivé?*
I've got to the first / second / third level.	*Je suis arrivé(e) au niveau un/deux/trois.*
I've got to the last / next to the last level.	*Je suis arrivé(e) au dernier/ à l'avant-dernier niveau.*

COMPUTER GAMES cont.   *LES JEUX VIDEO suite*

Level of difficulty cont.	*Niveau de difficulté suite*
Does it speed up at each level?	*Est-ce qu'il accélère à chaque niveau?*
It gets much quicker at the next level.	*Il va beaucoup plus vite au niveau suivant.*
You get a bonus life at each level.	*On gagne un vie à chaque niveau.*

What's your score?	***Quel est votre / ton score?***
What's your total now?	*Quel est votre / ton total maintenant?*
What did you score last time?	*Quel était votre / ton précédent score?*
What's the best you've ever scored?	*Quel est votre / ton meilleur score?*

USEFUL VERBS (abc)	***VERBES UTILES***
to accelerate	*accélérer*
to attack	*attaquer*
to avoid	*éviter*
to chase	*poursuivre*
to click	*cliquer*
to climb	*grimper*
to collect	*remporter/ accumuler*
to concentrate	*se concentrer*
to decrease	*diminuer*
to defend	*défendre*
to die	*mourir*
to duck	*esquiver*
to enter	*entrer*
to exit	*sortir*
to fly	*voler*
to follow	*suivre*
to get a bonus	*avoir un bonus*

COMPUTER GAMES - USEFUL VERBS cont.

LES JEUX VIDEO - VERBES UTILES suite

to hide	*se cacher*
to increase	*augmenter*
to insert	*insérer*
to jump	*sauter*
to kill	*tuer*
to leave	*partir*
to live	*vivre*
to load	*charger*
to lose	*perdre*
to lose concentration	*perdre sa concentration*
to pause	*interrompre*
to press	*appuyer*
to print	*imprimer*
to remember	*se souvenir*
to score	*marquer*
to shoot	*tirer*
to slow down	*ralentir*
to speed up	*accélérer*
to surprise	*surprendre*
to switch on / off	*allumer/ éteindre*
to take	*prendre*
to throw	*lancer*
to turn around	*tourner*
to type	*taper*
to win	*gagner*

DIRECTION WORDS	*LES ADVERBES DE DIRECTION*
in / on	*dans/ dessus*
over / under	*par-dessus/ par-dessous*
round / through	*autour/ à travers*
up / down	*en haut/ en bas*
before / after	*avant/ après*
left / right	*gauche/ droite*
near / far away	*près/ loin*

COMPUTER GAMES cont.   *LES JEUX VIDEO suite*

DESCRIPTIVE WORDS (abc)	*LES ADJECTIFS DESCRIPTIFS*
clumsy	*maladroit*
complicated	*compliqué*
correct	*correcte*
dangerous	*dangereux*
difficult	*difficile*
easy	*facile*
exposed	*découvert*
false	*faux*
flashing	*clignotant*
hidden	*caché*
highest	*le plus haut*
long	*long*
lowest	*le plus bas*
quick	*rapide*
round	*rond*
safe	*sain et sauf*
secret	*secret*
short	*court*
skilful	*habile*
slow	*lent*
tense	*tendu*
vulnerable	*vulnérable*

TELEVISION, VIDEO & RADIO
LA TELEVISION, LA VIDEO & LA RADIO

BASIC VOCABULARY	*VOCABULAIRE DE BASE*
a television	*une télévision*
the remote control	*une télécommande*
to point	*diriger*
a video player	*un magnétoscope*
a video cassette	*une cassette vidéo*
a video game	*un jeu vidéo*
a radio	*une radio*

WATCHING TELEVISION	*REGARDER LA TELEVISION*
Would you like to watch T.V.?	*Vous voulez / tu veux regarder la télé?*
What's on the television at the moment?	*Qu'est-ce qu'il y a à la télévision en ce moment?*
Is there anything good on the television?	*Il y a quelque chose de bien à la télévision?*
What's on the other channels?	*Qu'est-ce qu'il y a sur les autres chaînes?*
Shall we turn over?	*On change de chaîne?*
We have this programme in my country.	*On a cette émission dans mon pays.*
Do you like..?	*Vous aimez / tu aimes?*
Shall we stop watching television?	*On arrête de regarder la télévision?*
My family want to watch something else now.	*Ma famille veut regarder quelque chose d'autre maintenant.*
Shall we do something else instead?	*On fait quelque chose d'autre?*

TELEVISION cont   *TELEVISION suite*

THE CONTROLS FOR T.V., VIDEO AND RADIO (abc)	*LES COMMANDES POUR LA TELE, LA VIDEO ET LA RADIO*
the aerial point	*la prise d'antenne*
a channel	*une chaîne*
a counter	*un compteur*
counter reset	*un compteur de remise à zéro*
eject / to eject	*éjection/ éjecter*
fast forward / to fast forward	*avance rapide/ avancer rapidement*
indicator light / to flash	*le voyant / clignoter*
on / off	*allumé(e)/ éteint(e)*
pause / to pause	*pause/ mettre sur "pause"*
play / to play	*en marche/ marcher*
to press a button	*appuyer sur un bouton*
programme / to programme	*programme/ programmer*
record / to record	*enregistrement/ enregistrer*
to repeat	*rediffuser*
to reset	*remettre à zéro*
rewind / to rewind	*rembobinage/ rembobiner*
search	*chercher*
slow	*ralenti*
the speed	*la vitesse / la rapidité*
a switch / to flick a switch	*un bouton / actionner le bouton*
the timer	*le minuteur*
to tune	*régler*
to use the remote control	*utiliser la télécommande*
video / to insert	*cassette-vidéo/ insérer*
video in / video out	*cassette insérée/ cassette expulsée*

TELEVISION - USEFUL EXPRESSIONS cont

TELEVISION - EXPRESSIONS UTILES suite

Turning it on and off
How do you turn it on / off?
You turn it on / off here.

Allumer/ éteindre
Comment on l'allume/ l'éteint
On l'allume/ l'éteint ici.

Volume control
It's a bit too loud.
How do you turn it up / down?
I can't hear it properly.

La commande-son
C'est un peu trop fort.
Comment on l'augmente/ le diminue?
Je n'entends pas bien.

Playing a video
How do you insert the video?

The video needs rewinding.
How do you rewind it ?
How do you fast forward it?
Can you pause it for a moment, please?
How do you pause / eject it?

Regarder une cassette vidéo
Comment met-on la cassette vidéo?
Il faut rembobiner la cassette.
Comment on la rembobine?
Comment peut-on l'accélérer?
On peut la mettre sur "pause" un instant, s'il vous plaît?
Comment on la met sur pause/ l'éjecte?

Recording
How do you record something?
Is it recording properly?

Are you sure you are recording the right programme?

Can you programme the video to record while we are out?

Shall we record it and watch it some other tine?
Would you like to watch that programme we recorded?

Enregistrer
Comment on enregistre quelque chose?
Est-ce que l'enregistrement marche bien?
Vous êtes / tu es sûr que vous enregistrez / tu enregistres la bonne émission?
Vous pouvez / tu peux programmer l'enregistrement pendant que nous serons sortis?
Et si on l'enregistrait et le / la regardait une autre fois?
Vous aimeriez / tu aimerais regarder cette émission que l'on a enregistrée?

RECORDING ON VIDEOS

ENREGISTRER SUR UNE CASSETTE VIDEO

How does the remote control work?	*Comment marche la télécommande?*
Do you have Video Plus programming?	*Avez-vous / as-tu un programme Vidéo Plus?*
The tape has come to an end.	*La cassette est finie.*
Have you got another tape?	*Avez-vous / as-tu une autre cassette?*

Tuning the radio	***Régler la radio***
How do you tune the radio?	*Comment règle-t-on la radio?*
Can you find me the local radio station?	*Pouvez-vous / peux-tu me trouver la station de radio locale?*
Which is the best pop music programme?	*Quelle est la meilleure émission de musique pop?*
What wavelength do you tune it to?	*On la règle sur quelle fréquence?*

DIFFERENT TYPES OF T.V. PROGRAMMES

LES DIFFERENTS TYPES D'EMISSION DE TELEVISION

an advertisement	*une publicité / une pub*
a cartoon	*un dessin animé*
a chat show	*un talk-show*
a discussion programme	*un débat*
a documentary	*un documentaire*
an education programme	*une émission éducative*
a film	*un film*
a party political broadcast	*un débat politique*
a quiz	*un jeux*
a report	*un reportage*
a situation comedy	*une série humoristique / une comédie*
a sports programme	*une émission sportive*
a thriller	*un film à suspense*

DIFFERENT TYPES OF T.V. PROGRAMMES cont.

LES DIFFERENTS TYPES D'EMISSION DE TELEVISION suite

Soap operas	*Les séries télévisées*
Which soaps do you have in your country?	*Quelles séries avez-vous / as-tu dans votre pays?*
We watch this at home.	*On regarde cela chez nous.*
We are further behind / ahead of you.	*On est en retard/ avance sur vous.*

The news	*Les informations/ actualités*
the news headlines	*les titres de l'actualité*
I'd like to watch the headlines, please.	*J'aimerais regarder les titres s'il vous plaît / s'il te plaît.*
Did you see the news?	*As-tu/ avez-vous vu les informations?*
What was on the news?	*Qu'est-ce qu'il y avait aux informations?*
Was there any news about..?	*Il y a eu un reportage sur....?*
I didn't hear the news today.	*Je n'ai pas entendu les informations aujourd'hui.*
The news was boring / depressing / appalling.	*L'actualité était ennuyeuse/ déprimante/ horrible.*
What has happened?	*Que s'est il passé?*
Was there anything interesting on the news?	*Est-ce qu'il y avait quelque chose d'intéressant aux actualités?*

DIFFERENT TYPES OF T.V. PROGRAMMES cont.	*LES DIFFERENTS TYPES D'EMISSION DE TELEVISION suite*

The weather forecast	*La météo*
Did you hear the weather forecast?	*Avez-vous / as-tu entendu la météo?*
It's going to be….(abc)	*Il va...*

breezy	*frais*	rainy	*pleuvoir*
cloudy	*nuageux*	showery	*pleuvoir à verse*
cold	*faire froid*	snowy	*neiger*
freezing	*geler*	sunny	*faire beau / ensoleillé*
hot	*chaud*	thundery	*orageux*
icy	*glacé*	windy	*y avoir du vent / venté*
minus five	*faire moins cinq*		
When?		**Quand?**	
Later	*plus tard*	overnight	*pendant la nuit*
this morning	*ce matin*	tomorrow	*demain*
this afternoon	*cet après-midi*	the day after	*après-demain*
this evening	*ce soir*	next week	*la semaine prochaine*
tonight	*cette nuit*	soon	*bientôt*

THE VIDEO HIRE SHOP
LE MAGASIN DE LOCATION DE VIDEO

USEFUL EXPRESSIONS	*EXPRESSIONS UTILES*
Shall we go and get a video out?	*On se loue une cassette vidéo?*
Have you got your ticket?	*Vous avez / tu as votre /ta carte?*
You have to show your ticket.	*Il faut montrer votre / ta carte.*
Can you get any film out on your ticket?	*On peut louer n'importe quel film avec la carte?*
Are there some films you can't get out on your ticket?	*Y a-t-il des films qu'on ne peut pas louer avec la carte?*
How much does it cost to hire this video?	*Combien ça coûte de louer cette cassette?*
When does it have to be back by?	*Quand doit-on la rendre?*
How many videos can we get out?	*Combien de cassettes peut-on louer?*
What do you want to watch?	*Que voulez-vous / veux-tu regarder?*
I'd like to see this one.	*J'aimerais voir celui-là.*
Is this one good?	*Il / elle est bien celui-ci / celle-là?*
Is it very frightening?	*Cela fait très peur?*
Where is the comedy / thriller / cartoon / horror section?	*Où est la section "comédies" / "films à suspense" / "dessins animés" / "films d'horreur"?*
Where are the new releases?	*Où sont les nouvelles sorties?*
Is it out on video yet?	*C'est déjà sorti en vidéo?*
When is it going to be out on video?	*Quand sortira-t-il en vidéo?*
I've got that one on video at home.	*J'ai déjà la cassette à la maison.*

MUSIC
MUSIQUE

LISTENING TO MUSIC	***ECOUTER DE LA MUSIQUE***
HI FI STEREO SYSTEM	***LA CHAÎNE-STEREO***

A Compact Disc (C.D.) player	***Un lecteur-C.D.***
to play	*marcher*

A tape deck	***La platine à cassette***
a cassette tape	*une cassette*
to record on	*enregistrer sur*
to record over	*enregistrer par dessus*
to erase	*effacer*
to rewind	*rembobiner*
to fast forward	*accélérer*
to pause	*mettre sur "pause"*

A record turntable	***un tourne-disque / une platine***
a record	*un disque*
a short playing record	*un quarante-cinq tours*
a single	*un single*
a long playing record (an L.P.)	*un trente-trois tours*
a track	*une bande / une plage*
a stylus	*une point de lecture*
a scratch	*une rayure*
an old seventy eight	*un vieux soixante-dix-huit tour*

LISTENING TO MUSIC cont.

ECOUTER DE LA MUSIQUE suite

SOUND REPRODUCTION	*LA REPRODUCTION SONORE*
the amplifier	*les amplificateurs*
the speakers	*les haut-parleurs*
the headphones	*le casque*
the sound quality	*la qualité sonore*
to adjust	*régler*
the volume	*le volume*
the bass / the treble	*les basses / les aigus*
the balance	*la balance*
poor	*pauvre*
good	*bonne*
excellent	*excellente*
true	*vraie*
stereophonic	*stéréophonique*
quadrophonic	*quadrophonique*

AM / FM RADIO	*RADIO AM / FM*
the tuner	*le bouton de réglage*
to tune in	*régler*
to be out of tune	*n'être pas réglé*
to retune	*régler encore*
to crackle	*grésiller*
the band	*la bande*
the wavelength	*la longueur d'onde*

LISTENING TO MUSIC cont.

ECOUTER DE LA MUSIQUE suite

USEFUL VERBS AND COMMANDS (abc)	*VERBES UTILES ET COMMANDES*
to adjust the controls	*régler les commandes*
to decrease	*diminuer*
to erase	*effacer*
to fast forward	*accélérer*
to increase	*augmenter*
to listen	*écouter*
to pause	*mettre sur "pause"*
to play	*marcher / jouer*
to programme	*programmer*
to record	*enregistrer*
to record on	*enregistrer sur*
to record over	*enregistrer par dessus*
to repeat	*rediffuser*
to replay	*rejouer*
to retune	*régler encore*
to rewind	*rembobiner*
to skip a track	*sauter une plage*
to switch off	*éteindre*
to tune in	*régler*
to turn down	*baisser*
to turn on	*allumer*
to turn up	*monter*

LISTENING TO MUSIC	*ECOUTER DE LA MUSIQUE*
Would you like to listen to some music?	*Vous aimeriez / tu aimerais écouter de la musique?*
Shall we go and listen in my room?	*On va dans ma chambre écouter de la musique?*
What sort of music do you like?	*Quel genre de musique aimez-vous / aimes-tu?*

LISTENING TO MUSIC cont.

ECOUTER DE LA MUSIQUE suite

What would you like to listen to?	*Qu'est-ce que vous aimeriez / tu aimerais écouter?*
What's your favourite group?	*Quel est votre / ton groupe préféré?*
Who's your favourite singer?	*Quel est votre / ton chanteur préféré?*
What's number one in your country at the moment?	*Qui est numéro un dans votre / ton pays en ce moment?*
Did this stereo system cost a lot?	*Cette chaîne a coûté cher?*
It's very good reproduction.	*Elle a une très bonne reproduction.*
The quality of this recording isn't all that good.	*La qualité de cet enregistrement n'est pas si bon.*
It was recorded live.	*Il a été enregistré en direct.*
Is this group popular in your country?	*Est-ce que ce groupe est célèbre dans votre / ton pays?*
I've never heard of them before.	*Je n'avais jamais entendu parler d'eux avant.*
I play in a group.	*Je joue dans un groupe.*
I'm the lead singer / guitarist / drummer.	*Je suis le chanteur / guitariste / batteur.*
We formed a group a year ago.	*On a formé un groupe il y a un an.*

I LIKE..		**J'AIME**	
classical	*le classique*	pop	*le pop*
folk	*le folk*	rap	*le rap*
inde	*l'Indi*	reggae	*le reggae*
jazz	*le jazz*	soul	*la soul*
New Age	*le New Age*		

MUSIC LESSONS AND PRACTICE
COURS DE MUSIQUE ET PRATIQUE

MUSIC LESSONS	*LES COURS DE MUSIQUE*
a music teacher	*un professeur de musique*
a piano lesson	*un cours de piano*
How long have you had piano lessons?	*Depuis combien de temps prenez-vous / prends-tu des cours?*
I am only a beginner.	*Je suis seulement débutant.*
I've been learning for three years.	*J'apprends depuis trois ans.*

THE PIANO	*LE PIANO*
an upright piano	*un piano droit*
a grand piano	*un piano à queue*
Would it be O.K. if I played your piano?	*Ça ne vous dérange pas si je joue sur votre piano?*
Am I disturbing anyone?	*Je dérange quelqu'un?*
to put on the practice pedal	*utiliser la pédale d'exercice*
the loud pedal	*la pédale forte*
the soft pedal	*la pédale douce*
the piano stool	*le tabouret*
Is the stool the right height?	*Le tabouret est-il à la bonne hauteur?*
How do you make it a little higher / lower?	*Comment le hausse-t-on / le baisse-t-on?*
to raise	*hausser*
to lower	*baisser*
to adjust	*ajuster / régler*
a metronome	*un métronome*

MUSIC LESSONS AND PRACTICE cont.

COURS DE MUSIQUE ET PRATIQUE suite

THE VIOLIN	LE VIOLON
a violin case	*une boîte à violon*
a bow	*un archet*
a string	*une corde*
to tune the violin	*accorder le violon*
It sounds a bit out of tune.	*Il sonne un peu faux.*
Can you help me to tune it properly?	*Pouvez-vous / peux-tu m'aider à l'accorder, s'il vous plaît?*
to break a string	*casser une corde*
a music stand	*un pupitre à musique*
a music case	*un boîte à instrument de musique*

MUSIC PRACTICE	LA PRATIQUE MUSICALE
to practise the piano	*pratiquer le piano*
to practise one's pieces	*pratiquer ses morceaux*
to practise one's scales	*faire ses gammes*
Do you mind if I do my piano practice now?	*Ça vous ennuie si je pratique mon piano maintenant?*
I haven't done enough practice.	*Je n'ai pas fais assez d'exercices.*
I am supposed to do half an hour a day.	*En principe, je dois pratiquer une demi-heure par jour.*

EXAMINATIONS	LES EXAMENS
Do you take music exams?	*Vous passez / tu passes des examens de musique?*
What grade are you up to now?	*Vous êtes / tu es à quel niveau, maintenant?*
Which grade are you taking next?	*Vous choisirez / tu choisiras quel niveau ensuite?*
I failed my last exam.	*J'ai raté mon dernier examen.*
I got a pass / merit / distinction.	*J'ai eu mention passable / bien / très bien.*

READING
LA LECTURE

BOOKS   *LES LIVRES*

TYPES OF BOOKS	*LES TYPES DE LIVRES*
a hardback	*un livre cartonné*
a paperback	*un livre de poche*
a best seller	*un best-seller*
a prize winner	*un lauréat*
a novel	*un roman*
a book of poetry	*un recueil de poèmes*
a play	*une pièce*

FICTION	*FICTION*
a thriller	*un roman à suspense*
a romance	*un roman d'amour*
a mystery	*un roman policier*
science fiction	*science-fiction*
a horror story	*un roman fantastique*
a series	*une collection*
a sequel	*une suite*

NON-FICTION	*LA LITTERATURE NON-ROMANESQUE*
biography	*biographie (f)*
autobiography	*autobiographie (f)*
historical	*historique*
faction (mixture of fact and fiction)	*un docudrame*

READING cont.   *LA LECTURE suite*

REFERENCE BOOKS	*LIVRES DE REFERENCE*
a dictionary	*un dictionnaire*
to look a word up	*chercher un mot*
alphabetical order	*ordre alphabétique*
an atlas	*un atlas*
an encyclopaedia	*une encyclopédie*

CHILDREN'S BOOKS	*LIVRES POUR ENFANTS*
a fairy tale	*un conte de fée*
a picture book	*un livre d'images*
a cartoon	*une bande dessinée*

THE WRITERS OF BOOKS	*LES AUTEURS*
an author	*un auteur / un écrivain*
a biographer	*un biographe*
a poet	*un poète*
a playwright	*un dramaturge*

READING	*LA LECTURE*
to read	*lire*
Do you mind if I read for a while?	*Cela ne vous ennuyez / t'ennuie pas si je lis un peu?*
I am in the middle of a really good book at the moment.	*Je suis au milieu d'un très bon livre en ce moment.*
Do you feel like reading for a bit?	*Vous avez / tu as envie de lire un peu?*
Would you like to see what books I have?	*Vous aimerez / tu aimerais voir mes livres?*
What is this book like?	*Ce livre est bien?*
This book is excellent.	*Ce livre est excellent.*
Where are you up to?	*Vous en êtes où? Tu en es où?*
What has just happened?	*Qu'est-ce qu'il vient de se passer?*

READING cont.

LA LECTURE suite

My sister / brother has some books you might like to read.	*Ma soeur / mon frère a des livres qui pourraient vous / te plaire.*
I love reading.	*J'adore lire.*
I like to read in bed before I go to sleep.	*J'aime bien lire au lit avant de dormir.*
I don't read much.	*Je ne lis pas beaucoup.*
She is a real bookworm.	*Elle est un vrai rat de bibliothèque.*
to use a bookmark	*utiliser un marque-page*

NEWSPAPERS

LES JOURNAUX

TYPES OF NEWSPAPERS	***TYPES DE JOURNAUX***
a daily newspaper	*un quotidien*
a weekly newspaper	*un hebdomadaire*
a national newspaper	*un journal national*
a local newspaper	*un journal local*
the gossip columns	*les échos*
the gutter press	*la presse à scandale*

SECTIONS OF A NEWSPAPER	***LES SECTIONS DES JOURNAUX***
the headlines	*les titres*
a leading article	*un éditorial*
a report	*un reportage*
a letter	*une lettre*
the sports pages	*les pages "sport"*
the fashion pages	*les pages "Mode"*
the weather forecast	*la météo*
Births, Marriages and Deaths	*Naissances, Mariages et Décès*
a crossword	*un mot croisé*
the horoscope (See 165-166)	*l'horoscope*

READING cont.

LA LECTURE suite

PRODUCERS OF NEWSPAPERS	*L'EQUIPE DE LA REDACTION*
the editor	*le rédacteur en chef*
the sub-editor	*le sous-rédacteur*
the journalists	*les journalistes*
the foreign correspondent	*le correspondant étranger*
a freelance journalist	*un journaliste free-lance*
the photographer	*le photographe*
the press	*la presse*
the paparazzi	*les paparazzi*

MAGAZINES

LES MAGAZINES

TYPES OF MAGAZINES	*TYPES DE MAGAZINES*
a glossy magazine	*magazine de luxe*
a monthly	*un mensuel*
a weekly	*un hebdomadaire*
an expensive magazine	*un magazine cher*
a fashion magazine	*un magazine de mode*
a music magazine	*un magazine de musique*
a specialist magazine	*un magazine spécialisé*
children's magazines	*un magazine pour enfants*
comics	*une Bande Dessinée*

LENDING AND BORROWING BOOKS	*PRÊTER ET EMPRUNTER DES LIVRES*
to lend	*prêter*
to borrow	*emprunter*
This book is a good one.	*C'est un bon livre.*
I can lend it to you if you like.	*Je peux vous / te le prêter si vous voulez / tu veux.*
Would you like to borrow a book?	*Vous voudriez / tu voudrais emprunter un livre?*

LENDING AND BORROWING BOOKS cont.

PRÊTER ET EMPRUNTER DES LIVRES suite

Don't forget to return it, will you?	*N'oublie pas de le rendre, d'accord?*
I'll write my name in it.	*Je vais écrire mon nom dessus.*
You can take it back home with you if you want and post it back to me.	*Vous pouvez / tu peux l'emmener chez vous / toi si vous voulez / tu veux et me le retourner par la poste.*

THE LIBRARY

LA BIBLITHEQUE

a public library	*une bibliothèque municipale*
the librarian	*le (la) bibliothécaire*
a library ticket	*une carte de bibliothèque*
to take out a book	*prendre un livre*
Would you like to take out a book on my ticket?	*Vous pouvez / tu veux prendre un livre avec ma carte?*
How many books may I borrow at once?	*Combien de livres puis-je prendre en même temps?*
It has to be back by 3rd November.	*Il doit être rendu le 3 Novembre.*
My library books are due back today.	*Mes livres de bibliothèque doivent être rendus aujourd'hui.*
My books are overdue.	*J'ai rendu mes livres en retard.*
How much is the fine?	*L'amende est de combien?*
Can you also borrow films / cassettes?	*On peut aussi emprunter des films / cassettes?*

READING cont.　　　　　*LA LECTURE suite*

BUYING BOOKS AND MAGAZINES	*ACHETER DES LIVRES ET DES MAGAZINES*
a book shop	*une librairie*
a second-hand book shop	*un bouquiniste*
a bookstall	*un étalage de bouquiniste*
a news stand	*un kiosque à journaux*
Where can I buy English books and newspapers?	*Où puis-je acheter des livres et des journaux anglais?*
I have got a book token.	*J'ai un bon d'achat pour un livre / un chèque-livre.*
Can I use this token here?	*Puis-je utiliser ce bon d'achat ici?*
May I pay (partly) with this book token, please?	*Puis-je payer (en partie) avec le bon d'achat, s'il vous plaît?*
How much extra do I owe?	*Il me reste combien à payer?*

DESCRIBING BOOKS　　　　*DECRIRE UN LIVRE*

The plot is...　　　　　　*L'intrigue est...*
This book is about...　　　*Ce livre parle de...*
The characterisation is..　　*La peinture des caractères est...*
The language / setting is...　*La langue / le cadre est...*

boring	*ennuyeux(se)*	poetic	*poétique*
clever	*intelligent(e)*	predictable	*prévisible*
concise	*concis(e)*	pretentious	*prétentieux(se)*
contrived	*forcé(e)*	romantic	*romantique*
different	*différent(e)*	sad	*triste*
difficult	*difficile*	sarcastic	*sarcastique*
easy to read	*facile à lire*	slow	*lent(e)*
exciting	*saisissant(e)*	surprising	*surprenant(e)*
fast	*rapide*	tense	*tendu(e)*
funny	*amusant(e)*	typical	*typique*
gripping	*passionnant(e)*	unexpected	*inattendu(e)*
hysterical	*hilarant(e)*	untypical	*atypique*
long-winded	*lent(e)*	unusual	*inhabituel (le)*

HOROSCOPES
LES HOROSCOPES

THE SIGNS OF THE ZODIAC	*LES SIGNES DU ZODIAQUE*
• Aries (The Ram)	• *Bélier*
• Taurus (The Bull)	• *Taureau*
• Gemini (The Twins)	• *Gémeaux (les Jumeaux)*
• Cancer (The Crab)	• *Cancer (le Crabe)*
• Leo (The Lion)	• *Lion*
• Virgo (The Virgin)	• *Vierge*
• Libra (The Balance)	• *Balance*
• Scorpio (The Scorpion)	• *Scorpion*
• Sagittarius (The Archer)	• *Sagittaire (l'Archer)*
• Capricorn (The Goat)	• *Capricorne (la Chèvre)*
• Aquarius (The Water Bearer)	• *Verseau*
• Pisces (The Fishes)	• *Poisson*

THE HEAVENLY BODIES	*LES CORPS CELESTES*
the Sun	*le Soleil*
the Moon	*la Lune*
the Planets	*les Planètes*
• Mercury	• *Mercure*
• Venus	• *Venus*
• Mars	• *Mars*
• Jupiter	• *Jupiter*
• Saturn	• *Saturne*

HOROSCOPES cont.   *LES HOROSCOPES suite*

USEFUL EXPRESSIONS	*EXPRESSIONS UTILES*
What does your horoscope say?	*Que dit votre / ton horoscope?*
My horoscope sounds interesting.	*Mon horoscope a l'air intéressant.*
My horoscope sounds terrible.	*Mon horoscope a l'air horrible.*
Listen to what my horoscope says.	*Ecoutez / écoute ce que dit mon horoscope.*
Read me my horoscope.	*Lisez / lis-moi mon horoscope.*
What sign are you?	*De quel signe êtes-vous / es-tu?*
I am a Gemini.	*Je suis Gémeaux.*
I was born under the star sign of Aries.	*Je suis né(e) sous le signe du Taureau.*
What time of day were you born?	*A quelle heure du jour êtes-vous / es-tu né(e)?*
Where were you born?	*Où êtes-vous / es-tu né(e)?*
in conjunction with….	*en conjonction avec...*
under the influence of…	*sous l'influence de...*
on the cusp	*sur la corne*
position	*position*
house	*maison*
Do you believe in horoscopes?	*Vous croyez / tu crois aux horoscopes?*
I think they're rubbish.	*Je pense que c'est n'importe quoi.*
I think they are very accurate.	*Je pense qu'ils sont très exacts.*
Let me guess what star sign you are.	*Laissez / laisse-moi deviner votre / ton signe.*
Are you a Capricorn?	*Etes-vous / es-tu Capricorne?*

FOOD
LA NOURRITURE

MEALS , COURSES & SNACKS	*REPAS, PLATS ET COLLATIONS*
early morning tea / breakfast	*thé du matin(m)/petit déjeuner(m)*
elevenses	*pause-café (f)*
lunch	*déjeuner (m)*
afternoon tea	*thé de cinq heure (m)*
dinner / supper	*dîner (m) / souper (m)*
a snack	*une collation*
the first course / a starter	*l'entrée (f)*
the fish course	*le poisson*
the main course	*le plat principal*
the dessert	*le dessert*
cheese and biscuits	*le fromage*
coffee and mints	*café et mignardises*

SEATING ARRANGEMENTS	*LES DISPOSITIONS POUR LA TABLE*
Would you like to sit here?	*Voulez-vous vous asseoir ici?*
Sit next to me.	*Asseyez-vous / assieds-toi à côté de moi.*
Sit opposite me.	*Asseyez-vous / assieds-toi en face de moi.*
Sit anywhere.	*Asseyez-vous / assieds-toi où vous voulez / tu veux.*

FOOD PREFERENCES — *LES PREFERENCES CULINAIRES*

LIKES	*QUAND ON AIME:*
I thought that was..	*J'ai trouvé cela...*
gorgeous / delicious / really good	*succulent / délicieux / vraiment bon*
How did you make it?	*Comment avez-vous / as-tu fait cela?*
Would you give me the recipe?	*Vous me donnez / tu me donnes la recette?*
Is it difficult to cook?	*C'est difficile à faire?*

FOOD PREFERENCES cont.	*LES PREFERENCES CULINAIRES suite*
Shall we cook a meal for you tomorrow?	*Et si on cuisinait pour vous / toi demain?*
I love cooking.	*J'adore cuisiner.*
Would you like some more?	*En voulez-vous / veux-tu encore?*
Would you like a second helping?	*Vous voulez vous / tu veux te resservir?*
Only if no-one else wants it.	*Seulement si personne n'en veut.*

DISLIKES	*QUAND ON N'AIME PAS:*
Is there anything you don't like eating?	*Il y a des choses que vous n'aimez pas / tu n'aimes pas?*
Just say if you don't like it.	*Vous me dites / tu me dis si vous ne l'aimez pas / tu ne l'aime pas.*
I am just not very hungry.	*C'est seulement que je n'ai pas très faim.*
I'm afraid I don't eat...	*Je regrette mais je ne mange pas...*
I'm sorry but....disagrees with me.	*Je suis désolé(e) mais....je ne digère pas*
I can get you something else.	*Je peux vous / te donner autre chose.*
What do you feel like eating?	*Qu'avez-vous / as-tu envie de manger?*
Have you any...?	*Vous avez / tu as des...*

EXPERIMENTING WITH FOOD	*GOÛTER LA NOURRITURE*
This is typically English / French.	*C'est typiquement Anglais / Français.*
Have you ever tried this before?	*Vous avez / tu as déjà goûté cela?*
Can I try just a little bit, please?	*Je peux goûter un petit morceau, s'il vous / te plaît?*
What do you think of it?	*Qu'en pensez-vous / penses-tu ?*
How do you cook this?	*Comment cuisinez-vous / cuisines-tu cela?*
How do you prepare this?	*Comment préparez-vous / prépares-tu cela?*

FOOD cont.   *LA NOURRITURE suite*

EATING	MANGER
to eat	*manger*
to drink	*boire*
to bite	*mordre*
to chew	*mâcher*
to taste	*goûter*
to swallow	*avaler*
to digest	*digérer*
to choke	*s'étouffer*
to burn your mouth	*se brûler la bouche*

DIFFERENT DIETS	DIFFERENTS REGIMES
I am vegetarian.	*Je suis végétarien(ne).*
I am a vegan.	*Je suis végétalien(ne).*
I am diabetic.	*Je suis diabétique.*
I like junk food.	*J'aime la nourriture non diététique.*
I am allergic to…	*Je suis allergique à...*
I am trying to lose weight.	*J'essaie de perdre du poids.*
I am trying to gain weight.	*J'essaie de prendre du poids.*
I am trying to count my calories.	*J'essaie de compter mes calories.*
How many calories does this have?	*Combien de calories y a-t-il?*
I don't eat starch with protein.	*Je ne mange pas de féculent avec des protéines.*
I prefer my vegetables raw.	*Je préfère mes légumes crûs.*
I am on a low fat diet.	*Je suis un régime basse-calories.*
I can't eat fried food.	*Je ne peux pas manger de friture.*

TYPICALLY BRITISH FOOD

NOURRITURE TYPIQUEMENT BRITANNIQUE

Bangers and mash - sausages and mashed potatoes.	*Saucisse-Purée.*
Shepherd's pie - minced beef and onion, topped with mashed potato.	*Hachis parmentier - viande hachée avec des oignons recouvert de purée.*
Cornish pasty - an individual pie containing potatoes, vegetables and minced meat, typical of Cornwall.	*"Cornish Pasty" - une tourte individuelle fourrée aux pommes de terre, légumes et viande hachée, typique de Cornouaille.*
A full English breakfast - fried eggs, bacon, sausage, grilled tomato, mushrooms, fried bread and sometimes black pudding.	*Un petit-déjeuner anglais - œufs frits, bacon / lard, saucisse, des tomates grillées, champignons, pain frit, et quelquefois du boudin noir.*
Porridge - oats or oatmeal simmered with water and/or milk which the Scots eat with salt not sugar.	*Porridge - avoine ou flocons d'avoine cuit à feu doux avec de l'eau / ou du lait, que les Ecossais mangent avec du sel et non pas du sucre.*
Yorkshire pudding - made from batter and traditionally eaten with roast beef for Sunday lunch.	*"Yorkshire pudding" - fait avec de la pâte à frire et accompagnant traditionnellement le rôti du déjeuner dominical.*
Fish and chips - fish deep fried in batter with chips.	*Poisson - Frites - poisson pané frit avec des frites.*

TYPICALLY BRITISH FOOD
NOURRITURE TYPIQUEMENT BRITANNIQUE

A hot cross bun - a small bread like bun with currants in and a cross marked on top eaten on Good Friday.	*Un "cross bun" chaud - petit pain au lait avec des raisins secs, marqué d'une croix et dégusté le Vendredi Saint.*
Cheddar - a common British cheese often known as 'mousetrap'.	*Le Cheddar - un fromage britannique ordinaire.*
Lardy cake - a bread made with lard and dried fruit topped with a sticky sugary mixture.	*Un "Lardy Cake" - un gâteau fait avec du saindoux et des fruits secs recouvert d'un mélange sucré sirupeux.*
Bakewell tart - a tart filled with almond paste and jam created in Bakewell in Derbyshire.	*"Bakewell Tart" - une tarte à la frangipane et à la confiture créé à Bakewell dans le Derbyshire.*
Christmas pudding - a rich pudding made with a variety of dried fruit which can be kept for over a year.	*"Christmas pudding" - un pudding riche fait d'une variété de fruits secs qui peut se conserver pendant plus d'un an.*

TYPICALLY FRENCH FOOD

LA NOURRITURE FRANÇAISE TYPIQUE

Crudités - a selection of salad and raw vegetables cut into finger sized pieces and eaten with a dip.

Crudités - une sélection de salade et de légumes crûs coupés en morceaux de la taille d'un doigt et accompagnés d'une sauce.

Bouillabaisse - a fish soup.

Bouillabaisse - une soupe de poisson.

L'ailloli - a garlic mayonnaise

L'ailloli - une mayonnaise à l'ail.

Les escargots - snails

Les escargots

Les cuisses de grenouilles - frogs' legs.

Les cuisses de grenouilles

Cassoulet - a casserole of beans, sausage, garlic and goose fat.

Le Cassoulet - un ragoût de haricots, saucisse, ail, graisse d'oie et foie gras.

Chateaubriand - a steak.

Chateaubriand - un steak.

Un croque-monsieur - a toasted sandwich with ham and cheese.

Un croque-monsieur - un sandwich grillé au jambon et fromage.

Un croque-madame - a toasted sandwich with a fried egg on top.

Un croque-madame - un sandwich grillé recouvert d'un œuf sur le plat.

Crêpes - pancakes

Crêpes

Œufs à la neige / les îles flottantes - soft meringues in custard

Œufs à la neige / les îles flottantes - Des meringues molles dans une crème anglais

Sabayon - whipped egg yolks with liqueur

Sabayon - Jaunes d'œufs battus avec de la liqueur

Tarte tatin - an apple tart that is cooked upside down, with the pastry on top and caramelised apples underneath, and is turned over before serving

Tarte tatin - une tarte aux pommes cuite à l'envers avec la pâte au-dessus et des pommes caramélisées dessous, retournée au moment de servir

Vacherin - layers of meringue, cream and ice cream

Vacherin - des couches de meringues, de crème et de glace

Le citron pressé - fresh lemon drink

Le citron pressé - une boisson fraîche au citron

COOKING ## LA CUISINE

Cookery books	Les livres de cuisine
a recipe	une recette
to look up	regarder / chercher
to follow	suivre
instructions	instructions
method	méthode
ingredients	ingrédients
cooking time	temps de cuisson
Serves three to four people.	Plat pour trois ou quatre personnes.
an illustration	une illustration

COOKERY TERMS (abc) ## LES TERMES CULINAIRES

to add	ajouter	to grate	râper
to arrange	arranger	to grill	griller
to bake	cuire au four / faire de la pâtisserie	to grind	moudre
to blend	mélanger	to heat up	réchauffer
to boil	bouillir	to incorporate	incorporer
to casserole	faire cuire à la cocotte	to knead	pétrir
to chop	hacher	to liquidize	liquéfier
to combine	combiner	to mash	écraser
to cool	refroidir	to measure	mesurer
to cover	couvrir	to melt	fondre
to crimp	pincer	to mince	mâcher menu
to cut into cubes	couper en cubes	to peel	peler
to divide	diviser	to pour	verser
to drain	égoutter	to press	presser
to flip over	retourner	to rise	lever
to fold	plier	to roast	rôtir
to fold in	replier	to roll out	rouler
to fry	frire	to season	assaisonner
to garnish	garnir	to sift	tamiser

COOKERY TERMS (abc) cont.
LES TERMES CULINAIRES suite

to simmer	*mijoter*	to test	*essayer*
to skewer	*embrocher*	to time	*minuter*
to slice	*trancher*	to toss	*remuer*
to sprinkle	*saupoudrer*	to turn down	*rabattre*
to steam	*cuire à la vapeur*	to turn out	*démouler*
to stir	*remuer (en tournant)*	to turn up	*remonter*
to strain	*passer*	to whisk	*battre*
to taste	*goûter*		

COOKING MEASURES
LES MESURES

a teaspoonful	*une cuillerée à café*
a quarter / half a teaspoonful	*un quart / une demi-cuillérée à café*
three quarters of a teaspoonful	*les trois quart d'une cuillère à café*
a dessertspoonful	*une cuillerée à dessert*
a tablespoonful	*une cuillerée à soupe*
a cupful / half a cupful	*une tasse / une demi-tasse*
a pinch of	*une pincée de*

COOKING INGREDIENTS (AND HOW TO PREPARE THEM)
LES INGREDIENTS (ET COMMENT LES PREPARER)

DAIRY PRODUCTS
LES PRODUITS FRAIS

Milk	***Lait (m)***
whole milk	*lait entier*
semi-skimmed / skimmed milk	*lait demi-écrémé / écrémé*
long life milk	*lait stérilisé / longue conservation*
powdered milk	*lait en poudre*
a milk bottle	*une bouteille de lait*
a carton	*une brique*
a milk jug / to pour	*un pot de lait / verser*
a drink of milk	*un verre de lait*

COOKING INGREDIENTS cont.

LES INGREDIENTS suite

DAIRY PRODUCTS cont.

LES PRODUITS FRAIS suite

Cream	***Crème** (f)*
double cream	*crème fraîche épaisse*
single cream	*crème liquide*
clotted cream	*crème en grumeaux*
whipped cream	*crème fouettée*
soured cream	*crème aigre*
a jug of cream	*un pot de crème*
to whisk / to whip	*battre / fouetter*

Butter, margarine etc.	***Beurre** (m), **margarine** (f) etc.*
salted / unsalted butter	*salé / non salé*
margarine	*margarine*
soft / hard	*mou (molle) / dur(e)*
suet / lard / dripping	*graisse de rognon (f) / saindoux (m) / graisse de rôti (f)*
a butter dish	*un beurrier*
a butter knife	*un couteau à beurre*
to spread	*étaler*
to butter	*beurrer*

Yoghurt	***Yaourt** (m)*
set yoghurt	*yaourt ferme*
natural yoghurt	*yaourt naturel*
low fat yoghurt	*yaourt maigre*
fruit yoghurt	*yaourt aux fruits*
a pot of yoghurt	*un pot de yaourt*

COOKING INGREDIENTS cont.   *LES INGREDIENTS suite*

DAIRY PRODUCTS cont.   *LES PRODUITS FRAIS suite*

Cheese	*Fromage (m)*
hard / soft cheese	*fromage sec, dure / molle*
cream cheese	*fromage frais*
cottage cheese	*cottage-cheese*
goat's cheese	*fromage de chèvre*
Parmesan cheese	*Parmesan (m)*
cheese biscuits	*biscuits au fromage*
a cheese board / a cheese knife	*un plateau à fromage / un couteau à fromage*
to cut	*couper*
a cheese grater	*une râpe à fromage*
to grate	*râper*

EGGS	*LES ŒUFS*
a hen's egg	*un œuf de poule*
a quail's egg	*un œuf de caille*
brown / white	*un œuf brun / blanc*
fresh / old	*frais / vieux*
large / medium / small	*gras / moyen / petit*
size one / two / three etc.	*calibre un / deux / trois*
free range eggs	*des œufs fermiers*
farmyard	*ferme (f)*
battery	*batterie*
a dozen / half a dozen	*une douzaine / une demi-douzaine*
an egg box	*une boîte d'œufs*
the shell	*la coque*
to crack / to break	*craquer / casser*
the yolk / the white	*le jaune / le blanc*

COOKING INGREDIENTS cont. *LES INGREDIENTS suite*

Cooking eggs	*Cuisiner les œufs*
a boiled egg	*un œuf dur*
hard boiled / soft boiled	*un œuf dur / un œuf mollet*
cooked for four / five / six minutes	*cuit pendant quatre / cinq / six minutes*
an egg cup	*un coquetier*
soldiers	*des mouillettes*
to take the top off the egg	*décapuchonner un œuf*
scrambled egg	*œufs brouillés*
poached egg	*œufs pochés*

Preparing eggs	*Préparer les œufs*
to separate the whites from the yolks	*séparer les blancs des jaunes*
to whisk the whites	*battre les blancs en neige*
an egg whisk	*un fouet*
an electric beater	*un fouet électrique*
stiffly beaten	*battues fermement*
soft peaks	*battues légèrement*

BREAD	*LE PAIN*
wholemeal	*complet*
brown / white	*complet / blanc*
organic	*organique*
large / small	*grand / petit*
round / oblong	*rond / long*
unsliced / sliced	*non tranché / tranché*
thick / medium / thin sliced	*en tranches épaisses / moyennes / fines*
a bread bin	*une huche à pain*
a bread board / a bread knife	*une planche à pain / un couteau à pain*
to cut / to slice / a slice	*couper / trancher / une tranche*
to make breadcrumbs	*faire des miettes*

**COOKING INGREDIENTS
cont.**

LES INGREDIENTS suite

OTHER TYPES OF BREAD AND BAKED GOODS	*AUTRES TYPES DE PAINS ET DE PATISSERIES*
a French stick	*une baguette*
a roll	*une boule*
Ciabatta	*Ciabatte*
pitta bread	*pain pitta (m)*
crumpets	*une petite crêpe épaisse*
muffins / tea cakes	*muffins / des petits gâteaux*

**COFFEE, TEA AND OTHER
DRINKS**

*CAFE, THE ET AUTRES
BOISSONS*

Coffee	*Café (m)*
Do you like black or white coffee?	*Aimez-vous / aimes-tu / le café noir ou au lait?*
instant / decaffeinated coffee	*café instantané / café décaféiné*
real coffee / coffee beans	*vrai café / grains de café*
full / medium / light roast	*torréfaction (f) longue / moyenne / légère*
to grind / a coffee grinder	*moudre / un moulin à café*
fine / medium / coarse ground	*mouture (f) fine / normale*

Tea	*Thé (m)*
a tea pot / to pour	*une théière / verser*
to warm the pot	*chauffer la théière*
to let it brew	*laisser infuser*
tea bags / tea leaves	*sachets (m) / feuilles (f) de thé*
an infuser / a tea strainer	*un infuseur / une passoire à thé*
to strain	*passer*
Do you like your tea with milk and sugar?	*Vous prenez / tu prends votre / ton thé avec du lait et du sucre?*
Milk and no sugar, please.	*Avec du lait mais sans sucre, s'il vous plaît?*
No milk and one sugar, please.	*Sans lait et un sucre, s'il vous plaît.*

INGREDIENTS cont   *LES INGREDIENTS suite*

OTHER DRINKS   ***AUTRES BOISSONS***

tonic water	*Schweppes ®*
soda water	*eau gazeuse (f)*
ginger ale	*Canada Dry ®*
lemonade	*limonade (f)*
coca cola	*coca-cola ® (m)*
water	*eau*
squash / to dilute	*sirop (m) / diluer*
strong / weak / average	*fort / faible / moyen*

Fruit juice   ***Jus de Fruit (m)***

orange	*orange*	tomato	*tomates*
grapefruit	*pamplemousse*	vegetable	*légume*
pineapple	*ananas*	tropical juice	*fruits exotiques*
freshly squeezed		***fraîchement pressé***	

Additions to drinks   ***Suppléments (m)***

ice cubes	*glaçons (m)*
a slice of lemon	*une tranche de citron*
a cherry	*une cerise*

ALCOHOLIC DRINKS   *BOISSONS ALCOOLISEES*

---

cider	*cidre (m)*	rosé	*rosé*
beer	*bière (f)*	sparkling	*pétillant*
lager	*bière blonde*	Champagne	*Champagne (m)*
bottled	*bouteille (f)*	**Spirits**	*Spiritueux (m)*
draught	*pression*	gin	*gin (m)*
canned	*canette*	whisky	*whisky (m)*
Wine	*Vin (m)*	brandy	*cognac (m)*
a glass of	*un verre de*	vodka	*vodka (f)*
half a bottle of	*une demi-bouteille de*	rum	*rhum (m)*
red	*rouge*	a single	*un simple*
white	*blanc*	a double	*un double*

COOKING INGREDIENTS cont

LES INGREDIENTS suite

MEAT

VIANDE

How do you like your meat cooked?	Comment aimez-vous / aimes-tu la viande?
rare / medium rare	bleue / à point
well done / crispy	tendre / bien cuite

TYPES OF MEAT

LES TYPES DE VIANDE

beef	bœuf (m)	Parma ham	jambon de Parme
a steak	un steak	veal	veau (m)
pork	porc (m)	lamb	agneau (m)
bacon	bacon (m)	offal	abats (m)
smoked	fumé	liver	foie (m)
unsmoked	non fumé	kidney	rognons (m)
streaky	pas trop maigre	sweetbreads	ris (m) de veau / d'agneau
ham	jambon (m)	sausages	saucisse (f)

POULTRY AND GAME

VOLAILLE ET GIBIER

a chicken	un poulet	a guinea fowl	une pintade
a duck	un canard	a pheasant	un faisan
a goose	une oie	a hare	un lièvre
a turkey	une dinde	a rabbit	un lapin
venison	venaison		

COMMON FRUITS

FRUITS COURANTS

apple	pomme (f)	orange	orange (f)
apricot	abricot (m)	peach	pêche (f)
banana	banane (f)	pear	poire (f)
grapefruit	pamplemousse (m)	pineapple	ananas (m)
grapes	raisin (m)	plum	prune (f)
lemon	citron (m)	raspberry	framboise (f)
lime	citron vert (m)	satsuma	satsouma
melon	melon (m)	strawberry	fraise (f)

COOKING INGREDIENTS cont

LES INGREDIENTS suite

PREPARING FRUIT

LA PREPARATION DES FRUITS

to peel	*peler*
the peel	*la pelure*
the pith	*la peau blanche*
to quarter	*faire des quartiers*
to remove the pips	*enlever les pépins*
to take out the stone	*dénoyauter*

VEGETABLES & SALAD

LEGUMES & SALADE

aubergine	*aubergine (f)*	mushroom	*champignon (m)*
avocado	*avocat (m)*	onion	*oignon (m)*
broad beans	*haricots (m)*	Spring onion	*petit oignon*
French beans	*fève (f)*	parsnip	*panais (m)*
green beans	*haricots verts*	peas	*petit pois (m)*
runner beans	*haricots à rames*	red pepper	*poivre rouge (m)*
beetroot	*betterave (f)*	green pepper	*poivre vert*
broccoli	*broccoli (m)*	potato	*pomme de terre (f)*
Brussels sprouts	*choux de Bruxelles (m)*	jacket potato	*pomme de terre en robe des champs*
cabbage	*choux (m)*	boiled	*bouillie*
carrot	*carotte (f)*	mashed	*écrasée*
cauliflower	*chou-fleur (m)*	roasted	*rôties*
celeriac	*céleri-rave (m)*	chips	*frites*
celery	*céleri (m)*	spinach	*épinards (m)*
courgette	*courgette (f)*	swede	*rutabaga (m)*
cress	*cresson (m)*	sweetcorn	*maïs (m)*
cucumber	*concombre (m)*	radish	*radis (m)*
garlic	*ail (m)*	tomato	*tomate (f)*
leek	*poireau (m)*	turnip	*navet (m)*
lettuce	*laitue (f)*	watercress	*cresson (de fontaine) (m)*

COOKING INGREDIENTS cont
LES INGREDIENTS suite

SUGAR, HONEY, JAM etc.
SUCRE, MIEL & CONFITURE

white sugar	*sucre blanc (m)*	black treacle	*mélasse (f)*
granulated sugar	*sucre semoule*	molasses	*mélasse*
castor sugar	*sucre en poudre*	honey	*miel (m)*
icing sugar	*sucre glace*	runny honey	*miel liquide*
lump sugar	*sucre en morceau*	honeycomb	*miel d'abeille*
brown sugar	*sucre roux*	jam	*confiture (f)*
to sweeten	*sucrer*	orange marmelade	*marmelade d'orange*
syrup	*sirop (m)*	ginger marmelade	*marmelade (f) de gingembre*
golden syrup	*mélasse raffinée (f)*		

FLOUR etc.
FARINES

plain flour	*farine ordinaire (f)*	baking powder	*levure chimique (f)*
self-raising flour	*farine à gâteaux*	bicarbonate of soda	*bicarbonate de soude (m)*
white flour	*farine blanche*	cream of tartar	*crème de tartre (f)*
wholemeal flour	*farine complète*	arrowroot	*marante*
buckwheat flour	*farine de Blé Noir*	gelatine	*gélatine*
cornflour	*farine de maïs*	yeast	*levure*

PREPARING NUTS
LA PREPARATION DES NOIX

to crack	*casser*	ground nuts	*noix en poudre*
the shell	*l'écorce (f)*	salted nuts	*noix salées*
nutcrackers	*casse-noisettes*	unsalted nuts	*noix non salées*
whole nuts	*noix entières (f)*	roasted nuts	*noix grillées*
chopped nuts	*en morceaux noix / noisettes*		

COOKING INGREDIENTS cont
LES INGREDIENTS suite

SALT AND PEPPER etc.
POIVRE (m) ET SEL (m)

table salt	*sel de table*	to sprinkle	*verser / saupoudrer*
sea salt	*sel de mer*	a pinch of salt	*une pincée de sel*
crystal rock salt	*fleur de sel*	peppercorns	*grains (m) de poivre*
celery salt	*sel de céleri*	black / white / green	*noir / blanc / vert*
a salt mill	*un moulin à sel*	a pepper mill	*un moulin à poivre*
to grind	*moudre*	to fill	*remplir*
to season	*assaisonner*	tomato sauce	*Ketchup*

BARBECUES
BARBECUES

SHOULD WE HAVE A BARBECUE?	*ON FAIT UN BARBECUE?*
Should we eat outside?	*On mange dehors?*

LIGHTING THE BARBECUE	*ALLUMER LE BARBECUE*
Have we got..?	*Avons-nous…?*
• aluminium foil	• *du papier aluminium*
• charcoal	• *charbon (m)*
• lighter fluid	• *liquide plus léger (m)*
to squirt	*verser quelques gouttes (f)*
to pour over	*verser par dessus*
to soak	*tremper*
to light	*allumer*
a match	*une allumette*
to stand back	*reculer*
to get going well	*bien entretenir*
to go out	*sortir*

COOKING ON A BARBECUE	*CUISINER AU BARBECUE*
to be ready to cook	*être prêt pour la cuisson*
to barbecue	*cuire au barbecue*
to grill	*griller*
tongs	*pinces (f)*
skewers	*brochettes (instrument) (f)*
to turn over	*retourner*

BARBECUES cont.

BARBECUES suite

FOOD

NOURRITURE (f)

sausages	*saucisses (f)*	spare ribs	*côtelettes (dans*
bacon	*bacon (m)*		*l'échine) (f)*
steaks	*steaks (m)*	marinade	*marinade (f)*
chops	*joues (f)*	sauce	*sauce (f)*
kebabs	*brochettes (de*	to brush over	*dorer*
	viande) (f)		
chicken	*pilons de poulet*	marshmallows	*chamallow (m)*
drumsticks			*/ guimauve (f)*

COMMON EXPRESSIONS FOR BARBECUES

EXPRESSIONS USUELLES POUR LE BARBACUE

Is it ready yet?	*C'est prêt maintenant?*
Are they ready yet?	*Ils / elles sont prêt(es) maintenant?*
They won't be long now.	*Cela ne sera pas long maintenant.*
Another few minutes.	*Encore quelques minutes.*
This isn't cooked properly.	*Ce n'est pas bien cuit.*
I'm afraid this is a bit burnt.	*Je crains que cela ne soit un peu brûlé.*

EATING AT McDONALD'S

MANGER AU McDONALD'S

ROYAL CHEESE
A wheatroll, 100% beef, cheese spread, onions, slices of gherkins, ketchup and mustard sauce.

ROYAL CHEESE
Pain, 100% bœuf, fromage, oignons, cornichons, ketchup et moutarde.

BIG MAC
A wheatroll, 100% beef, onions, slices of gherkins, iceberg lettuce, cheese spread and Big Mac-sauce.

BIG MAC
Pain, 100% bœuf, oignons, cornichons, laitue, fromage, sauce Big Mac.

CHICKEN McNUGGETS
Chicken in breadcrumbs with:-
- mustard sauce
- sweet and sour sauce
- barbecue sauce
- curry sauce

CHICKEN McNUGGETS
Poulet pané avec:-
- *moutarde sauce*
- *sweet and sour sauce*
- *barbecue sauce*
- *curry sauce*

MAC CHICKEN
A wheatroll with chicken.

MAC CHICKEN
Pain et poulet.

MENU BIG MAC =
Big Mac, French Fries, Fizzy Drink.

MENU BIG MAC =
Big Mac, Frites, Boisson Gazeuse.

MENU BACON =
Mac Bacon, French Fries, Fizzy Drink

MENU BACON =
Mac Bacon, Frites, Boisson Gazeuse.

SALADS
Salmon and shrimp salad
Crudité salad

SALADES
Salade saumon-crevettes
Salade crudité

EATING AT MᶜDONALD'S
cont.

MANGER AU MCDONALD'S
suite

DESSERTS
Brownies
Muffins
Apple turnover
Cookies

DESSERTS
Brownies
Muffins
Chausson au Pommes
Cookies

MILK SHAKES
vanilla
strawberry
banana

MILK-SHAKES
vanille
fraise
banane

SUNDAES
Hot fudge
Caramel
Strawberry

SUNDAES
Hot fudge
Caramel
Fraise

CINEMA & THEATRE

CINEMA & THEATRE

THE CINEMA

LE CINEMA

USEFUL EXPRESSIONS

EXPRESSIONS UTILES

Would you like to go to the cinema..?	*Vous aimeriez / tu aimerais aller au cinéma...?*
• this afternoon?	• *cet après-midi?*
• this evening?	• *ce soir?*
• tomorrow?	• *demain?*
• one day?	• *un jour?*
• while you are here?	• *pendant que vous êtes / tu es ici?*
There's a very good film on at the moment.	*Il y a un très bon film en ce moment.*
It starts at...	*Il commence à...*
It ends at...	*Il finit à...*
Is there a supporting film first?	*Y a-t-il un court-métrage avant?*
Is there an interval?	*Y a-t-il une entracte?*
Who's in the film?	*Qui joue dans le film?*
The star of the film is..	*La vedette du film est...*
It's starring...	*Les acteurs sont...*
It's that man who was in..	*C'est cet homme qui était dans...*
Wasn't she in..?	*Elle n'était pas dans...?*
Who is the director?	*Qui est le réalisateur?*

THE CINEMA cont. BUYING TICKETS AND GOING IN
LE CINEMA suite L'ACHAT DES TICKETS ET L'ENTREE

Could we have two tickets, please?	*On peut avoir deux tickets, s'il vous plaît?*
Can you reserve seats?	*Pouvez-vous réserver des places?*
Do you give a reduction to students?	*Vous faites des réduction-étudiants?*
We are …..years old.	*On a…ans.*
Would you like some pop corn?	*Vous voulez / tu veux des pop corns?*
Would you like an ice cream or a drink?	*Vous voulez / tu veux une glace ou une boisson?*
Do you want to go to the loo first?	*Vous voulez / tu veux aller aux toilettes avant?*
Where are the toilets?	*Où sont les toilettes?*
We'd better hurry - the film's just starting.	*On ferait mieux de se dépêcher: le film vient de commencer.*
Where would you like to sit?	*Où voulez-vous vous/ veux-tu t'asseoir?*
Do you like to be near the front or not?	*Vous aimez / tu aimes être devant ou non?*
Can you see O.K.?	*Vous voyez / tu vois bien?*
I can't see because of the person in front of me.	*Je ne peux pas voir à cause de la personne devant moi.*
Can we try to sit somewhere else?	*On peut essayer de s'asseoir autre part?*

FOLLOWING THE PLOT
SUIVRE L'INTRIGUE

Does it have subtitles?	*Est-ce qu'il y a des sous-titres?*
It has subtitles.	*Il a des sous-titres.*
It's dubbed.	*C'est doublé.*
Can you understand what's going on?	*Vous comprenez / tu comprends ce qu'il se passe?*
I don't understand it.	*Je ne comprends pas.*
What just happened?	*Qu'est-ce qu'il vient de se passer?*
What did he say?	*Qu'est-ce qu'il a dit?*

THE THEATRE

LE THEATRE

BOOKING SEATS

RESERVER LES PLACES

the booking office	*le bureau de location*
to reserve seats	*les places réservées*
Which performance?	*Quelle représentation?*
the matinée	*la matinée*
the evening performance	*la représentation du soir*
Where do you want to sit?	*Où voulez-vous vous / veux-tu t'asseoir?*
in the stalls	*dans l'orchestre*
in the circle	*au balcon*
What seats are available?	*Quelles sont les places disponibles?*
How much are the seats?	*Combien sont les places?*

BUYING A PROGRAMME

ACHETER UN PROGRAMME

to buy a programme	*acheter un programme*
to look at the programme	*regarder le programme*
to see who is in the play	*voir qui est dans la pièce*
to study the plot	*étudier l'intrigue*
to read about the actors' backgrounds	*lire à propos de l'origine des acteurs*

HAVING SOMETHING TO EAT OR DRINK

PRENDRE QUELQUE CHOSE A MANGER OU A BOIRE

the bar	*le bar*
the restaurant	*le restaurant*
to have a drink	*boire quelque chose*
before the performance	*avant la représentation*
in the interval	*pendant l'entracte*
to book a table	*réserver une table*

THE THEATRE cont.

LE THEATRE suite.

THE AUDITORIUM

LA SALLE

an aisle	*une aile*
a box	*une loge*
the toilets	*les toilettes*
a fire exit	*une sortie de secours*
the acoustics	*l'acoustique*

THE SEATING

LES PLACES

to show your ticket	*montrer son ticket*
row A, B etc.	*rangée A, B etc.*
an usher	*un placeur*
to be shown to your seat	*se faire montrer les places*
the stalls	*l'orchestre (emplacement)*
the circle	*le balcon*

BEFORE THE PERFORMANCE

AVANT LA REPRESENTATION

to read the programme	*lire le programme*
to have a chocolate	*prendre un chocolat*
to let someone past	*laisser passer quelqu'un*
to stand up	*se lever*
to sit down	*s'asseoir*
to take your coat off	*enlever son manteau*
to get a good view	*avoir une bonne vue*
to be able to see	*être capable de voir*
to use the opera glasses	*utiliser les lunettes d'opéra*
to insert a coin	*insérer une pièce*
to borrow	*emprunter*

THE THEATRE cont.   *LE THEATRE suite.*

THE STAGE   *LA SCENE*

a theatre in the round	*un théâtre*
a raised stage	*une scène surélevée*
the wings	*les coulisses*
the scenery	*le décor*
a scene-change	*un changement de décor*
the props	*les accessoires*
to make an entrance	*faire son entrée*
to come on stage	*venir sur scène*
to exit	*sortir*
to leave	*quitter / partir*

THE LIGHTING   *L'ECLAIRAGE*

spotlights	*les spots (m)*
floodlights	*les projecteurs (m)*
coloured	*colorés*
to dim	*réduire / tamiser*
to go down	*baisser*
to go off	*s'éteindre*
to come back on	*revenir*
the lighting effects	*les effets de lumière*

THE CURTAIN   *LE RIDEAU*

to open	*ouvrir*
to shut	*fermer*
to raise	*lever*
to fall	*tomber*
a safety curtain	*un rideau de sûreté*

THE THEATRE cont. *LE THEATRE suite.*

THE PERFORMERS *LES ACTEURS*

the cast	*la troupe*
the lead	*le rôle principal*
the star	*la vedette*
the hero / the heroine	*le héros / l'héroïne*
the villain	*le méchant*
the actors	*les acteurs*
the actresses	*les actrices*
the understudy	*la doublure*

THE WRITERS *LES AUTEURS*

the playwright	*le dramaturge*
the composer	*le compositeur*
the librettist	*le librettiste*
the choreographer	*le chorégraphe*
the musical director	*le chef d'orchestre*

THE TECHNICAL STAFF *LE PERSONNEL TECHNIQUE*

the stage manager	*le régisseur*
the technical director	*le directeur technique*
the lighting technicians	*les techniciens de lumière*

THE PLAY *LA PIECE*

a Shakespeare play	*une pièce de Shakespeare*
a play by Pinter	*une pièce de Pinter*
a comedy	*une comédie*
a farce / slapstick	*une farce / une farce bouffonne*
a tragedy	*une tragédie*
a history	*une histoire*
a thriller	*une pièce à suspense*
a whodunnit	*une pièce policière*
a romance	*une histoire d'amour*
a pantomime	*une pantomime*
the plot	*l'intrigue*

THE THEATRE cont.   *LE THEATRE suite.*

REHEARSALS   *LES REPETITIONS*

to rehearse	*répéter*
to have a dress rehearsal	*avoir une répétition en costume*
a final rehearsal	*une dernière répétition*

THE SET DESIGN   *LA CONCEPTION DU DECOR*

abstract	*abstrait*	functional	*fonctionnel*
artistic	*artistique*	eccentric	*excentrique*
realistic	*réaliste*	unusual	*inhabituel*

THE COSTUME DESIGN   *LA CONCEPTION DES COSTUMES*

historical	*historique*	masked	*masqué*
period costume	*d'époque*	bold	*audacieux*
contemporary	*contemporain*	extravagant	*extravagant*
imaginative	*imaginatif*		

THE MAKEUP   *LE MAQUILLAGE*

to be made up	*être maquillé*	to emphasize	*souligner*
to exaggerate	*exagérer*	to remove	*enlever*
to conceal	*dissimuler*	greasepaint	*fard gras*
to distort	*déformer*		

THE SPECIAL EFFECTS   *LES EFFETS SPECIAUX*

sound effects	*les effets sonores (m)*	battle noises	*les bruits de combat (m)*
music	*musique (f)*	lighting effects	*effets de lumière (m)*
thunder	*tonnerre (m)*	smoke	*fumée (f)*

THE THEATRE cont.   *LE THEATRE suite.*

THE PARTS OF THE PLAY   *LES PARTIES D'UNE PIECE*

a scene	*une scène*	an act	*un acte*
the first scene	*la première scène*	the last act	*le dernier acte*
second	*seconde / deuxième*	a speech	*un discours*
third	*troisième*	a soliloquy	*un soliloque*
a change of scene	*changement de scène*	an aside	*un aparté*

THE INTERVAL   *L'ENTR'ACTE*

a brief interval	*une courte entracte*
a long interval	*une longue entracte*
to go to the bar	*aller au bar*
a long queue	*une longue queue*
to go to the toilet	*aller aux toilettes*
to ring the bell	*sonner la cloche*
to return to your seat	*retourner à sa place*

THE END OF THE PLAY   *LA FIN DE LA PIECE*

to applaud	*applaudir*
the applause	*les applaudissements*
to clap	*applaudir*
a standing ovation	*une ovation debout / une standing ovation*
to give a curtain call	*faire un rappel*
to bow / to curtsy	*faire la révérence*
to be given a bouquet	*recevoir un bouquet*

AFTER THE PLAY   *APRES LA PIECE*

to go to the stage door	*aller à l'entrée des artistes*
to try to get an autograph	*essayer d'obtenir un autographe*
a signature	*une signature*
to sign an autograph book	*signer un carnet d'autographe*

THE THEATRE cont. | *LE THEATRE suite.*

DISCUSSING THE PERFORMANCE (abc) | *PARLER DE LA PIECE*

amateur	amateur	realistic	réaliste
convincing	convaincant(e)	sad	triste
excellent	excellent(e)	sensitive	sensible
funny	amusant(e)	spectacular	spectaculaire
hysterical	très drôle	tense	tendu(e)
imaginative	imaginatif(ve)	terse	concis(e)
impressive	impressionnant(e)	theatrical	théâtral(e)
ironic	ironique	tragic	tragique
moving	émouvant(e)	true to life	véridique
professional	professionnel(le)	unconvincing	pas convaincant(e)
psychological	psychologique		

OPERA | *L'OPERA*

TYPES OF OPERA | *LES TYPES D'OPERA*

an opera	un opéra	a comic opera	un opéra comique
an operetta	une opérette	a rock opera	un opéra-rock

TYPES OF SONG | *LES TYPES DE CHANT*

a solo	un solo	an aria	une aria
a duet	un duo	a recitative	un récital
a chorus	un chœur	a part-song	chant (m) polyphonique

197

OPERA cont.		L'OPERA suite	

THE SINGERS		LES CHANTEURS / LES CHANTEUSES	
soprano	*soprano (m)*	falsetto	*fausset (m)*
contralto	*contralto (m)*	baritone	*baryton (m)*
alto	*alto (m)*	bass	*basse (m)*
tenor	*ténor (m)*	a prima donna	*une prima donna*

THE MUSIC		LA MUSIQUE	
the score	*la partition*	the overture	*l'ouverture*
the libretto	*le libretto*		

THE BALLET — *LE BALLET*

THE DANCERS etc.	LES DANSEURS / LES DANSEUSES etc.
a ballerina	*une ballerine*
a prima ballerina	*une danseuse étoile*
the corps de ballet	*le corps de ballet*
the choreographer	*le chorégraphe*
the composer	*le compositeur*

GETTING READY TO DANCE	LA PREPARATION
to do exercises at the barre	*s'exercer à la barre*
to warm up	*s'échauffer*
to limber	*faire des exercices d'assouplissement*
to stretch the muscles	*étirer les muscles*
to loosen the joints	*détendre les articulations*

THE BALLET cont.   *LE BALLET suite*

THE POSITIONS   *LES POSITIONS*

the position of..	*la position de*	third position	*troisième position*
the head	*la tête*	fourth position	*quatrième position*
the arms	*les bras*	fifth position	*cinquième position*
the body	*le corps*	turned out	*en canard*
the legs	*les jambes*	in line	*en ligne*
the feet	*les pieds*	in the air	*en l'air*
first position	*première position*	pointed	*pointé*
second position	*deuxième position*		

THE MOVEMENTS   *LES MOUVEMENTS*

to jump	*sauter*
to leap	*bondir*
to turn	*tourner*
to beat the feet	*frapper du pied*
to change the leg position	*changer la position des jambes*
to do pointe work	*faire des pointes*
to mime	*mimer*
to gesture	*mimer*
an arabesque	*une arabesque*
a pirouette	*une pirouette*
a fouetté	*un Fouetté*
an entrechat	*un entrechat*
a jeté	*un jeté*
a pas de deux	*un pas de deux*
to partner	*s'accoupler*
a partner	*un partenaire*

THE BALLET cont.   *LE BALLET suite*

BALLET CLOTHES etc.   *LES COSTUMES DE BALLET etc.*

ballet shoes	*des chaussons de danse (m)*
blocked shoes	*des pointes (f)*
to darn	*repriser*
tights	*collants (m)*
a tutu	*un Tutu*
a hair net	*un filet à cheveux*
to put one's hair up	*remonter ses cheveux*
to tie one's hair back	*attacher ses cheveux*
to plait one's hair	*faire une natte*

THE BALLET ITSELF   *LE BALLET EN LUI-MÊME*

the music	*la musique*	the plot	*l'intrigue (f)*
the composer	*le compositeur*	the libretto	*le libretto*
the steps	*les pas*	the scenario	*le scénario*
the choreographer	*le chorégraphe*	the orchestra	*l'orchestre*
the conductor	*le chef d'orchestre*	the pit	*l'orchestre (fauteuils)*

PARTIES & CLUBS
LES SOIREES ET LES BOITES

GETTING IN	*L'ENTREE*
a nightclub	*une boîte de nuit*
a bouncer	*un videur*
How old do you have to be to get in?	*Quel est l'âge-limite pour rentrer?*
Have you got an identity card?	*Avez-vous / as-tu une carte d'identité?*
Have you got anything that proves your age?	*Avez-vous /as-tu quelque chose pour prouver votre/ ton âge?*
How much does it cost to get in?	*C'est combien l'entrée?*

PARTIES	*LES SOIREES*
Have you got an invitation?	*Avez-vous /as-tu une invitation?*
I am / am not invited.	*Je ne suis pas invité(e)?*
a gatecrasher	*un intrus*
to give a party	*faire une soirée*
to draw up a list of people to invite	*faire la liste des invités*
to take a bottle	*apporter une bouteille*

THE MUSIC	*LA MUSIQUE*
What's the music like?	*Comment est la musique?*
It's just a disco.	*C'est seulement un disco.*
There's live music.	*Il y a un groupe.*
The group is good.	*Le groupe est bon.*
What sort of music do you like?	*Quelle sorte de musique aimez-vous / aimes-tu?*
This music isn't my sort of thing.	*Cette musique n'est pas mon genre de musique.*
I prefer...	*Je préfère...*
Which groups do you like?	*Quels sont les groupes que vous aimez / tu aimes?*
Should we ask them to play..?	*On leur demande de jouer...?*

CLUBS AND PARTIES cont.

LES BOÎTES DE NUIT ET SOIREES suite

INTRODUCTIONS

PRESENTATIONS

What nationality are you?	*De quelle nationalité êtes-vous / es-tu?*
Are you English / French / German / Spanish?	*Etes-vous / es-tu Anglais / Français / Allemand / Espagnol?*
Can you speak English?	*Vous savez / tu sais parler Anglais?*
What are you called? I'm called..	*Comment vous appelez-vous / tu t'appelles? Je m'appelle...*
What's your name? My name is..	
This is my friend….	*Voici mon ami(e)...*
Where do you live?	*Où habitez-vous / habites-tu?*
Where are you staying?	*Où séjournez-vous / séjournes-tu?*
How old are you?	*Quel âge avez-vous / as-tu?*
I'm sixteen.	*J'ai seize ans.*
Have you been here before?	*Vous êtes / tu es déjà venu(e) ici?*
Are you at school / college / working?	*Vous êtes / tu es au lycée / à l'université? / Vous travaillez / tu travailles?*
Which school / college do you go to?	*A quelle école / quelle université allez-vous / vas-tu?*
Where do you work?	*Où travaillez-vous / travailles-tu?*
What do you do?	*Que faites-vous / fais-tu?*
Do you know those people over there?	*Vous connaissez / tu connais ces gens là-bas?*
How old are they?	*Quel âge ont-ils?*
What's he / she like?	*Comment est-il / elle?*
Shall we go and talk to …?	*On va parler à...?*
Do you like dancing?	*Vous aimez / tu aimes danser?*
She's a really good dancer.	*Elle danse vraiment très bien.*
The music is so loud.	*La musique est si forte.*
I can't hear what you're saying.	*Je n'entends pas ce que vous dites / tu dis.*

CLUBS AND PARTIES cont.

DRINKS

LES BOÎTES DE NUIT ET SOIREES suite
BOISSONS

Shall we go to the bar?	*On va au bar?*
Which bar shall we go to?	*A quel bar allons-nous?*
Would you like a drink?	*Vous voulez / tu veux boire quelque chose?*
What would you like to drink?	*Qu'est-ce que vous voulez / tu veux boire?*
I'd like a coke / a beer.	*J'aimerais bien un Coca / une bière.*
I'll have what you're having.	*La même chose que vous / toi.*
You have to be eighteen.	*Il faut avoir dix-huit ans.*
The drinks are very expensive.	*Les boissons sont très chères.*

GETTING HOME AFTERWARDS

RENTRER CHEZ SOI

What time do you have to leave?	*A quelle heure devez-vous / dois-tu partir?*
What time does the club shut?	*A quelle heure la boîte ferme-t-elle?*
What time does the party finish?	*A quelle heure la soirée finit-elle?*
Are you being picked up?	*On vient vous / te chercher?*
Yes, I'm being picked up at one.	*Oui, on vient me chercher à une heure.*
How are you getting home?	*Comment rentrez-vous / rentres-tu?*
Do you want a lift with us?	*Vous voulez / tu veux qu'on vous / te ramène?*
Could I possibly have a lift in your car?	*Vous pouvez / tu peux me ramener?*
Should we share a taxi?	*On partage un taxi?*
Which bus / train are you getting?	*Vous prenez / tu prends quel bus / train?*
Can I see you again sometime?	*On peut se revoir un de ces jours?*
Should we go somewhere together tomorrow night?	*On va quelque part ensemble demain soir?*
Would you like to go to the cinema with us tomorrow?	*Vous voudriez / tu voudrais aller au cinéma avec nous demain?*
Shall we go and get something to eat?	*On va manger quelque chose?*

FAIR, CIRCUS & ZOO
LES FÊTES FORAINES, LE CIRQUE ET LE ZOO

THE FAIR

LA FÊTE FORAINE

USEFUL EXPRESSIONS

EXPRESSIONS UTILES

There is a fair on - would you like to go?	*Il y a une fête foraine, voudriez-vous / voudrais-tu y aller?*
What rides do you like?	*Quels manèges aimez-vous / aimes-tu?*
Which rides would you like to go on?	*Sur quels manèges voudriez-vous / voudrais-tu aller?*
How much money have you got to spend?	*Combien d'argent avez-vous / tu as?*
How much is it to go on the dodgems?	*C'est combien pour aller sur les autos-tamponneuses?*
Should we have another go on that?	*On recommence celui / celle-ci?*
What would you like to go on next?	*Vous voulez / tu veux aller où après?*
What time do we have to be home by?	*A quelle heure devez-vous / dois-tu rentrer à la maison?*
If we get separated, shall we meet by the big wheel?	*Si on se perd, on se rejoint à la grande roue?*

THE RIDES

LES MANEGES

The Ferris Wheel	*La Grande Roue*
Shall we sit together?	*On s'assoit ensemble?*

THE FAIR - RIDES cont.

LA FÊTE FORAINE - LES MANEGES suite

The Ghost Train	*Le Train Fantôme*
It's very dark.	*Il fait très noir.*
I can't see.	*Je ne vois rien.*
I am frightened.	*J'ai peur.*
Hold my hand.	*Tenez / tiens ma main.*
It will be over in a minute.	*Ce sera fini dans une minute.*

The Dodgems	*Les Autos-tamponneuses (f)*
to wait for them to stop	*attendre qu'elles s'arrêtent*
to climb in	*grimper dans*
to put your seat belt on	*mettre sa ceinture*
to steer	*diriger / conduire*
to turn the wheel	*tourner le volant*
to the left / to the right	*vers la gauche / vers la droite*
to go round in circles	*tourner en rond*
to go the other way	*aller en sens inverse*
to accelerate	*accélérer*
to chase	*poursuivre*
to get stuck	*être coincé*
to hit / to bump	*taper / tamponner*
Let's try to bump them.	*Essayons de les tamponner.*
Please don't bump us.	*S'il vous plaît ne nous tamponnez pas.*

The Waltzers	*Les Monts-Blancs (m)*
Where do you want to sit?	*Où voulez-vous vous / veux-tu t'asseoir?*
Can I sit in the middle, please?	*Je peux m'asseoir au milieu, s'il vous plaît?*
You're squashing me.	*Vous me serrez / tu me serres.*
Please twirl us some more.	*S'il vous plaît / s'il te plaît faites nous encore tourner.*
Please don't do that.	*S'il vous plaît / s'il te plaît ne faites pas cela.*

THE FAIR - RIDES cont.   *LA FÊTE FORAINE - LES MANEGES suite*

The Merry-go-Round	*Le Manège (de chevaux de bois)*
Which horse / animal would you like to go on?	*Sur quel cheval / animal voulez-vous / veux-tu aller?*
Do you like to be on the inside or the outside?	*Vous voulez / tu veux être à l'intérieur ou à l'extérieur?*

The Rollercoaster	*Les Montagnes Russes*
to scream	*crier*
to feel sick	*avoir envie de vomir*
to hate it / to love it	*les détester / les adorer*
to loop the loop	*faire un looping*
to be upside down	*être retourné*

The Helter Skelter	*Le Toboggan*
to take a mat	*prendre un tapis*
to climb to the top	*grimper tout en haut*
to slide down	*glisser*

A Centrifuge	*Un Centrifugeur*
the centrifugal force	*la force centrifuge*
to be pinned to the side	*être collé sur les côtés*

A Simulator	*Un Simulateur*
realistic	*réaliste*
not very realistic	*pas très réaliste*

THE FAIR - RIDES cont.

LA FÊTE FORAINE - LES MANEGES suite

Darts and the rifle range	Les Fléchettes et le tir à la carabine
a dart	une fléchette
a dartboard	un tableau de fléchette
to throw	lancer
to aim	viser
to score	marquer
a gun / a rifle	un pistolet / une carabine
to point	pointer
to shoot	tirer
the target	la cible
to hit / to miss	atteindre / manquer
to hit the bull's eye	atteindre le mille
I need twenty more.	Il m'en faut encore vingt.
I have to score one hundred.	Je dois marquer cent.

Hoopla	Le Jeu d'anneaux
to throw the ring	lancer l'anneau
to get the ring over	encercler
nearly	presque
to win	gagner

A Coconut Shy	Un Jeu de Massacre
to throw a ball	lancer une balle
to try to hit	essayer de toucher
to throw harder	lancer plus fort
to make it wobble	le faire trembler
to knock it down	l'assommer
to fall off	tomber
to win a coconut	gagner une noix de coco

THE FAIR cont.

LA FÊTE FORAINE suite.

WINNING PRIZES

GAGNER DES PRIX

Well done!	*Bravo!*
What prize would you like?	*Quel prix aimeriez-vous / aimerais-tu?*
I would like a..	*J'aimerais un...*
• goldfish	• *poisson rouge*
• a teddybear	• *nounours*
• one of those	• *un comme ceux-là*
Have you won anything yet?	*Vous avez / tu as gagné quelque chose?*
Yes, I've won this.	*Oui, j'ai gagné ceci.*
No, I never win anything.	*Non, je ne gagne jamais rien.*

THE GAMES ARCADE

LA SALLE DE JEUX

I haven't any change.	*Je n'ai pas de monnaie.*
Where do you get change from?	*Où peut-on faire de la monnaie?*
There is a change machine over there.	*Il y a une machine à monnaie là-bas.*
What coins does this game take?	*Quelles pièces cette machine prend-elle?*
a fruit machine	*une machine à sous*
a pinball machine	*un Flipper*
Where do you put the money in?	*Où on met l'argent?*
How do you play?	*Comment on joue?*
You have to…	*Il faut...*
to roll a coin	*faire rouler une pièce*
to make it land on..	*le faire atterrir sur...*
to pull this handle	*tirer la poignée*
to press this button	*appuyer sur le bouton*

THE FAIR cont. *LA FÊTE FORAINE suite*

FOOD *LA NOURRITURE*

Candy Floss	*La Barbe à Papa*
on a stick	*sur un bâtonnet*
in a bag	*dans un sac*
pink	*rose*
yellow	*jaune*

Hot Dogs	*Hot Dogs*
Do you want your hot dog with..?	*Vous voulez / tu veux votre ton hot dog avec...*
• mustard	• *de la moutarde*
• tomato ketchup	• *du Ketchup*
• fried onions	• *des oignons frits*
• plain	• *nature*
• a lot of	• *beaucoup de*
• just a little	• *juste un peu*
• no onions, thanks.	• *sans oignons, merci.*

Popcorn	*Pop Corn*
a bag of	*un sachet de*
a carton of	*un pot de*
large / medium / small	*grand / moyen / petit*
sweet	*sucré*
salted	*salé*
Would you like some of my popcorn?	*Vous voulez / tu veux un peu de mes popcorns?*

THE FAIR cont.

LA FÊTE FORAINE suite.

PROBLEMS

LES PROBLEMES

a pickpocket	*un pickpocket / voleur*
My money has been stolen.	*Mon argent a été volé.*
Take care of your money.	*Attention à votre argent.*
My purse / wallet has disappeared.	*Mon porte-monnaie / portefeuille a disparu.*
I feel dizzy / a bit sick.	*J'ai la tête qui tourne / envie de vomir.*
It's rather noisy.	*C'est assez bruyant.*
Can we go home soon?	*On peut rentrer à la maison bientôt?*

USEFUL ADJECTIVES

ADJECTIFS UTILES

awful	*affreux*	fun	*drôle, marrant*
dizzy	*étourdissant*	funny	*amusant*
excellent	*excellent*	horrible	*horrible*
fantastic	*fantastique*	terrible	*terrible*
frightening	*effrayant*	terrifying	*terrifiant*

THE CIRCUS

LE CIRQUE

THE BIG TOP

LE GRAND CHAPITEAU

the ring	*la piste*
sawdust	*la sciure de bois*
the seats	*les gradins*

THE PEOPLE

LES GENS DE CIRQUE

The Ring Master	**"Monsieur Loyal"**
a top hat	*un haut-de-forme*
a whip	*un fouet*
to crack the whip	*faire claquer le fouet*

THE CIRCUS - THE PEOPLE cont.	LE CIRQUE - LES GENS DE CIRQUE suite

The Clown	*Le Clown*
a red nose	*un nez rouge*
big feet	*grands pieds*
to walk on stilts	*marcher sur des échasses*
to ride a monocycle	*faire du monocycle / de la moto*
to trip up	*trébucher*
to fall down	*tomber parterre*
to squirt water	*gicler de l'eau*
to make people laugh	*faire rire les gens*

The Acrobats	*Les Acrobates*
a trapeze artist	*un trapéziste*
the high wire	*la corde raide*
a safety net	*un filet*
a ladder	*une échelle*
a swing / to swing	*une balançoire / se balancer*
to balance	*être en équilibre*
to wobble	*chanceler*
to fall	*tomber*

Other Circus Performers	*Autres Gens de Cirque*
a bareback rider	*un cavalier (qui monte à crû)*
a lion tamer	*un dresseur de lions*

CIRCUS ANIMALS	*LES ANIMAUX DE CIRQUE*
a horse	*un cheval*
a lion	*un lion*
an elephant	*un éléphant*

THE ZOO   *LE ZOO*

PARTS OF THE ZOO   *LES PARTIES DU ZOO*

the elephant house	*la maison aux éléphants*
the aquarium	*l'aquarium*
a tank	*un réservoir*
the cages / the monkeys' cage	*les cages / les cages à singe*
the reptile house	*la maison aux reptiles*
the model train	*le train modèle*
Can we have a ride on the model train?	*Peut-on monter dans le train modèle?*
Do you want to go to the adventure playground?	*Vous voulez / tu veux aller dans l'aire de jeux?*
a lake / an island	*un lac / une île*
the cafeteria / the toilets	*le cafétéria / les toilettes*

THE ANIMALS (abc)   *LES ANIMAUX*

a bat	*une chauve-souris*	a monkey	*un singe*
a bear	*un ours*	an ostrich	*une autruche*
a crocodile	*un crocodile*	a panda	*un Panda*
a dolphin	*un dauphin*	a pelican	*un pélican*
an elephant	*un éléphant*	a penguin	*un pingouin*
an emu	*un émeu*	a rhinoceros	*un rhinocéros*
a fish	*un poisson*	a seal	*un phoque*
a pink flamingo	*un flamand rose*	a snake	*un serpent*
a giraffe	*une girafe*	a tarantula	*une tarentule*
a hippopotamus	*un hippopotame*	a tiger	*un tigre*
a kangaroo	*un kangourou*	a tortoise	*une tortue*
a leopard	*un léopard*	a turtle	*une tortue marine*
a lion	*un lion*	a zebra	*un zèbre*

SIGHTSEEING
FAIRE DU TOURISME

STATELY HOMES & CASTLES	*MANOIRS ET CHATEAUX*

OPENING HOURS	*HEURES D'OVERTURE*
What are your opening hours?	*Quelles sont vos heures d'ouverture?*
Are you open every day of the week?	*Etes-vous ouverts tous les jours?*
How much is it to go round?	*Cela coûte combien de faire le tour?*
Is there a guided tour?	*Y a-t-il une visite guidée?*
What time is the tour?	*A quelle heure est la visite?*
Is there a commentary one can listen to?	*Y a-t-il un commentaire?*
Do you have the commentary in English / French / Spanish / German?	*Y a-t-il un commentaire en Anglais / Français / Espagnol / Allemand?*
How do the headphones work?	*Comment marchent les écouteurs?*
Could I have a guide book, please?	*Je peux avoir un guide, s'il vous plaît?*

COULD I HAVE A TICKET FOR...?	*PUIS-JE AVOIR UN BILLET POUR...*
• the house only	• *la maison seulement*
• the gardens only	• *les jardins seulement*
• one adult	• *un adulte*
• one student	• *un étudiant*
Is there a reduction for students / groups?	*Y a-t-il une réduction-étudiants / groupe?*

STATELY HOMES & CASTLES cont.

MANOIRS ET CHÂTEAUX suite

ARCHITECTURAL STYLES		LES STYLES ARCHITECTURUAX	
Who was the architect?		*Qui était l'architecte?*	
What style was this built in?		*Dans quel style a-t-il / elle été construit(e)?*	
Norman	*Roman*	Baroque	*Baroque*
medieval	*médiéval*	Classical	*Classique*
gothic	*gothique*	Georgian	*Géorgien*
Tudor	*Tudor*	Regency	*Régence*
Renaissance	*Renaissance*	Victorian	*Victorien*

TYPES OF BUILDINGS (in approximately descending size)		LES TYPES D'EDIFICES (du plus grand au plus petit)	
a palace	*un palais*	a folly	*une folie*
a castle	*un château*	a conservatory	*une verrière*
a mansion	*un hôtel particulier*	a coach house	*une remise*
manor house	*manoir(m)*	(a coach)	*un carrosse*
the court	*la cour*	(a royal coach)	*un carrosse royal*
a priory	*un prieuré*	a thatched cottage	*une maison à toit de chaume*
the chapel	*la chapelle*	a stable	*une étable*
the lodge	*le pavillon*	a greenhouse	*une serre*
the gatehouse	*la loge*		

STATELY HOMES & CASTLES cont.

MANOIRS ET CHATEAUX suite

EXTERNAL DETAILS

(top downwards)

LES DETAILS EXTERIEURS

(de haut en bas)

a turret	*une tourelle*	the door	*la porte*
battlements	*remparts*	a flight of steps	*une volée d'escalier*
the parapet	*le parapet*	a portcullis	*une herse*
a facade	*une façade*	a drawbridge	*un pont-levis*
a balcony	*un balcon*	a moat	*une douve*
the windows	*les fenêtres*	a rampart	*un rempart*
French windows	*portes-fenêtres*	the gateway	*le portail*
the porch	*le porche*	floodlighting	*illumination*

THE PARK AND GARDENS

LE PARC ET LES JARDINS

the park	*le parc*	a path	*une allée*
the garden	*le jardin*	a terrace	*une terrasse*
a formal garden	*un jardin à la française*	an informal garden	*un jardin simple*
a rose garden	*un jardin à rosier*	a wild flower garden	*un jardin en friche*
a knot garden	*un jardin "Tudor"*	a ha-ha	*une clôture en contrebas*

A MAZE

UN LABYRINTHE

to go in	*y aller / entrer*	to find your way out	*trouver la sortie*
to get lost	*se perdre*	to be gone ages	*être parti depuis très longtemps*
to turn back	*faire demi-tour*		
to try to get out	*essayer de sortir*		

STATELY HOMES cont.　　　　*LES MANOIRS suite*

GARDEN BUILDINGS AND ORNAMENTS		*LES EDIFICES ET ORNEMENTS DE JARDIN*	
a conservatory	*une verrière*	(a dove)	*une colombe*
an orangery	*une orangerie*	a statue	*une statue*
a greenhouse	*une serre*	an urn	*une urne*
a dovecote	*un colombier*	a pedestal	*un piedestal*

WATER FEATURES		*LES POINTS D'EAU*	
a lake	*un lac*	an ornamental pond	*un bassin ornemental*
an island	*un îlot*		
a river	*une rivière*	water lilies	*nénuphars (m)*
a fountain	*une fontaine*	goldfish	*poisson rouge (m)*
a waterfall	*une chute d'eau*	a water garden	*un jardin aquatique*
When are the fountains turned on?		*Quand les fontaines sont-elles en marche?*	

HIRING BOATS	*LOUER LES BATEAUX*
a boat	*un bateau*
a motorboat	*un bateau à moteur*
to go for a trip	*faire un tour (de bateau)*
to start the engine	*démarrer le moteur*
a canoe / to go canoeing	*un canoë / aller faire du canoë*
a paddle / to paddle	*une rame / ramer*
on the right / left	*à droite / à gauche*
to steer	*diriger*
to row	*faire de l'aviron*
to moor	*amarrer*
to collide with someone	*heurter quelqu'un*
to try to avoid someone	*essayer d'éviter quelqu'un*

STATELY HOMES & CASTLES cont.

*MANOIRS ET CHATEAUX
suite*

THE TEA ROOM
Where is the tea room?
Shall we have a cup of tea?
Shall we take it into the garden?
Shall we stay inside?

LE SALON DE THE
Où est le salon de thé?
On prend une tasse de thé?
On le prend dans le jardin?
On reste à l'intérieur?

THE GIFT SHOP
Can I look round the gift shop?

Do you want to buy something for
your family?

Would you like to buy some
postcards?

LA BOUTIQUE DE CADEAUX
*Est-ce que je peux faire un tour
dans la boutique de cadeaux?*
*Vous voulez / tu veux acheter
quelque chose pour votre / ta
famille?*
*Vous voulez / tu veux acheter des
cartes postales?*

INTERNAL DETAILS

DETAILS INTERIEURS

THE MAIN ROOMS
(in descending importance)

LES PIECES PRINCIPALES
*(dans l'ordre décroissant de leur
importance)*

THE MAIN HALL
a suit of armour

LE HALL D'ENTREE
une armure complète

chain mail	*cotte de maille*	guns	*fusils (m)*
heraldry	*un blason*	pistols	*pistolets (m)*
a coat of arms	*une armoire*	swords	*épées (f)*
weapons	*armes*	shields	*boucliers (m)*

**STATELY HOMES &
CASTLES cont.**

*MANOIRS ET CHATEAUX
suite*

THE STATEROOM

*LA GRANDE SALLE DE
RECEPTION*

the paintings		*les peintures (f) / tableaux (m)*
a mural		*une peinture murale*
a fresco	*une fresque*	the ceiling	*le plafond*
the portraits	*les portraits (m)*	the plasterwork	*les plâtres (m)*
the mirrors	*les miroirs (m)*	the carpet	*le tapis*
a bust	*un buste*	the curtains	*les rideaux (m)*
the fireplace	*la cheminée*	the furniture	*le mobilier*

THE BALLROOM

LA SALLE DE BAL

the chandelier	*le lustre*
the mirrors	*les miroirs (m)*

THE BANQUETING HALL

LA SALLE DE BANQUET

the dining table	*la table*	the silver	*l'argenterie (f)*
the chairs	*les chaises (f)*	the tureens	*les soupières (f)*
a dinner service	*un service à dîner*	a banquet	*un banquet*

THE DRAWING ROOM

LE SALON

a grandfather clock		*une horloge de parquet*
the panelling	*les lambris (m)*	a tapestry	*une tapisserie*
the sofas	*les canapés (m)*	porcelain	*porcelaine (f)*
the armchairs	*les fauteuils (m)*		

THE LIBRARY

LA BIBLIOTHEQUE

valuable / antique books	*les livres de valeur / anciens*
a family tree	*un arbre généalogique*
the bookcases	*les étagères*

**STATELY HOMES &
CASTLES cont.**

*MANOIRS ET CHATEAUX
suite*

THE MUSIC ROOM *LA SALLE DE MUSIQUE*

| a harpsichord | *un clavecin* | a harp | *une harpe* |

THE STAIRCASE & GALLERY *LES ESCALIERS ET LA GALARIE*

a spiral staircase	*un escalier en colimaçon*	a servants' staircase	*l'escalier des domestiques*
a back staircase	*un escalier de service*	a secret staircase	*un escalier secret*
a minstrels' gallery	*la tribune des musiciens*	to look down on	*regarder en bas*

THE NURSERY *LA CHAMBRE D'ENFANTS*

a rocking horse		*un cheval à bascule*
a dolls' house		*une maison de poupée*
a cradle	*un berceau*	toys	*jouets (m)*
a cot	*un lit d'enfant*	a desk	*un bureau*

THE KITCHEN *LA CUISINE*

a kitchen table		*une table de cuisine*
the range		*un fourneau de cuisine*
a dumb waiter		*un monte-charge*
the cold store		*un entrepôt frigorifique*
a fireplace	*une cheminée*	to smoke	*fumer*
an inglenook	*le coin du feu*	pots and pans	*les casseroles*
a hook	*un crochet*	the utensils	*les ustensiles*
a rotisserie	*une rôtisserie*	copper	*cuivre (m)*
a spit	*une broche*	pewter	*les étains (m)*
to turn	*tourner*	the sink	*l'évier (m)*
to cook	*cuisiner*	the cook	*le cuisinier*

STATELY HOMES cont.　　*LES MANOIRS suite*

OTHER ROOMS　　*AUTRES PIÈCES*

Servants' accommodation　*Le logement des domestiques*
the servants' rooms　*les pièces des domestiques (f)*
the attic　*le grenier*

The cellar　*la cave*
a wine cellar　*une cave à vin*

The dungeons　*les donjons (m)*
the torture chamber　*la chambre des tortures*
a chamber of horrors　*la chambre d'épouvante*

THE ROYAL FAMILY	*LA FAMILLE ROYALE*		
a King	*un Roi*	a Prince	*un Prince*
a Queen	*une Reine*	a Princess	*une Princesse*
the Queen Mother	*la Reine-Mère*	a Duke / Duchess	*un Duc / Duchesse*

THE SERVANTS	*LES DOMESTIQUES*		
the butler	*le majordome*	the footmen	*les valets de pied*
the chef	*le chef cuisinier*	a maidservant	*une servante*
the cook	*le cuisinier*	a manservant	*un valet de chambre*

STATELY HOMES & CASTLES cont.

MANOIRS ET CHATEAUX suite

USEFUL DESCRIPTIVE WORDS (abc)

DESCRIPTIONS UTILES

added on	*ajouté*	dilapidated	*dilapidé*
ancient	*antique*	dusty	*poussiéreux*
attractive	*attrayant*	elegant	*élégant*
austere	*austère*	expensive	*cher*
authentic	*authentique*	faded	*décoloré(e)*
baroque	*baroque*	gold	*doré(e)*
beautiful	*beau*	gothic	*gothique*
built by	*construit par*	imposing	*imposant(e)*
burnt down	*brûlé*	in ruins	*en ruine*
century	*siècle*	luxurious	*luxueux(se)*
eleventh	*onzième*	modern	*moderne*
twelfth	*douzième*	modernised	*modernisé(e)*
thirteenth	*treizième*	old	*vieux / vieille*
fourteenth	*quatorzième*	ornate	*orné(e)*
fifteenth	*quinzième*	over-restored	*trop restauré(e)*
sixteenth	*seizième*	rare	*rare*
seventeenth	*dix-septième*	rebuilt	*reconstruit(e)*
eighteenth	*dix-huitième*	reclaimed	*reconquis(e)*
nineteenth	*dix-neuvième*	restored by	*restauré(e) par*
twentieth	*vingtième*	ruined	*ruiné(e)*
twenty first	*vingt-et-unième*	splendid	*splendide*
charming	*charmant*	sumptuous	*somptueux*
commonplace	*commun*	valuable	*de grande valeur*
designed by	*crée par*	wonderful	*merveilleux(se)*

CHURCHES   *LES EGLISES (f)*

ARCHITECTURAL CLASSIFICATIONS		*CLASSIFICATIONS ARCHITECTURALES*	
Romanesque	*Roman*	Flamboyant	*flamboyant(e)*
Saxon	*Saxon*	Jacobean	*de l'époque de Jacques I*
Norman	*Roman*	Renaissance	*Renaissance*
Gothic	*Gothique*	Baroque	*Baroque*
Early English	*Premier Gothique Anglais*	Classical	*Classique*
Decorated	*Décore(e)*	Georgian	*Géorgien(ne)*
Perpendicular	*Perpendiculaire*	Victorian	*Victorien(ne)*
Tudor	*Tudor*		

EXTERNAL DETAILS		*DETAILS EXTERIEURS*	
a buttress	*un conte fort*	the churchyard	*le cimetière*
a flying buttress	*arc-boutant (m)*	a grave	*une tombe*
a gargoyle	*une gargouille*	a tombstone	*une pierre tombale*
a pinnacle	*un pinacle*	an inscription	*une inscription*
a spire	*une flèche*	to read	*lire*
a tower	*une tour*	Roman	*les chiffres*
a weathercock	*une girouette*	numerals	*romains (m)*

CHURCHES cont. *LES EGLISES suite*

INTERNAL DETAILS		**DETAILS INTERIEURS**	
the Lady Chapel		*la chapelle de la Sainte Vierge*	
alabaster	*albâtre (m)*	a fresco	*une fresque*
an arcade	*une arcade*	the lectern	*le lutrin*
an arch	*un arc*	marble	*marbre (m)*
the aisle	*l'aile (f)*	a mural	*une peinture murale*
the altar	*l'autel (m)*	the nave	*la nef*
(to kneel at)	*s'agenouiller à*	a niche	*une niche*
(to pray)	*prier*	the organ	*l'orgue (m)*
the bell tower	*le clocher*	(to play the organ)	*jouer de l'orgue*
a bell	*une cloche*	(the organist)	*l'organiste*
to ring the bells	*sonner les cloches*	a pew	*un banc*
a candle	*un cierge*	a pillar	*un pilier*
(to buy)	*acheter*	the porch	*le porche*
(to light)	*allumer*	the pulpit	*la chaire*
the chancel	*le chœur (place*	(to give a sermon)	*faire un sermon*
the choir	*le chœur (singers)*	(to preach)	*prêcher*
a choir stall	*la stalle*	the roof	*le toit*
a column	*une colonne*	(a vault)	*une voûte*
The Cross	*la Croix*	(a beam)	*une poutre*
the crypt	*la crypte*	a statue	*une statue*
the door	*la porte*	a tomb	*une tombe*
the font	*les fonts baptismaux*	the transept	*le transept*
(a Baptism)	*un baptême*	a window	*un vitrail*
(a Christening)	*un baptême*	(stained glass)	*des vitraux*

CHURCHES cont.   *LES EGLISES suite*

USEFUL DESCRIPTIVE WORDS (abc)		*DESCRIPTIONS UTILES*	
cold	*froid(e)*	musty	*qui sent le renfermé*
dark	*sombre*	open	*ouvert(e)*
dilapidated	*délabré(e)*	ornate	*ornée*
elegant	*élégant(e)*	peaceful	*paisible*
humble	*humble*	rich	*riche*
intricate	*complexe*	rural	*rural(e)*
locked-up	*fermée*	sombre	*sombre*

ART GALLERIES & EXHIBITIONS
LES GALERIES D'ART ET EXPOSITIONS

ART GALLERIES	*LES GALERIES D'ART*
an art collection	*une collection*
an artist	*un artiste*
a work of art	*une œuvre d'art*
a painting	*une peinture*
a private view	*un vernissage*
an invitation	*une invitation*

MUSEUMS	*LES MUSEES*
an exhibition	*une exposition*
an exhibit	*une pièce exposée*

USEFUL EXPRESSIONS	*EXPRESSIONS UTILES*
There is an interesting exhibition on at the moment.	*Il y a un exposition intéressante en ce moment.*
Would you like to go to it?	*Vous aimeriez / tu aimerais y aller?*
Is there a catalogue?	*Y a-t-il un catalogue?*
How much is an entrance ticket?	*Combien est le billet d'entrée?*
Is there a reduction for students?	*Y a-t-il une réduction-étudiants?*
Entrance is free.	*L'entrée est gratuite.*
How much do guide books cost?	*Combien coûtent les guides?*
How much are these postcards?	*Combien coûtent ces cartes postales?*
Do you have a guide book in English / French / German / Spanish?	*Avez-vous un guide en Anglais / Français / Allemand / Espagnol?*
Shall we split up and meet here in half an hour?	*On se sépare et on se retrouve ici dans une demi-heure?*

ART GALLERIES & EXHIBITIONS cont.

LES GALERIES D'ART ET EXPOSITIONS suite

WHO / WHAT IS YOUR FAVOURITE..?		*QUI / QUEL EST TON / TA...PREFERE(E)?*	
artist	*artiste (m/f)*	painting	*peinture (f)*
sculptor	*sculpteur (m)*	piece of sculpture	*sculpture (f)*

WHAT TYPE OF ART DO YOU LIKE MOST? (abc)		*QUEL ART PREFEREZ VOUS / PREFERES-TU ?*	
abstract art	*art abstrait (m)*	post-impressionism	*post-impressionnisme*
art deco	*art-déco*	Pre-Raphaelite	*préraphaélite*
classical art	*classique (m)*	primitive art	*art primitif (m)*
cubism	*cubisme (m)*	prints	*estampes (f)*
engravings	*gravures (f)*	realism	*réalisme (m)*
etchings	*eaux-fortes (f)*	religious art	*art religieux*
expressionism	*expressionnisme (m)*	romantic art	*art roman (m)*
impressionism	*impressionnisme (m)*	seascapes	*paysages maritimes (m)*
landscapes	*paysages (m)*	self portraits	*autoportraits*
life drawings	*peinture vivantes (f)*	sporting works	*tableaux de chasse*
miniatures	*miniatures (f)*	still life	*nature morte (f)*
nudes	*nus (m)*	surrealism	*surréalisme (m)*
oil paintings	*peintures à l'huile (f)*	symbolism	*symbolisme (m)*
pastels	*pastels (m)*	townscapes	*paysages urbains (m)*
pop art	*pop-art (m)*	water colours	*aquarelles (f)*
portraits	*portraits (m)*	wood cuttings	*gravures sur bois (f)*

ART GALLERIES cont.   *LES GALERIES D'ART suite*

WHAT IS YOUR FAVOURITE PERIOD?	*QUELLE EST VOTRE / TA PERIODE PREFEREE?*
My favourite period is..	*Ma période préférée est...*
medieval	*le Moyen-Age*
Renaissance	*la Renaissance*
High Renaissance	*la Haute Renaissance*
Baroque	*le Baroque*

eighteenth century	*le dix-huitième siècle*
nineteenth century	*le dix-neuvième siècle*
twentieth century	*le vingtième siècle*

WHAT IS YOUR FAVOURITE MEDIUM?	*QUEL GENRE PREFEREZ-VOUS / PREFERES-TU?*
I particularly like..	*J'aime surtout...*
acrylics	*les acryliques*
chalk	*la craie*
charcoal	*le fusain*
crayon	*le crayon*
gouache	*la gouache*

oil	*l'huile (f)*
pastels	*les pastels (m)*
tempera	*une détrempe*
water colours	*la peinture à l'eau*

USEFUL EXPRESSIONS	*LES EXPRESSIONS UTILES*
the allegorical meaning	*le sens allégorique*
the background / the foreground	*l'arrière plan / le premier plan*
the colour	*la couleur*
the delicacy	*la délicatesse*
the effect on the viewer	*l'effet sur le spectateur*
the emotion	*l'émotion*
the focus	*la mise au point*
the grouping	*le regroupement*
the light and shade	*la lumière et l'ombre*
the meaning	*le sens*
the obscurity	*l'obscurité (f)*

ART GALLERIES cont. *LES GALERIES D'ART suite*

USEFUL EXPRESSIONS cont. *LES EXPRESSIONS UTILES suite*

the poses	*les poses (f)*
the power	*la puissance*
the structure	*la structure*
the subtlety	*la subtilité*
the suffering	*la souffrance*
the symbolism	*le symbolisme*
the technique	*la technique*
the use of perspective	*l'utilisation (f) de la perspective*
the vanishing point	*le point de fuite*

BASIC ART EQUIPMENT *LE MATERIEL ARTISTIQUE DE BASE*

an easel	*un chevalet*	a palette knife	*un couteau (à) palette*
paper	*du papier*	a pencil	*un crayon*
canvas	*une toile*	a rubber	*une gomme*
paints	*de la peinture*	a water pot	*un pot d'eau*
a paintbrush	*un pinceau*	white spirit	*du white spirit*

PAINTING METHODS *LES METHODES DE PEINTURE*

to blend	*mélanger*	to mix	*mélanger*
to copy	*copier*	to re-paint	*repeindre*
to dab	*appliquer par petites touches*	to paint over	*peindre par dessus*
to dip	*tremper*	to sketch	*ébaucher*
to glaze	*vernir*	to varnish	*vernir*
to imitate	*imiter*	to wash	*laver*

ART GALLERIES cont.   *LES GALERIES D'ART suite*

ART CLASSIFICATIONS	LES CLASSIFICATIONS DE L'ART
Fine Art	*Les Beaux-Arts (m)*
Applied Art	*Art appliqué*
jewellery	*joaillerie (f)*
silversmithing	*orfèvrerie (f)*
porcelain making	*fabrication (f) de la porcelaine*
metalwork	*ferronnerie (f)*
pottery	*poterie (f)*
Decorative Art	*Art Décoratif*
embroidery	*broderie (f)*
tapestry	*tapisserie (f)*

VINEYARDS
LES VIGNES

THE VINEYARD	LA VIGNE
a château	*un château*

THE VINES	LES VIGNES
a grapevine	*une vigne*
a bunch of grapes	*une grappe de raisin*
a grape	*un raisin*
green / purple	*blanc / rouge*

VINEYARDS cont.

LES VIGNES suite

PICKING THE GRAPES	*LA CUEILLETTE DU RAISIN*
ripe	*mûr*
unripe	*vert / pas mûr*
to harvest	*récolter*
to pick	*cueillir*
to gather	*rassembler*
to press	*presser*
the juice	*le jus*

STORING THE WINE		*CONSERVER LE VIN*	
a barrel	*un tonneau*	to ferment	*fermenter*
wooden	*en bois (m)*	fermentation	*fermentation (f)*
oak	*chêne (m)*	to bottle	*mettre en bouteille*
steel	*acier*	a bottle	*une bouteille*
a vat	*une cuve*	to label	*étiqueter*
a vatful	*une cuvée*	a label	*une étiquette*

CLASSIFYING WINE		*CLASSIFIER LE VIN*	
an officially classified wine		*Appellation d'origine contrôlée*	
country of origin		*pays d'origine (m)*	
a good year		*une bonne année*	
a bad year		*une mauvaise année*	
alcoholic content		*alcoolique*	
vintage	*millésime (m)*	dry wine	*vin sec*
region	*région (f)*	sparkling wine	*vin pétillant*
a table wine	*un vin de table*	champagne	*champagne (m)*
red wine	*vin rouge*	fortified wine	*vin bonifié*
white wine	*vin blanc*	an aperitif	*un apéritif*
rosé wine	*rosé*	sherry	*xérès / sherry*
sweet wine	*vin sucré*	vermouth	*vermouth (m)*

VINEYARDS cont.   *LES VIGNES suite*

SERVING WINE		SERVIR LE VIN	
to serve at the right temperature		*servir à la bonne température*	
to keep at room temperature		*conserver à température ambiante*	
to open a bottle		*ouvrir une bouteille*	
to allow to breathe		*laisser respirer*	
to chill	*rafraîchir*	to decant	*décanter*
to uncork	*déboucher*	sediment	*la lie*
a corkscrew	*un tire-bouchon*	to pour	*verser*

TASTING WINE	GOUTER LE VIN
a wine tasting	*une dégustation de vin*
to savour	*savourer*
the bouquet	*le bouquet*
the colour	*la couleur / robe*
to hold up to the light	*élever à la lumière*
to hold in the mouth	*garder en bouche*
to spit	*cracher*
a spittoon	*un crachoir*
to sample	*un échantillon*
to identify	*identifier*
to appreciate	*apprécier*
to have a good palate	*avoir un bon palais*

WALKS   *LES PROMENADES*

A WALK	**UNE PROMENADE**
Would you like to go for a walk?	*Vous voulez / tu veux aller vous / te promener?*
How far do you feel like going?	*Vous voulez / tu veux aller jusqu'où?*
Where would you like to go to?	*Où voulez-vous / veux-tu aller?*
Do you like walking?	*Vous aimez / tu aimes marcher?*

TAKING THE DOG	**SORTIR LE CHIEN**
I'm taking the dog for a walk.	*Je sors le chien.*
Would you like to come?	*Vous voulez / tu veux venir?*
Where is its lead?	*Où est sa laisse?*
How do you put on its lead?	*Où met-on sa laisse?*
May I hold the lead?	*Je peux tenir la laisse?*
Don't let it off the lead here.	*Gardez-le / garde-le en laisse ici.*
You can let it off the lead now.	*Vous pouvez / tu peux enlever la laisse maintenant.*
Dogs must be kept on the lead.	*Les chiens doivent être gardés en laisse.*

CLOTHES   *LES VETEMENTS*

Footwear	**Se chausser**
socks / shoes	*chaussettes / chaussures*
boots / wellingtons	*bottines / bottes en caoutchouc*
Have you any walking shoes / boots / wellingtons with you?	*Vous avez / tu as des chaussures de marche / des bottines / des bottes avec vous / toi?*
Would you like to borrow a pair of wellingtons?	*Vous voulez / tu veux emprunter une paire de bottes?*
We may have some that fit you.	*Nous en avons peut être qui vous iront / t'iront.*
Try these.	*Essayez / essaie celles-ci.*
Are they comfortable?	*Elles sont confortables?*
Do they fit?	*Elles vous / te vont?*
They are too small / big.	*Elles sont trop petites / grandes.*

WALKS cont.   *LES PROMENADES suite*

Clothes for bad weather	*Les vêtements pour mauvais temps*
Bring...	*Apportez / apporte...*
a coat	*un manteau*
a jacket	*une veste*
a mackintosh	*un imperméable*
a pullover / a sweater	*un pull / un sweater*
trousers	*un pantalon*
a hat	*un chapeau*
a scarf	*une écharpe*
a pair of gloves	*une pair de gants*
an umbrella	*un parapluie*
spare clothes	*un vêtement de rechange*

PICNICS	*LES PIQUE-NIQUES*
Shall we take a picnic?	*On prend un pique-nique?*
Help me pack the picnic.	*Aidez-moi / aide-moi à préparer le pique-nique.*
What would you like to eat and drink?	*Qu'aimeriez-vous / qu'aimerais-tu boire et manger?*
Shall we stop for something to eat and drink now?	*On s'arrête pour manger et boire quelque chose?*
Shall we take a rug?	*On prend une nappe?*
to sit down for a while	*se reposer un moment*

PICNIC FOOD & DRINK	*LA NOURRITURE ET BOISSON POUR PIQUE-NIQUES*
a flask / to fill	*une bouteille Thermos / remplir*
to pour	*verser*
a hot drink	*une boisson chaude*
a cold drink	*une boisson fraîche*
to be thirsty	*avoir soif*
to be hungry	*avoir faim*

WALKS cont. *LES PROMENADES suite*

PICNIC FOOD & DRINK cont. *LA NOURRITURE ET BOISSON POUR PIQUE-NIQUES suite*

sandwiches	*sandwiches (m)*
What do you want on your sandwiches?	*Que voulez-vous / veux-tu dans votre / ton sandwich?*
ham / chicken /	*jambon (m) / poulet (m) /*
salami / cheese /	*saucisson (m) / fromage (m) /*
fish / salad / tomato	*poisson (m) / salade (f) / tomate (f)*
/ egg / mayonnaise	*/ œuf (m) / mayonnaise (f)*
a packet of crisps	*un paquet de chips*
a piece of cake	*un morceau de gâteau*
some fruit	*des fruits*
an apple / a banana / an orange / some grapes	*une pomme / une banane / une orange / du raisin*
a bar of chocolate	*une barre de chocolat*
Would you like a piece of chocolate?	*Vous voulez / tu veux un morceau de chocolat?*

DISCUSSING THE ROUTE	*DECIDER DE LA ROUTE A SUIVRE*
a plan / a sketch	*un plan / un croquis*
a map / directions	*une carte / directions (f)*
Where are we?	*Où sommes-nous?*
Show me where we are going to go.	*Montrez-moi / montre-moi où nous allons.*
How far is that? / Are we lost?	*C'est loin? / On est perdu?*
Are we going in the right / wrong direction?	*On va dans la bonne / mauvaise direction?*
Shall we ask someone?	*On demande à quelqu'un?*
to use a compass	*utiliser une boussole*
the needle / to point	*l'aiguille (f) / pointer*
North / South / East / West	*Nord / Sud / Est / Ouest*
We need to go in this direction.	*Il faut aller dans cette direction.*

WALKS cont.   *LES PROMENADES suite*

PROBLEMS	*LES PROBLEMES*
Is there a telephone box?	*Y a-t-il une cabine téléphonique?*
Could we possibly use your telephone, please?	*On peut utiliser votre téléphone, s'il vous plaît?*
We are lost.	*On est perdu.*
We are trying to get to…	*On essaie d'aller à…*
Where is the pub?	*Où est le café?*
Is there a village shop?	*Y a-t-il une boutique dans le village?*
I am tired.	*Je suis fatigué(e),*
My legs are aching.	*Mes jambes me font mal.*
I have a blister.	*J'ai une ampoule.*
My shoes are rubbing.	*Mes chaussures frottent.*
I fell over.	*Je suis tombé(e).*
It's just a graze.	*C'est seulement une écorchure.*
Have you a sticking plaster / an Elastoplast ®?	*Avez-vous / as-tu un pansement?*
I hurt my foot / leg / hand / arm / back.	*Je me suis fait mal au pied / à la jambe / à la main / au bras / au dos.*
I have sprained my ankle.	*Je me suis tordu la cheville.*
I have been stung.	*J'ai été piqué(e).*
I have been bitten by something.	*J'ai été mordu par quelque chose.*
Have you anything to put on a sting?	*Avez-vous / as-tu quelque chose pour mettre sur ma piqûre?*
Have you any fly repellent?	*Avez-vous / as-tu des anti-mouches?*

WALKS cont.   *LES PROMENADES suite*

LANDMARKS   *POINTS DE REPERE (m)*

BUILDINGS etc (abc)	*LES EDIFICES etc. (m)*
a chemist's shop	*une pharmacie*
the church	*l'église (f)*
a cottage	*une maison de campagne*
the graveyard	*le cimetière*
a house	*une maison*
the manor house	*le manoir*
a newsagent's shop	*une buraliste*
the playground	*le terrain de jeux*
the police station	*le commissariat / la station de police*
a post box	*une boîte à lettres*
the post office	*la poste*
the railway station	*la gare*
the recreation ground	*le terrain de jeux*
a shop	*un magasin*
the telephone box	*la cabine téléphonique*
the village green	*la place du village*
the village hall	*la mairie / la salle paroissiale*
the village school	*l'école (f) du village (m)*
the village shop	*la boutique du coin*

TYPES OF ROAD	*LES TYPES DE ROUTE*
a signpost	*une borne*
to point the way to..	*pointer dans la direction...*
a road	*une route*
a main road	*une grand-route*
a "B" road / a minor road	*une route de campagne*
a lane	*une petite route*
a bridleway	*une piste cavalière*
a rough track	*un chemin*
a footpath	*un sentier*

WALKS cont.   *LES PROMENADES suite*

OBSTACLES / *OBSTACLES*

a stile	*un échalier*	a bog	*un marécage*
a gate	*une grille / barrière*	a cowpat	*une bouse de vache*
a wall	*un mur*	a railway	*un chemin de fer*
a cattle grid	*un grillage*	a railway bridge	*un pont de chemin de fer*

FARMS / *LES FERMES*

a farmhouse	*une ferme*	an egg	*un œuf*
a farmyard	*une ferme / basse-cour*	to collect the eggs	*ramasser les œufs*
the farmer	*le fermier*	a basket	*un panier*
the dairy	*la laiterie*	the barn	*la grange*
the cowshed	*l'étable (f)*	a hayloft	*le fumier*
a hen coop	*un poulailler*	a stable	*une étable*
a hen	*une poule*	a trough	*un abreuvoir*

WATER / *L'EAU (f)*

a river	*une rivière*	an island	*une île*
a stream	*un courant*	a pond	*un bassin*
a ford	*un gué*	a puddle	*une flaque*
a canal	*un canal*	a waterfall	*une chute d'eau*
a barge	*une péniche*	rapids	*des rapides (m)*
a lock	*une écluse*	the current	*les courrants (m)*
the lock keeper	*un éclusier*	strong	*forts*
the towpath	*le chemin de halage*	fast	*rapides*
a lake	*un lac*	dangerous	*dangereux*

WALKS cont.　　　　　　　　　*LES PROMENADES suite*

CROSSING WATER		***TRAVERSER DES POINTS D'EAU***	
stepping stones	*marchepieds (m)*	a bridge	*un pont*
slippery	*glissant*	to cross	*traverser*
wobbly	*branlant*	a footbridge	*un pont*
to tread on	*marcher sur*		*piétonnier*
to jump	*sauter*		

PADDLING	***BARBOTER***
Shall we paddle?	*On barbote?*
Take off your socks and shoes.	*Enlevez vos / enlève tes chaussettes (f) et chaussures (f).*
Have you got a towel?	*Avez-vous / as-tu une serviette?*
Dry your feet here.	*Séchez vos / sèche tes pieds ici.*
It's freezing / quite warm.	*C'est glacé / assez chaud.*
It's deep / shallow.	*C'est profond / c'est ne pas profond.*
It's pebbly / muddy.	*C'est rocailleux / boueux.*

HIGH GROUND		***LES TERRAINS EN ALTITUDE***	
a mountain	*une montagne*	a steep slope	*une pente raide*
to climb	*grimper*	to be careful	*faire attention*
to go to the top	*aller au sommet*	a hill	*une colline*
to see the view	*voir la vue*	a gentle slope	*une pente douce*
panoramic	*panoramique*	a valley	*une vallée*
spectacular	*spectaculaire*	a tunnel	*un tunnel*
Can you see..?	*Vous pouvez / tu peux voir...?*	a cave	*une cave*
		dark	*sombre*
on the horizon	*à l'horizon*	to echo	*résonner*
in the distance	*au loin*	an echo	*un écho*
over there	*là-bas*	to hide	*cacher*

WALKS cont.   *LES PROMENADES suite*

FIELDS etc.		*LES CHAMPS*	
a meadow	*une prairie*	unploughed	*non-labouré(e)*
a field	*un champ*	sown	*semé(e)*
ploughed	*labouré(e)*	a valley	*une vallée*

WALKING CONDITIONS		*LES CONDITIONS (f)*	
muddy	*boueux(se)*	tiring	*fatigant(e)*
slippery	*glissant(e)*	boring	*ennuyeux(se)*
steep	*en pente*	good	*bon(ne)*
flooded	*inondé(e)*	perfect	*parfait(e)*

WEATHER CONDITIONS   *LES CONDITIONS (f) METEOROLOGIQUES*

Hot	*Chaud*
It's very sunny.	*Il fait très beau.*
It's stuffy.	*Il fait lourd.*
It may thunder.	*Il va peut être y avoir de l'orage.*
It is too hot for me.	*Il fait trop chaud pour moi.*
Can we go into the shade for a bit?	*On peut aller à l'ombre un moment?*
I am boiling.	*Je bous.*

Cold	*Froid*
It's freezing.	*Il gèle.*
It's icy.	*Il y a du verglas.*
It's rather slippery.	*C'est assez glissant.*
Shall we slide on the ice?	*On peut glisser sur la glace?*
I am frozen.	*Je suis gelé(e).*

WALKS cont.

WEATHER CONDITIONS cont.

LES PROMENADES suite

LES CONDITIONS METEOROLOGIQUES suite.

Wet	Humide
It's beginning to rain.	Il commence à pleuvoir.
It's drizzling.	Il bruine.
It's pouring down.	Il pleut à verse.
Everywhere is very muddy.	C'est boueux partout.
I am soaked.	Je suis trempé(e).
My feet are wet.	Mes pieds sont tout mouillés.
It may stop raining soon.	Il va peut être arrêter de pleuvoir bientôt.
Shall we shelter here until it stops raining?	On s'abrite ici jusqu'à ce que la pluie s'arrête?

Thunder	La tonnerre
Did you hear the thunder?	Avez-vous / as-tu entendu le tonnerre?
I think there's going to be a thunderstorm.	Je crois qu'il va y avoir de l'orage.
It just lightened.	Il vient d'y avoir un éclair.
Count how long between the flash and the thunder.	Comptez / compte le temps entre l'éclair et le tonnerre.
It's a long way away.	Il est très loin.
It's very close.	Il est très proche.
We had better get back.	On ferait mieux de repartir.

TREES

LES ARBRES

a forest	une forêt
a wood	un bois
a tree	un arbre
a bush	un buisson

WALKS cont.   *LES PROMENADES suite*

Parts of Trees		Les éléments de l'arbre	
the trunk	le tronc	strong	fort(e)
a hollow trunk	un tronc creux	rotten	pourri(e)
massive	massif(ve)	a twig	une brindille
a branch	une branche	a leaf	une feuille

Climbing trees		Grimper aux arbres	
to climb up	grimper	to grasp	s'agripper
to swing from	se balancer de	to get a foothold	prendre pied

TYPES OF TREES		LES TYPES D'ARBRE	
deciduous	à feuilles caduques	ivy	lierre (m)
evergreen	à feuilles persistantes	mountain ash	un sorbier
ash	frêne (m)	oak	chêne (m)
beech	hêtre (m)	pine	pin (m)
birch	bouleau (m)	silver birch	bouleau argenté (m)
Christmas	sapin de noël	spruce	un épicéa
fir	sapin (m)	sycamore	sycomore (m)
hawthorn	une aubépine	weeping willow	un saule pleureur
holly	du houx	yew	if (m)

WALKS cont.   *LES PROMENADES suite*

ANIMALS (abc)		*LES ANIMAUX*	
a badger	*un blaireau*	a rabbit	*un lapin*
a cow	*une vache*	(a rabbit hole)	*un terrier*
(a bull)	*un taureau*	(a burrow)	*un terrier*
(a bullock)	*un bœuf*	(a rabbit warren)	*un terrier*
(a calf)	*un veau*	a sheep	*un mouton*
(a herd of cows)	*un troupeau de vaches*	(a ram)	*un bélier*
a dog	*un chien*	(a ewe)	*une brebis*
a fox	*un renard*	(a lamb)	*un agneau*
a goat	*une chèvre*	(a flock)	*un troupeau*
a hare	*un lièvre*		

BIRDS (abc)		*LES OISEAUX*	
a blackbird	*un merle*	a peacock	*un paon*
a duck	*un canard*	(a peahen)	*une paonne*
(a drake)	*une cane*	(tail feathers)	*les plumes de la queue*
(a duckling)	*un caneton*	(to display)	*déplier*
a goose	*une oie*	a robin	*un rouge-gorge*
(a gosling)	*un oison*	a swallow	*une hirondelle*
a hen	*une poule*	a swan	*un cygne*
(a cock)	*un coq*	(a cygnet)	*un cygnet*
(a chicken)	*un poulet*	a thrush	*une grive*
a kingfisher	*un martin-pêcheur*		

WALKS cont.   *PROMENADES suite*

BIRDS & THEIR ACTIONS		LES OISEAUX ET LEURS ACTIVITES	
to fly	*voler*	to build a nest	*construire un nid*
to sing	*chanter*	to lay an egg	*pondre un œuf*
to whistle	*siffler*	to hatch out	*couver*
to chirp	*pépier/gazouiller*	to learn to fly	*apprendre à voler*

FEEDING BIRDS	NOURRIR LES OISEAUX
Shall we take some bread for the birds?	*On prend du pain pour les oiseaux?*
Did you bring some bread?	*Vous avez / tu as apporté du pain?*
Would you like to give them some?	*Vous voulez / tu veux leur en donner?*
to throw	*jeter*

INSECTS		INSECTES	
an ant	*une fourmi*	a spider	*une araignée*
a bee	*une abeille*	a spider's web	*une toile d'araignée*
to sting	*piquer*	a fly	*une mouche*
to buzz	*bourdonner*	a wasp	*une guêpe*

FRUIT PICKING	LA CUEILLETTE DES FRUITS
Would you like to go fruit picking?	*Vous voulez / tu veux aller cueillir des fruits?*
I want to make jam.	*Je veux faire de la confiture.*
to pick	*cueillir*
Pick one's that are ripe/ sweet / sour.	*En cueillez / cueille un(e) mûr(e) / sucré(e) / aigre.*
I don't want them too ripe / unripe.	*Je ne veux pas qu'ils soient trop mûrs / verts.*

WALKS cont.   *LES PROMENADES suite*

FRUIT PICKING cont.   *LA CUEILLETTE DES FRUITS suite*

to put in a basket	*mettre dans un panier*
How many have you got?	*Combien en avez-vous / as-tu?*
I think we need a few more.	*Je crois qu'il en faut encore un peu.*
That is probably enough now.	*C'est assez maintenant je crois.*
There are a lot over here.	*Il y en a plein ici.*
Don't eat too many.	*N'en mangez / mange pas trop*

Kinds of Fruit		*Les catégories de fruits*	
apples	*pommes (f)*	gooseberries	*groseilles vertes - f*
blackberries	*mûres (f)*	raspberries	*framboises (f)*
blackcurrants	*cassis (m)*	redcurrants	*groseilles rouges*
cherries	*cerises (f)*	strawberries	*fraises (f)*

PHOTOGRAPHY
LA PHOTOGRAPHIE

TAKING PHOTOGRAPHS	***PRENDRE DES PHOTOS***
May I take a picture of you, please?	*Je peux prendre une photo de vous / toi, s'il vous / te plaît?*
Could you take a picture of me, please?	*Vous pouvez / tu peux me prendre en photo?*
Can you wait for a second while I take a photograph?	*Vous pouvez / tu peux attendre une seconde pendant que je prends une photo?*
Can you stand / sit over there, please?	*Vous pouvez vous / tu peux te mettre là-bas?*
Could you move a little closer together, please?	*Vous pouvez vous rapprocher un peu, s'il vous plaît?*
Could you try to smile?	*Vous pouvez / tu peux essayer de sourire?*
Can you try to keep still, please?	*Vous pouvez / tu peux essayer de ne pas bouger?*
Should I bring my camera with me?	*J'emporte mon appareil avec moi?*
Could you look after my camera for me, please?	*Vous pouvez / tu peux surveiller mon appareil-photo, s'il vous / te plaît?*
Don't you like having your photo taken?	*Vous n'aimez pas / tu n'aimes pas être pris(e) en photo?*
I like / hate having my photo taken.	*J'aime bien / je déteste être pris(e) en photo.*
I am not photogenic.	*Je ne suis pas photogénique.*
I would like to take a photo of you all to show my family.	*J'aimerais prendre une photo de vous tous pour montrer à ma famille.*
May I take a photo of your house?	*Je peux prendre une photo de votre maison?*

PHOTOGRAPHY cont.

LA PHOTOGRAPHIE suite

LOOKING AT PHOTOS	*REGARDER LES PHOTOS*
Have you any photos of when you were young?	*Vous avez / tu as des photos de vous / toi quand vous étiez / tu étais plus jeune(s)?*
Can I look at your photo album?	*Je peux regarder votre / ton album?*
That photo of you is very good.	*Cette photo de vous / toi est très bonne.*
That one doesn't look at all like you.	*Celle-ci ne vous / te ressemble pas du tout.*
You have changed a lot.	*Vous avez / tu as beaucoup changé.*
You haven't changed much.	*Vous n'avez pas / tu n'a pas beaucoup changé*
Have you got photos of your holiday?	*Vous avez / tu as des photos de vos / tes vacances?*
Are you in the photo?	*Vous êtes / tu es sur la photo?*
It's a very good photo.	*C'est une très bonne photo.*
in the foreground / background	*au premier plan / à l'arrière plan*
This photograph is of..	*La photo est de...*
This photo was taken two years ago.	*La photo a été prise il y a deux ans.*
That's where we used to live.	*C'est là qu'on habitait.*
That one is of me as a baby.	*Celle-là, c'est moi quand j'étais petit(e).*

CAMERAS

LES APPAREILS PHOTOS

TYPES OF CAMERA	*LES TYPES D'APPAREILS PHOTO (m)*
Polaroid	*Polaroid*
instant	*instantané*
automatic / manual	*automatique / manuel*
disposable	*jetable*

PHOTOGRAPHY cont.

LA PHOTOGRAPHIE suite

USING A CAMERA	*L'UTILISATION D'UN APPAREIL PHOTO*
a button / to press	*un bouton / appuyer*
a lever / to pull	*un levier / tirer*
a switch / to switch	*un bouton / actionner*
the lens cap / to remove / to replace	*le bouchon d'objectif / enlever / remplacer*
the lens / normal / wide angle / zoom	*la lentille / normale / grand angle / zoom*
to clean	*nettoyer*
the viewfinder	*le viseur*
to focus	*mettre au point / focus*
in focus / out of focus	*au point / pas au point*
auto-focus	*auto-focus*
clear / blurred	*net(te) / flou*
the aperture / the aperture setting	*l'ouverture (f) / le réglage de l'ouverture*
the shutter / the shutter speed	*l'obturateur (m) / la vitesse d'obturation*
the flash	*le flash*
Did you use a flash?	*Avez-vous / as-tu utilisé le flash?*
I need a new flash bulb.	*Il me faut un nouveau flash.*

CAMERA ACCESSORIES	*LES ACCESSOIRES*
a camera case	*un étui d'appareil photo*
a camera bag	*un sac*
a strap	*une sangle / une bandeau lière*
a camera stand	*une support d'appareil photo*
a tripod	*un trépied*
a photo album	*un album photo*

PHOTOGRAPHY cont.

LA PHOTOGRAPHIE suite

BUYING FILMS

ACHETER DES PELLICULES

Do you sell films here?
Vous vendez des pellicules ici?

Could I have a colour / black and white film, please?
Je peux avoir une pellicule couleur / noir et blanc, s'il vous plaît?

What sort would you like?
Quelle sorte de pellicule voulez-vous?

Two hundred / three hundred / four hundred?
Deux cents / trois cents / quatre cents?

How many would you like?
Combien de poses voulez-vous?

Twelve / twenty four / thirty six, please.
Douze / vingt-quatre / trente-six s'il vous plaît.

thirty five millimetre format
format trente-cinq millimètres

to load
changer

How do you load the film?
Comment charge-t-on la pellicule?

Could you help me to load the film, please?
Vous pouvez / tu peux m'aider à charger la pellicule, s'il vous plaît?

to rewind
rembobiner

automatic rewind
rembobinage automatique

to remove the film
enlever la pellicule

Could you develop these for me, please?
Vous pouvez les développer, s'il vous plaît?

I would like them in one hour if possible.
J'aimerais les avoir dans une heure, si possible.

I would like to collect them in four hours / tomorrow.
J'aimerais les avoir dans quatre heures / demain.

Can you develop black and white film here?
Pouvez-vous développer une pellicule noire et blanc ici?

Do you want just one set of prints?
Vous les voulez en un exemplaire?

I would like an extra set of prints.
J'aimerais un deuxième exemplaire.

These are under-exposed / over-exposed.
Celles-ci sont sous-exposées / sur-exposées.

VIDEO CAMERA RECORDERS (CAMCORDERS)
LES CAMERAS VIDEO

THE VIDEO CAMERA	*LA CAMERA VIDEO*
a camcorder case	*un étui à caméra*
to get the video camera out	*sortir la caméra*
a grip strap	*la sangle*
to hold	*tenir*

TAPES		*LES CASSETTES*	
a tape	*une cassette*	to insert	*insérer*
a cassette	*une cassette*	to eject	*éjecter / sortir*
a blank tape	*une cassette vierge*	to label	*coller une étiquette*
a used tape	*une cassette utilisée*	to record on	*enregistrer sur*

BATTERIES	*LES PILES (f)*
a battery pack	*un paquet de piles*
a battery charger	*un rechargeur*
to charge up the battery	*recharger la batterie*
Plug it into the mains.	*brancher sur un générateur*
The battery is fully charged.	*La batterie est rechargée.*
It is getting weak.	*Elle commence à faiblir.*
The battery has run down.	*La batterie est vide.*
Do you have an adaptor for this?	*Avez-vous / as-tu un adaptateur pour ceci?*
to attach the battery to the camcorder	*relier les piles à la caméra*
to slide / to push	*glisser / pousser*
to click into place	*mettre en place (avec un déclic)*

CAMCORDERS cont.   *LES CAMERAS VIDEO suite*

THE LENS	*LA LENTILLE*
a lens hood	*le capuchon de la lentille*
to remove	*enlever*
to replace	*remplacer*
to clean the lens	*nettoyer la lentille*

TURNING THE CAMCORDER ON AND RECORDING	*METTRE LA CAMERA EN MARCHE ET ENREGISTRER*
the power switch	*le bouton "power"*
to switch on / off	*allumer / éteindre*
a flashing light	*un clignotant*
a warning light	*l'avertisseur lumineux*
ready to record	*prêt à enregistrer*
standby	*"standby"*
record mode	*le mode d'enregistrement*
Are you ready?	*Etes-vous / es-tu prêt(e)(s)?*
I am about to record now.	*Je vais bientôt enregistrer.*
the viewfinder	*le viseur*
to focus	*mettre au point*
to adjust	*régler*
to zoom	*zoomer*

GETTING THE SOUND RIGHT	*OBTENIR LE BON SON*
the microphone	*le micro*
Can you speak up a bit, please?	*Pouvez-vous / peux-tu parler plus fort, s'il vous plaît?*
That wasn't loud enough.	*Ce n'était pas assez fort.*
That was too loud.	*C'était trop fort.*

CAMCORDERS cont. *LES CAMERAS VIDEO suite*

PLAYING BACK	**MARCHE ARRIERE**
to switch between camera and player	*passer de l'enregistrement au visionnement*
to playback	*faire marche arrière*
the playback switch	*le bouton de marche arrière*
to rewind	*rembobiner*
to fast forward	*avancer rapidement*
to stop	*arrêter*
to pause	*pauser / appuyer sur "pause"*

EDITING	**LE MONTAGE**
to edit	*monter*
to cut	*couper*
to record over	*enregistrer par dessus*
the counter reset button	*le bouton du compteur de remise à zéro*
to zero the counter	*remettre le compteur à zéro*
to insert a marker	*insérer un marqueur*

SPORT
LE SPORT

TENNIS   ## *LE TENNIS*

DO YOU PLAY TENNIS?	*VOUS JOUEZ / TU JOUES AU TENNIS?*
Would you like to play tennis?	*Vous voulez / tu veux jouer au tennis?*
Shall we just knock up for a while?	*On fait des balles, un moment?*
Is the net the right height?	*Le filet est-il à la bonne hauteur?*
Shall we check the height of the net?	*On vérifie la hauteur du filet?*
It's too low / too high.	*Il est trop bas / trop haut.*
Up a bit / down a bit / O.K.	*Un peu en haut / en bas / c'est bon.*

EQUIPMENT	*L'EQUIPEMENT*
a tennis racket	*une raquette de tennis*
Which racket would you prefer?	*Quelle raquette préférez-vous / préfères-tu?*
What weight of racket would you like?	*Quel poids de raquette préférez-vous / préfères-tu?*
a tennis ball	*une balle de tennis*
new balls	*des balles neuves*
a racket press	*un presse-raquette*
a holdall	*un fourre-tout*
a sportsbag	*un sac de sport*
a towel	*une serviette*

TENNIS cont.   *LE TENNIS suite*

CLOTHES		*LA TENUE*	
I haven't got any tennis clothes with me.		*Je n'ai pas ma tenue avec moi.*	
You can borrow some clothes.		*Vous pouvez / tu peux emprunter des vêtements.*	
You can wear anything.		*Vous pouvez / tu peux porter ce que vous voulez / tu veux.*	
shorts	*un short*	socks	*des chaussettes*
a T shirt	*un tee-shirt*	a sweatband	*un bandeau*
a tennis skirt	*une jupe*	a sun visor	*une visière*
a tennis dress	*une robe*	a headband	*bandeau*
tennis shoes	*des chaussures de tennis*	a track suit	*un jogging*

THE TENNIS COURT	*LE COURT DE TENNIS*
the net	*le filet*
the base line	*la ligne de fond*
the service line	*la ligne de service*
the centre line	*la ligne centrale*
the tramlines	*les lignes de côté*
the side netting	*les filets de côté*
the service box	*le carré de service*
the changing room	*le vestiaire*
a locker	*un casier*

STARTING A GAME	*COMMENCER UNE PARTIE*
Do you want to carry on knocking up?	*Vous voulez / tu veux continuer à faire quelques balles?*
Shall we start to play now?	*On commence à jouer maintenant?*
How many sets shall we play?	*Combien de sets joue-t-on?*

TENNIS cont.   *LE TENNIS suite*

STARTING A GAME cont.   *COMMENCER UNE PARTIE*
                                  suite

to toss up	*tirer à pile ou face*
Let's toss for it.	*Tirons à pile ou face.*
to toss a coin.	*faire pile ou face*
Heads or tails? It's heads / tails.	*Pile ou face? C'est face / pile*
Spin your racket.	*Tournez votre / tourne ta raquette.*
Rough or smooth?	*Rêche ou lisse?*
It's rough / it's smooth.	*Elle est rêche / lisse?*
You serve first.	*Vous commencez / tu commences à servir.*
Which end do you prefer?	*Quel côté vous préférez / tu préfères?*
I prefer this / that end.	*Je préfère ce côté-ci / là.*
The sun is in my / your eyes.	*J'ai / vous avez / tu as le soleil dans les yeux.*

SERVING	**LE SERVICE**
to serve	*servir*
to hold one's serve	*défendre son service*
to break someone's serve	*faire le break*
to serve an ace	*faire un ace*
first / second service	*premier / deuxième service*
It's your service.	*C'est votre / ton service.*

TENNIS cont.	LE TENNIS suite

IN OR OUT?	DEDANS OU DEHORS?
Was that in / out?	C'était dedans ou dehors?
Out! The ball was definitely out.	Dehors! La balle était vraiment dehors.
In! The ball was just in.	Dedans! La balle était juste dedans.
I'm not sure.	Je ne suis pas sûr(e)
I didn't see it land.	Je ne l'ai pas vue tomber.
It touched the line.	Elle a touché la ligne.
Shall we play it again?	On la rejoue?

FAULTS	FAUTES
a fault	une faute
a double fault	une double faute
a foot fault	une faute de pied

LET BALLS	LES BALLES "LET"
to play a let	faire un "let"
Should we play a let?	On fait un "let"?

KEEPING THE SCORE	TENIR LES POINTS
What's the score?	Quel est le score?
I've forgotten what the score is.	J'ai oublié le score.
The score is	Le score est
• love all	• zéro partout
• love fifteen	• zéro-quinze
• fifteen love	• quinze-zéro
• fifteen all	• quinze partout

TENNIS cont.	*LE TENNIS suite*
KEEPING THE SCORE cont.	*TENIR LES POINTS suite*

- thirty forty
- deuce
- That's deuce.
- Advantage.
- My / our / your advantage.
- Game.
- Game to you.
- That's game.
- Change ends

Three games to two, first set.
Match point!
Game, set and match.
a tie-breaker
a sudden-death-tie-breaker
Shall we play another game?

- *trente-quinze*
- *égalité*
- *C'est une égalité.*
- *avantage*
- *Mon / notre / votre / ton avantage*
- *Jeu.*
- *Jeu pour vous / toi.*
- *Cela fait jeu.*
- *On change de côté.*

Trois jeux à deux, premier set.
Balle de match!
Jeu, set et match.
un tie-break
une prolongation de tie-break
On fait un autre jeu?

STROKES — *LES COUPS*

forehand / a forehand drive	*un coup droit / un coup droit*
a forehand volley	*une volée de face*
backhand / a backhand drive	*un revers / un revers*
a backhand volley	*une volée de revers*
to lob / a high lob / a top spin lob	*un lob / un grand lob / un lob lifté*
a smash / an overhead smash	*un smash / un smash lobé*
first / second service	*premier / deuxième service*
an ace	*un ace*
a drop shot	*un amorti*
a slice	*un slice*
a volley / a half volley	*une volée / une demi-volée*
a slam	*un chelem*

TENNIS cont.   *LE TENNIS suite*

LOSING THE BALL	*PERDRE LA BALLE*
Did you see where the ball went?	*Avez-vous / as-tu vu où la balle est tombée?*
We've lost the ball.	*On a perdu la balle.*
It went somewhere here.	*Elle est allée quelque part par là.*
I can't find it.	*Je ne la trouve pas.*
I've found it.	*Je l'ai trouvée.*
Let's look for it later.	*On l'a cherchera après.*
Have you any more balls?	*Avez-vous / as-tu d'autres balles?*

THE OFFICIALS	*LES OFFICIELS*
an umpire	*un juge de chaise*
Will you be umpire?	*Voulez-vous / veux-tu être juge de chaise?*
the referee	*le juge-arbitre*
the net judge	*le juge au filet*
the foot-fault judge	*le juge de fond*
the line judge	*le juge de ligne*
a ball boy / a ball girl	*une ramasseur de balle*

DIFFERENT GAMES	*LES JEUX DIFFERENTS*
singles	*simples*
ladies' singles / men's singles	*simples-dames / simples-messieurs*
doubles	*doubles*
ladies' doubles / men's doubles	*doubles-dames / doubles-messieurs*
mixed doubles	*doubles mixtes*
lawn tennis	*tennis sur gazon*
tennis on a hard surface	*tennis sur surfaces dures*
to play tennis on grass	*jouer au tennis sur gazon*

TENNIS cont. *LE TENNIS suite*

TENNIS TOURNAMENTS	LES TOURNOIS DE TENNIS
the first round	*le premier tour*
the second round	*le second tour*
the quarter final	*le quart de finale*
a semi final	*la demi-finale*
the final	*la finale*
the championship	*le championnat*
the grand slam	*le grand chelem*
a seeded player	*une tête de série*
first seed	*tête de série numéro un*
He was seeded third.	*Il était classé troisième tête de série.*

HOW WELL YOU PLAYED	COMMENT VOUS AVEZ JOUE
You play well.	*Vous jouez / tu joues bien.*
Well played! / Good shot!	*Bien joué! / Bonne balle!*
Bad luck!	*Pas de chance!*
I haven't played for ages.	*Je n'ai pas joué depuis des années.*

RIDING   *L'EQUITATION*

CAN YOU RIDE?	*SAVEZ-VOUS MONTER?*
How long have you ridden?	*Il y a combien de temps que vous montez?*
I have ridden for five years.	*Je monte depuis cinq ans.*
Would you like to have a riding lesson with me?	*Vous aimeriez / tu aimerais prendre une leçon d'équitation avec moi?*
Shall we go for a ride?	*On monte?*
You ride well.	*Vous montez / tu montes bien.*
Who are you riding?	*Vous montez / tu montes qui?*
What is your horse's name?	*Comment s'appelle votre / ton cheval?*

CLOTHES AND EQUIPMENT		*LA TENUE ET L'EQUIPEMENT*	
a riding hat	*une bombe*	riding boots	*des bottes d'équitation*
a riding jacket	*une veste d'équitation*	a whip	*une cravache*
jodhpurs	*un pantalon d'équitation*	gloves	*des gants*

THE STABLE	*LES ETABLES*
the stable yard / the tackroom	*une étable / la sellerie*
a gate	*une barrière*
a mounting block	*un mounting block*
the school	*l'école*
a barn	*une grange*
a horse box	*un box*

RIDING TERMS	*LES TERMES D'EQUITATION*
to hold the reins	*tenir les reines*
to give someone a leg up	*faire la courte-échelle à quelqu'un*

RIDING TERMS cont.

LES TERMES D'EQUITATION suite

to mount	*monter*	to kick (rider)	*talonner (cavalier)*
to dismount	*démonter*	to rein back	*faire reculer*
to ride	*monter*	to fall off	*tomber*
to walk	*au pas*	to rear	*se cabrer*
to trot	*au trot / trotter*	to buck	*lancer une ruade*
to canter	*au petit galop*	to shy	*refuser*
to gallop	*galoper*	to neigh	*hennir*
to jump	*sauter*	to walk a horse	*conduire un*
to kick (horse)	*botter (cheval)*		*cheval à pied*

HACKING	*PROMENADE A CHEVAL*
a hack / to go for a hack	*une promenade / se promener à cheval*
a road	*une route*
a lane	*une voie*
a bridleway	*une piste cavalière*
a footpath	*un sentier*
a ditch	*un fossé*
a field	*un champ*
a gate / to open / to shut / to jump	*une barrière / ouvrir / fermer / sauter*
private land	*terres privées*

RIDING cont.   ## L'EQUITATION suite

TACK   ### LA SELLERIE

to saddle up	monter en selle	the stirrups	les éperons (m)
the saddle	la selle	to lengthen	rallonger
the flaps	les claquements (m)	to shorten	raccourcir
the girth	la sangle	even	égal
to tighten	resserrer	uneven	inégal
to loosen	desserrer	the bridle	la bride
a buckle	une boucle	the bit	le mors
a hole	un trou	the headstall	la têtière
the fasten	l'attache (f)	the reins	les rênes (f)
the seat	le siège	a leading rein	la longe
the pommel	le pommeau	a head collar	le collier
the cantle	le troussequin	a blanket	une couverture

GROOMING A HORSE   ### LE PANSAGE

to groom	panser	soft / hard	souple / dure
to rub down	bouchonner	a bucket	un seau
to brush	brosser	water	eau (f)
a currycomb	une étrille	a tap	un robinet
a dandybrush	une brosse (de pansage)	a sponge	une éponge
		to sponge	éponger

HOOF PROBLEMS   ### LES PROBLEMES AVEC LES SABOT

a hoof pick	un cure-pied	to shoe	ferrer
a horseshoe	un fer à cheval	to lose a shoe	perdre un fer
a stone	un caillou	lame	boiteux
the blacksmith	le maréchal-ferrant		

RIDING cont.   *L'EQUITATION suite*

TYPES OF HORSE	LES TYPES DE CHEVAUX
a thoroughbred	*un pur sang*
a mare	*une jument*
a stallion	*un étalon*
a foal / a colt	*un poulain*
a pony	*un poney*
a Shetland pony	*un poney Shetland*
a carthorse	*un cheval de trait*
a shirehorse	*un shire*
a racehorse	*un cheval de course*

DESCRIBING HORSES	DESCRIPTION DES CHEVAUX
How old is your horse?	*Quel âge a votre / ton cheval?*
He / she is three years old.	*Il / elle a trois ans.*
How tall is he / she?	*Quelle est sa taille?*
She is … hands.	*Elle fait…paumes.*
What colour is your horse?	*De quelle couleur est votre / ton cheval?*

grey	*gris*	the mane	*la crinière*
bay	*bai*	the tail	*la queue*
chestnut	*châtaigne*	the hindquarters	*la croupe*
palomino	*alezan*	the temperament	*le tempérament*
dappled	*miroité*	frisky	*sémillant(e)*
piebald	*pie*	gentle	*gentil(le)*
skewbald	*pie*	lazy	*paresseux(se)*
broken	*dompté*	fast	*rapide*
unbroken	*indompté*	nervous	*nerveux(se)*
the coat	*la robe*	temperamental	*capricieux*

RIDING cont.   *L'EQUITATION suite*

COMPETITIONS	*CONCOURS HIPPIQUES*
hunter trials	*les épreuves de chasse (f)*
a three day event	*un événement de trois jours*
equitation	*équitation (f)*
dressage	*dressage (m)*
collection / collected trot	*le rapprochement / petit trot (m)*
extension / extended trot	*allongement (m) / trop allongé*
cross country	*cross-country*
show jumping	*saut d'obstacle (m)*
to jump / a jump	*sauter / un saut*
height / three feet high	*hauteur (f) / un mètre de haut*
a water jump / a ditch	*un obstacle d'eau / un fossé*
a fence / a pole / a gate	*une haie / une barre / une barrière*
a double	*un double*
a fault / a double fault	*une faute / une double faute*
a time fault	*une faute de temps*
a penalty / a time limit	*un penalty / une limite de temps*
a race against time	*une course contre la montre*
to start the clock	*déclencher le chronomètre*
a refusal / three refusals	*un refus / trois refus*
to disqualify	*disqualifier*
to have a clear round	*faire un parcours sans faute*
a jump-off	*une épreuve finale*

RIDING cont.   *L'EQUITATION suite*

USEFUL EXPRESSIONS	EXPRESSIONS UTILES
You can borrow a hat at the riding school.	*Vous pouvez / tu peux emprunter une bombe au club d'équitation.*
Does that hat fit you properly?	*Est-ce que cette bombe vous / te va?*
Put your feet in the stirrups.	*Mettez vos / mets tes pieds dans les étriers.*
Use your whip.	*Utilisez votre / utilise ta cravache.*
Kick harder.	*Talonnez / talonne plus fort.*
Can you trot / canter / gallop?	*Vous savez / tu sais trotter / galoper?*
Would you like to try a jump?	*Vous voulez / tu veux essayer de sauter?*
What height can you jump?	*Quelle hauteur pouvez-vous / peux-tu sauter?*

SKIING
LE SKI

CLOTHES		*LA TENUE*	
a ski suit		*une combinaison de ski*	
thermal underwear		*des dessous thermolactyl*	
sunglasses		*des lunettes de soleil*	
a salopette	*une salopette*	gloves	*des gants (m)*
a ski jacket	*un anorak*	mittens	*des mitaines*
a hood	*une cagoule*		

EQUIPMENT		*L'EQUIPEMENT*	
ski boots	*des chaussures de ski*	ski poles	*des bâtons de ski (m)*
skis	*des skis (m)*	straps	*les lanières (f)*
ski bindings	*les fixations (f)*	handgrips	*les poignées (f)*
fastens	*les attaches (f)*	a ski pass	*un forfait*
clasps	*les boucles (f)*	a photo	*une photo*
to tighten	*resserrer*	suntan cream	*une crème solaire*
to loosen	*desserrer*		

USEFUL EXPRESSIONS	*EXPRESSIONS UTILES*
Don't forget your…	*N'oubliez pas vos / n'oublie pas ton / ta / tes ….*
Have you got your…?	*Avez-vous vos / as-tu ton / ta / tes…?*
May I borrow..?	*Puis-je emprunter…?*
I can't find my..	*Je ne trouve pas mon / ma / mes…*
I've forgotten where I left my…	*J'ai oublié où j'ai laissé…*

SKIING cont.   *LE SKI suite.*

SKI HIRE	*LA LOCATION DE SKIS*
I would like to hire boots / skis / poles, please?	*J'aimerais louer des chaussures / des skis /des bâtons, s'il vous plaît?*
What size boots are you?	*Quelle est votre pointure?*
Try these.	*Essayez celles-ci.*
Are those comfortable?	*Celles-là sont confortables?*
Where do they feel tight / loose?	*Où serrent-elles / sont-elles trop larges?*
How do you adjust them?	*Comment on les règle?*
You can adjust the fastens like this..	*On peut régler les attaches comme ceci...*
What length skis do you normally wear?	*Vous prenez / tu prends quelle longueur de ski en général?*
How tall are you?	*Quelle est votre / ta taille?*
What do you weigh? I weigh..	*Combien pesez-vous / pèses-tu? Je pèse...*
How experienced are you?	*Vous avez de l'expérience?*
I'm a beginner.	*Je suis débutant.*
I'm intermediate.	*J'ai un niveau moyen.*
I'm experienced.	*J'ai un niveau avancé.*
Try these poles.	*Essayez ces bâtons.*
Choose poles with yellow handles.	*Choisissez des bâtons à poignées jaunes.*
These poles are too short / too long.	*Ces bâtons sont trop courts / longs.*
Bring the boots back if the are uncomfortable.	*Rapportez les chaussures si elles ne sont pas confortables.*
Can I change my boots, please?	*Je peux changer mes chaussures, s'il vous plaît?*
They are too narrow.	*Elles sont trop étroites.*
They squash my toes.	*Elles m'écrasent les pieds.*
They hurt here.	*Elles me font mal ici.*
Can you sharpen my skis, please?	*Vous pouvez aiguiser mes skis, s'il vous plaît?*

SKI HIRE cont.   *LA LOCATION DE SKIS suite.*

Can you wax my skis, please?	*Vous pouvez cirer mes skis, s'il vous plaît?*
Can I hire..?	*Je peux louer...?*
• a monoski	• *un monoski*
• a toboggan	• *une luge*
• skating boots	• *des patins (m)*
• a crash helmet	• *un casque*
• a ski board	• *une planche de ski*

WEATHER CONDITIONS	*LES CONDITIONS METEOROLOGIQUES (f)*
Have you heard the weather forecast?	*Avez-vous / as-tu entendu le bulletin météorologique?*
It's raining.	*Il pleut.*
It's cloudy.	*Il y a des nuages.*

SNOW	*LA NEIGE*
It's snowing.	*Il neige.*
There's no snow.	*Il n'y a pas de neige.*
It's snowing heavily.	*Il neige beaucoup.*
The snow is a metre deep.	*Il y a un mètre de neige.*
fresh snow / powder	*la neige fraîche / la poudreuse*
The snow is powdery.	*La neige est poudreuse.*
It's very icy.	*C'est très verglacé.*
The snow is slushy.	*La neige est fondue.*
a blizzard	*le blizzard*
danger of avalanche	*danger d'avalanche*

TEMPERATURE	*LA TEMPERATURE*
It's below freezing point.	*Il fait en dessous de zéro.*
It's six degrees below zero.	*Il fait six degrés en dessous de zéro.*
It's freezing / It's thawing.	*Il gèle / Il dégèle.*
The snow is melting.	*La neige fond.*

SKIING cont. *LE SKI suite.*

VISIBILITY	*VISIBILITE (f)*
The visibility is poor.	*La visibilité est faible.*
It's foggy.	*Il y a du brouillard.*
It's misty.	*C'est brumeux.*
It's difficult to see far.	*C'est difficile de voir au loin.*
freezing fog	*brouillard givrant (m)*

THE SKI RUNS	*LES PISTES DE SKI (f)*
a map of the ski area	*une carte du domaine skiable*
the level of difficulty	*le niveau de difficulté*
nursery slopes	*les pistes pour débutants*
easiest runs	*les pistes les plus faciles*
easy runs	*les pistes faciles*
average runs	*les pistes moyennes*
most difficult runs	*les pistes les plus dures*
off-piste / dangerous	*hors-piste / dangereux*
narrow / wide	*étroit(e) / large*
gentle	*doux(ce)*

SKI LIFTS	*LES REMONTE-PENTES (m)*
What time do the lifts open / close?	*A quelle heure ouvrent / ferment les remonte-pentes?*
Where do I buy a ski pass?	*Où dois-je acheter mon forfait?*
You will need a photograph.	*Il vous / te faut une photo.*
Where is there a photo booth?	*Où y a-t-il un photomaton?*
What coins does it take?	*Quelles pièces accepte-t-il?*
It takes...	*Il accepte...*
a tow bar	*un tire-fesse / un téléski*
a button lift	*un téléski à perche*
a drag lift / a chair lift	*un téléski / un télésiège*
a cable car	*un funiculaire*
a gondola	*une gondole*
a safety bar	*une barre de sécurité*
a foot rest	*un repose-pied*
a ski rack	*un porte-ski*

SKIING cont.   *LE SKI suite.*

QUEUEING	***FAIRE LA QUEUE***
to form a queue	*faire une queue*
to queue up	*faire la queue*
crowded	*plein(e)*
a short / long queue	*une courte / longue queue*
a queue jumper	*un(e) resquilleur(se)*
Wait your turn.	*Attendez votre / attends ton tour.*
He pushed in front of me.	*Il a poussé devant moi.*

SKI SCHOOL	***L'ECOLE DE SKI***
Where is the ski school meeting place?	*Où est le point de rendez-vous de l'école de ski?*
a ski instructor	*un moniteur de ski*
a ski class	*une classe de ski*
Which class are you in?	*Dans quelle classe / à quel niveau êtes-vous / es-tu?*
Which class should I join?	*Dans quel groupe dois-je aller?*
How much skiing have you done?	*Avez-vous / as-tu fait beaucoup de ski?*
I have been skiing three times.	*J'ai fait trois fois du ski.*
I have only been skiing on a dry ski slope.	*J'ai seulement skié sur une piste artificielle.*
I am a beginner / intermediate / experienced.	*Je suis débutant(e) / moyen(ne) / expérimenté(e).*
I only began skiing last year.	*J'ai seulement commencé à skier l'année dernière.*
You have to do a ski test.	*Il faut que vous passez / tu passes un examen.*
Show me how you ski.	*Montrez-moi / montre-moi comment vous skiez / tu skies..*
Go and join that group over there.	*Allez / va rejoindre ce groupe là-bas.*
Join that class.	*Allez / va dans ce groupe.*

LEARNING TO SKI   *APPRENDRE A SKIER*

Put on your skis.	*Chaussez vos / chausse tes skis.*
The bindings need to be open.	*Les fixations doivent être ouvertes.*
Sidestep up the hill.	*Montez / monte la pente en escalier.*
Have you ever used a drag lift?	*Avez-vous / as-tu déjà utilisé un téléski?*
to ski	*skier*
to fall down	*tomber*
to get up	*se relever*
to turn round	*tourner*
to traverse	*traverser*
to snow plough	*faire un chasse-neige*
a snowplough turn	*un virage en chasse-neige*
a stem turn	*un stem*
a parallel turn	*un virage parallèle*
Can you ski over / round moguls?	*Vous pouvez / tu peux skier sur des bosses?*
a mogul field	*une piste à bosses*
hot dogging	*ski acrobatique (m)*
to mono-ski	*faire du monoski*
to ski board	*faire du surf des neiges*
slalom racing	*course (f) de slalom (m)*
the course	*le parcours*
the poles / the flags	*les piquets (m) / les drapeaux (m)*
the gates	*les portes (f)*

FALLING DOWN   *LES CHUTES (f)*

Can you do an emergency stop?	*Vous savez vous / tu sais t'arrêter?*
to fall down	*tomber*
Are you hurt?	*Vous vous êtes / tu t'es fait mal?*
I'm fine.	*Je vais bien.*
I hurt here..	*Ca me fait mal ici.*
I can't get up.	*Je ne peux pas me lever.*

LEARNING TO SKI cont. *APPRENDRE A SKIER suite*

FALLING DOWN cont. *LES CHUTES suite*

How do you get up from a fall?	*Comment se relève-t-on d'une chute?*
Sort out your skis.	*Déchaussez vos / déchausse tes skis.*
Edge your skis.	*Mettez vos / mets tes skis en amont.*
Plant your poles and push.	*Plantez vos / plante tes bâtons et poussez / pousse.*
Stand up.	*Debout!*
Take your skis off.	*Enlevez vos / enlève tes skis.*
Put the lower ski on first.	*Mettez / mets le ski en aval d'abord.*
Push the inside edge into the snow.	*Poussez / pousse l'arrête interne dans la neige.*

APRES SKI *L'APRES-SKI*

a bar / a restaurant	*un bar / un restaurant*
a disco / a nightclub (See 201-203)	*une boîte de nuit*
expensive / cheap	*cher(e) / pas cher(e)*
a skating rink (See 282-283)	*une patinoire*
to ice skate	*faire du patin à glace*
to toboggan	*faire de la luge*
to go for a sleigh ride	*faire un tour de traîneau*
a sleigh	*un traîneau*

ACCIDENTS *LES ACCIDENTS*

There has been an accident.	*Il y a eu un accident.*
Someone is hurt.	*Quelqu'un est blessé.*
Where do you hurt? (See 237, 411, 420)	*Où avez-vous / as-tu mal?*
Don't move him / her.	*Ne le / la bougez / bouge pas.*
Can you stand up?	*Pouvez-vous vous / peux-tu te lever?*
Fetch the rescue service.	*Allez / va chercher les services de secours.*
Help / Get help.	*Aide / allez / va chercher de l'aide.*
Warn other people.	*Avertissez / avertis les autres personnes.*

SKIING cont.   *SKIER suite*

RESCUE SERVICES   ***LES SERVICES DE SAUVETAGE (m)***

a helicopter	*un hélicoptère*
to air lift	*emmener par pont aérien (m)*
a doctor	*un médecin*
a stretcher / a blood wagon	*un brancard / une civière*
a broken arm / leg	*un bras / une jambe cassé(e)*
What is your name?	*Comment vous appelez-vous?*
Where are you staying?	*Quel est votre / ton lieu de séjour?*
Are you insured?	*Etes-vous / es-tu assuré(e)(s)?*

HOW ARE YOU FEELING?   ***COMMENT VOUS-SENTEZ-VOUS?***

I am cold / hot.	*J'ai froid / chaud.*
I am tired / feel fine.	*Je suis fatigué(e) / je vais bien.*
I am thirsty / hungry.	*J'ai soif / faim.*
I want to stop now.	*Je veux arrêter maintenant.*
I want to carry on.	*Je veux continuer.*
I can't do this.	*Je ne peux pas faire cela.*
This is good fun.	*C'est vraiment drôle.*
I am scared.	*J'ai peur.*
Can we do it again?	*On le refait?*
My legs hurt.	*J'ai mal aux jambes.*
My boots are rubbing.	*Mes chaussures frottent.*
Can we stop for lunch soon?	*On peut s'arrêter pour manger bientôt?*
I would like a drink.	*J'aimerais bien boire quelque chose.*
I need the toilet.	*J'ai besoin d'aller aux toilettes.*
Let's go to that mountain café.	*Allons dans ce bar d'altitude.*
Shall we stop for a few minutes?	*On s'arrête quelques minutes?*
I'd like to go back to the hotel / chalet now.	*J'aimerais retourner à l'hôtel / au chalet maintenant.*
I have to be back at four o'clock.	*Je dois être de retour à quatre heures.*
Shall we meet again after lunch?	*On se retrouve après le déjeuner?*
Where / when shall we meet?	*Où / quand se retrouve-t-on?*

FOOTBALL
LE FOOTBALL

THE PITCH	*LE TERRAIN*
the goal / the goal posts	*le goal / les poteaux (m)*
the cross bar	*la barre transversale*
the netting	*les filets (m)*
the goal area / the goal line	*les buts (m) / la ligne de but*
the penalty area	*la surface de réparation*
the touch line	*la ligne de touche*
the corner	*le coin*
offside / mid field	*hors-jeu / milieu de terrain*
the terrace / a stand	*le gradin / une tribune*
the bench	*le banc de touche*
floodlighting	*l'éclairage (m)*
muddy	*boueux*

THE PLAYERS (abc)	*LES JOUEURS*
an amateur	*un amateur*
to award a free kick	*accorder un coup franc*
the away team	*les visiteurs*
to be on the bench	*être sur le banc*
to blow the whistle	*siffler*
a coach	*un entraîneur*
a defender	*un défenseur*
the favourites	*les favoris*
a footballer	*un footballeur*
a forward	*un avant*
a goal keeper	*un goal*
home team	*l'équipe qui reçoit*
a manager	*un directeur*
a mid-fielder	*un milieu de terrain*

FOOTBALL cont.   *LE FOOTBALL suite*

THE PLAYERS cont. (abc)   *LES JOUEURS suite*

an opponent	*un opposant*
a penalty	*une pénalité*
a professional	*un professionnel*
a referee	*un arbitre*
a striker	*un attaquant*
the strong side	*l'aile forte (f)*
a substitute	*un remplaçant*
to be substituted on / off	*être remplacé*
a sweeper	*un libéro*
the teams	*les équipes (f)*
a transfer	*un transfert*
a transfer fee	*un prix de transfert*
the weak side	*l'aile faible*

THE SPECTATORS	***LES SPECTATEURS***
a spectator	*un spectateur*
a fan	*un fan*
a supporter	*un supporteur*
the crowd	*la foule*
a ticket holder	*un détenteur de ticket*
a tout	*un revendeur de billet*
to cheer	*saluer*
to shout	*crier*
to chant	*scander*
to sing	*chanter*
the national anthem	*l'hymne national (m)*
a football hooligan	*un hooligan*

FOOTBALL cont.

LE FOOTBALL suite

PLAY	*LE JEU*
a kick / to kick off	*un coup / donner le coup d'envoi*
a free kick / a corner kick	*un coup franc / un corner*
a goal kick	*un coup de pied de renvoi*
an indirect free kick	*un coup franc indirect*
to pass / to dribble	*passer / dribbler*
to head / a header	*faire une tête / une tête*
to throw in	*remettre en jeu*
to tackle / a tackle	*tackler / un tackle*
to intercept / to challenge	*intercepter / faire un challenge*
a good / bad challenge	*un bon / un mauvais challenge*
to take a corner	*faire un corner*
to be offside	*être hors-jeu*
to be sent off	*être expulsé*
to be shown the red / yellow card	*avoir le carton rouge / jaune*
tactics	*les tactiques (f)*
the rules / the rule book	*les règles (f) / le règlement*
against the rules	*contraire au règlement*
foul play / a foul	*jeu déloyal (m) / une faute*
a penalty	*un penalty*
the penalty spot	*le point de réparation*
a penalty goal	*but sur pénalité*
a penalty shoot out	*les tirs (m) au but*

THE SCORE	*LES POINTS (m)*
an aggregate score	*le score final*
What is the score?	*Quel est le score?*
to score an own goal	*marquer contre son camp*
to equalize	*égaliser*
to win	*gagner*

FOOTBALL cont.   *LE FOOTBALL suite*

THE RESULT	***LES RESULTATS (m)***
a win / to win / a victory	*un gain / gagner / une victoire*
a walk over	*une victoire facile*
a draw / to draw	*un match nul / faire match nul*
a defeat	*une défaite*
to be defeated / to lose	*être battu / perdre*
a tie / to tie	*une égalité / faire match nul*
a replay	*le fait d'être rejoué*
a match	*un match*
a friendly	*un match amical*
no score	*score nul / zéro-zéro*

STAGE OF THE GAME	***LES ETAPES (f) DU JEU***
first half	*première mi-temps (f)*
second half	*deuxième mi-temps*
half time	*mi-temps*
full time	*fin (f) de match (m)*
extra time	*prolongation (f)*
injury time	*arrêts de jeu (m)*

GENERAL TERMS	***TERMES GENERAUX (m)***
soccer	*football (m)*
the football season	*la saison football*
the football league	*le championnat de football*
divisions	*divisions (f)*
first / second / third division	*première / deuxième / troisième division*
League Division One	*Championnat de première division*
the Premier League	*la "Premier League" (la toute première division) N'a pas d'équivalent en France.*
a cup	*une coupe*
a trophy	*un trophée*

FOOTBALL cont.   *LE FOOTBALL suite*

EQUIPMENT	LA TENUE
a football	*un ballon de football*
kit	*les affaires (f) de sport / tenue (f)*
home kit	*la tenue de l'équipe qui reçoit*
away kit	*la tenue des visiteurs*
team strip	*la tenue de l'équipe*
shorts	*un short*
a shirt	*un maillot "de foot"*
socks	*des chaussettes (f)*
football boots	*des chaussures (f) de foot*
a sweatband	*un bandeau*

USEFUL EXPRESSIONS	EXPRESSIONS UTILES
Who's playing?	*Qui joue?*
What's the score?	*Quel est le score?*
There's no score yet.	*Il n'y a pas eu de points marqués encore.*
to play injury time	*jouer les arrêts de jeu*
They won by five goals to nil.	*Ils ont gagné à cinq buts à zéro.*
They failed to score.	*Ils n'ont marqué aucun point.*
It was a draw.	*C'était un match nul.*
They took the lead in the second half.	*Ils ont mené dans la deuxième mi-temps.*

RUGBY
RUGBY

THE PLAYERS	*LES JOUEURS*
the forwards	*les avants (m)*
the back / front row	*la troisième / la première ligne*
the second row	*la deuxième ligne*
a hooker / a flanker	*un talonneur/ un ailier*
the half backs	*les demis (m)*
scrum half / fly half	*demi de mêlée / demi d'ouverture*
three quarter backs	*trois-quart arrière*
fullback	*arrière*
wing three quarter	*trois-quart aile*

THE FIELD	*LE TERRAIN*
the goal / the goal posts	*le but / les poteaux (m)*
the uprights	*les montants (m)*
the cross bar	*la barre transversale*
halfway line / goal line	*la ligne médiane / la ligne d'essai*
dead-ball line	*ligne du ballon mort*
the twenty two line	*ligne des vingt-deux mètres*

THE PLAY (abc)	*LE JEU*
to bounce	*rebondir*
converted	*transformé*
a drop kick / to drop kick	*un drop / dropper*
a free kick	*un coup franc*
to hook	*talonner*
a line out	*une touche*
mark	*arrêt (m) de volée*
a penalty / a penalty try	*un penalty / un essai de pénalité*
a scrummage / scrum	*une mêlée*
to touch down	*marquer un essai*

ICE SKATING
LE PATIN A GLACE

WOULD YOU LIKE TO GO ICE SKATING?	*VOUS AIMERIEZ / TU AIMERAIS FAIRE DU PATIN A GLACE?*
Can you skate?	*Vous savez / tu sais patiner?*
How long have you skated?	*Cela fait combien de temps que vous patinez / tu patines?*
Would you like to have a go at it?	*Vous voulez / tu veux essayer?*

THE ICE RINK	*LA PATINOIRE*
the ticket office	*le guichet*
Could we have four tickets, please?	*On peut avoir quatre billets, s'il vous plaît?*
Have you got your own boots?	*Vous avez vos/ tu as tes propres chaussures?*
Do you want to hire boots?	*Vous voulez / tu veux louer des chaussures?*
Could I have two tickets for the ice rink and we would like to hire boots, please.	*Je peux avoir deux billets pour la patinoire et on voudrait louer des chaussures, s'il vous plaît.*

BOOT HIRE	*LA LOCATION DE CHAUSSURES*
What size of shoe do you take?	*Quelle est votre / ta pointure?*
I am size six.	*Je fais du trente-sept.*
I am a continental size forty.	*Je fais du quarante.*
You take your shoes off and hand them in at the boot hire shop.	*On enlève ses chaussures et on les donne au magasin de location.*
Try your skates on.	*Essayez vos / essaies tes patins.*
How do you fasten them?	*Comment on les attache?*
You fasten them like this.	*On les attache comme ceci.*
Are they comfortable?	*Ils sont confortables?*
These boots hurt.	*Ces chaussures font mal.*
Can I change my boots, please?	*Je peux changer mes chaussures, s'il vous plaît?*

ICE SKATING cont.   *LE PATIN A GLACE suite*

ON THE ICE	*SUR LA GLACE*
Hold on to the handrail at first.	*Tenez-vous / tiens toi à la rampe d'abord.*
Should we skate round the edge until you're used to it?	*On patine autour du bord jusqu'à ce que vous vous habituez / tu t'habitues?*
to fall over	*tomber*
to get knocked down	*se faire bousculer*
Someone pushed me over.	*Quelqu'un m'a poussé.*
Can you help me to get up, please?	*Vous pouvez / tu peux m'aider à me lever, s'il vous plaît / s'il te plaît?*
Are you O.K.?	*Ca va?*
You're doing really well.	*Vous vous débrouillez / tu te débrouilles très bien.*
I think I'll just watch for a bit.	*Je pense que je vais juste regarder un moment.*

TYPES OF SKATING	*LES TYPES DE PATINAGE*
speed skating	*patinage (m) de vitesse*
figure skating	*patinage artistique*
ice dancing	*danse (f) sur glace (f)*
solo skating	*patinage individuel*
pair skating	*patinage en couple*
a leap	*un bond*
a spiral	*une spirale*
a jump	*un saut*
a spin	*une toupie*

TABLE TENNIS
LE TENNIS DE TABLE / LE PING-PONG

CAN YOU PLAY TABLE TENNIS?	*VOUS JOUEZ / TU JOUES AU TENNIS DE TABLE?*
Would you like to play table tennis / ping pong?	*Vous voulez / tu veux jouer au tennis de table / ping-pong?*
Do you have a table tennis table?	*Vous avez / tu as une table de ping-pong?*
Do you play much?	*Vous jouez / tu joues souvent?*
I haven't played for ages.	*Je n'ai pas joué depuis des années.*
I've forgotten how to play.	*J'ai oublié comment jouer.*
Shall I teach you how to play?	*Je vous / t'apprends comment jouer?*

EQUIPMENT	*LE MATERIEL*
a table tennis table	*une table de ping-pong*
the white line	*la ligne blanche*
the net	*le filet*
the edge of the table	*le bout de la table*
a bat	*une raquette de ping-pong*
Which bat do you prefer?	*Quelle raquette préférez-vous / préfères-tu?*
I'll take this one.	*Je prends celle-ci.*
a table tennis ball	*une balle de ping-pong*
Have you got any more balls?	*Vous avez / tu as d'autres balles?*
This ball isn't bouncing properly.	*Cette balle ne rebondit pas bien.*

PLAYING	*LE JEU*
Let's choose ends.	*Choisissons les côtés (m).*
Spin the racket.	*Tournez / tourne la raquette.*
Toss for it.	*Faisons pile ou face.*
We change ends every game.	*On change de côté à chaque jeu.*

TABLE TENNIS cont.   *LE PING-PONG suite*

DOUBLES	*LES DOUBLES (m)*
In doubles the players take alternate shots.	*Dans les doubles les joueurs jouent en alternance.*
You have to serve from the right to the right.	*Il faut servir à droite sur la droite.*
Each player receives service for five points.	*Chaque jouer reçoit un service pour cinq points.*

SINGLES	*LES SIMPLES (m)*
You serve first.	*Vous servez / tu sers d'abord.*
You change service every five points.	*Il faut donner le service tous les cinq points.*
Whose service is it?	*A qui est-ce de servir?*
It's mine / yours.	*C'est à moi / à vous/ à toi.*
It's your service now because five points have been scored.	*C'est à vous / à toi de servir maintenant car cinq points ont été marqués.*

SHOTS	*LES COUPS (m)*
to hit forehand	*frapper du coup droit*
to hit backhand	*frapper du revers*
to serve	*servir*
You hit the net.	*Vous avez / tu as mis dans le filet.*
Where did the ball land?	*Où est tombée la balle?*
Was it in or out?	*Elle était bonne ou mauvaise?*
It was in / out.	*Elle était bonne / mauvaise.*
It didn't land on the table.	*Elle n'est pas retombée sur la table.*
It was a let.	*C'était un let.*
Play it again.	*Rejouez-la / rejoue-la.*
Can you find the ball?	*Vous trouvez / tu trouves la balle?*
Did you see exactly where it went?	*Avez-vous / as-tu vu où elle est tombée exactement?*

TABLE TENNIS cont.   *LE TENNIS DE TABLE suite*

SCORING	LES POINTS (m)
What's the score?	*Quel est le score?*
Love all.	*Zéro partout.*
One love.	*Un-zéro.*
Three, two.	*Trois-deux.*
Twenty, twenty.	*Vingt-vingt.*
The service changes every point now.	*Le service change à tous les points maintenant.*
The winner is the first person to score twenty one points.	*Le vainqueur est le premier joueur qui marque vingt-et-un.*
You have to get two points ahead of me to win.	*Vous devez / tu dois avoir deux points d'avance sur moi pour gagner.*
You won easily.	*Vous avez / tu as gagné haut-la-main.*
Well played! / Bad luck!	*Bien joué! Pas de chance!*
It was a close game.	*C'était une partie serrée.*
Shall we play the best of three games?	*On fait la belle?*

GOLF
LE GOLF

THE GOLF COURSE		*LE TERRAIN DE GOLF*	
the links	*les links*	thirteenth	*treizième*
a hole	*un trou*	fourteenth	*quatorzième*
first	*premier*	fifteenth	*quinzième*
second	*deuxième*	sixteenth	*seizième*
third	*troisième*	seventeenth	*dix-septième*
fourth	*quatrième*	eighteenth	*dix-huitième*
fifth	*cinquième*	a tee	*un tee*
sixth	*sixième*	the fairway	*le Fairway*
seventh	*septième*	the rough	*le rough*
eighth	*huitième*	the green	*le green*
ninth	*neuvième*	the putting green	*le green*
tenth	*dixième*	a flag	*un drapeau*
eleventh	*onzième*	the hole	*le trou*
twelfth	*douzième*		

OBSTACLES		*LES OBSTACLES (m)*	
a hazard	*un hasard*	sand	*sable (m)*
long grass	*herbe haute (f)*	a ditch	*fossé (m)*
bushes	*buissons (m)*	a pond	*bassin (m)*
trees	*arbres (m)*	a lake	*lac (m)*
a bunker	*un bunker*		

OTHER PARTS OF THE GOLF CLUB	*LES AUTRES PARTIES DU GOLF*
the club house / the bar	*le pavillon / le bar*
the practice ground / green	*le terrain de practice / le green*
miniature golf	*mini golf (m)*
crazy golf	*mini golf*

GOLF cont.   *LE GOLF suite*

THE EQUIPMENT		*LE MATERIEL*	
a golf bag	*un sac de golf*	the irons	*les fers (m)*
a caddie	*un Caddie*	the long irons	*les longs fers*
to caddie	*être le Caddie*	six / seven	*six / sept*
a set of golf clubs	*un club de golf*	eight / nine	*huit / neuf*
the woods	*les bois (m)*	the putter	*le Putter*
a driver	*un Driver*	the sand wedge	*le sand wedge*
one / two	*un / deux*	the pitching wedge	*le pitching wedge*
three / four	*trois / quatre*	a golf ball	*une balle de golf*
five	*cinq*	a tee	*un tee*

THE STROKES	*LES COUPS (m)*
You must shout "Fore!".	*Il faut crier "Attention".*
to tee up	*placer la balle sur le tee*
to strike	*frapper*
to drive	*driver*
a beautiful drive	*un beau drive*
to hook	*faire un coup hooké*
to slice	*slicer*
to make an approach shot	*faire une approche*
to putt	*putter*
a putt	*un putt*
to tap	*taper*
to hole	*faire un trou*
a shot	*un coup*
a long shot	*un long coup*
a chip shot	*un coup coché*
a low / high shot	*un coup bas / haut*
to swing	*faire un swing*
a short / long swing	*un swing court / long*

GOLF cont.   *LE GOLF suite*

THE SCORING	LES POINTS (m)
par / under par / over par	*par / sous le par / au dessus du par*
a birdie	*un Birdie*
an eagle / a double eagle	*un Eagle / un albatros*
a hole in one	*un trou en un*
a bogey / a double bogey	*un Bogey / un double Bogey*
a handicap	*un handicap*
What is your handicap?	*Quel est votre / ton handicap?*

MOTOR RACING
LES COURSES AUTOMOBILES

THE COURSE	*LA COURSE*
the starting line	*la ligne de départ*
the finishing line	*la ligne d'arrivée*
the chequered flag	*le drapeau à damier*
the track	*l'autodrome*
a lane	*un couloir*
the inside / outside lane	*le couloir de droite / le couloir de gauche*
a lap / to do a lap	*un tour de piste / faire un tour de piste*
to lap someone	*prendre un tour d'avance sur quelqu'un*
to do a lap of honour	*faire un tour d'honneur*
a five lap course	*une course à cinq tours*
a circuit	*un circuit*
a bend	*un virage*
a double bend	*un double virage*
a hairpin bend	*un virage en épingle à cheveux*
He took the bend too fast.	*Il a pris le virage trop vite.*
a chicane	*une chicane*
the pits	*les stands (m)*
a crash barrier	*une barrière de sécurité*

THE PEOPLE	*LES PERSONNES EN PRESENCE*
a racing driver	*un coureur automobile*
a champion	*un champion*
an ex-champion	*un ex-champion*
a winner	*un vainqueur*
a runner-up	*un(e) second(e)*
a loser	*un perdant*
a spectator	*un spectateur*
a mechanic	*un mécanicien*
a co-driver	*un copilote*

MOTOR RACING cont.

LES COURSES
AUTOMOBILES suite

THE RACING CAR	*LES VOITURES (f) DE COURSES*
the steering wheel	*le volant*
the accelerator	*l'accélérateur (m)*
the brakes	*les freins (m)*
the tyres / new tyres	*les pneus / pneus neufs (m)*
a puncture / to change the tyres	*une crevaison / changer les pneus*
the bumper	*le pare-chocs*
the chassis	*le châssis*
the body	*la carrosserie*
the make of car	*l'écurie (f)*
the engine size	*la taille du moteur*
the horse power	*la puissance (en chevaux)*
the speed	*la vitesse*

THE VERBS (abc)	*LES VERBES*
to accelerate	*accélérer*
to be out of control	*perdre le contrôle*
to brake	*freiner*
to collide / to crash	*entrer en collision / s'écraser*
to correct a skid	*rétablir un dérapage*
to drive	*conduire*
to finish	*arriver*
to lap	*faire un tour de piste*
to lose	*perdre*
to overtake / to race	*doubler / courir*
to show the chequered flag	*agiter le drapeau à damier*
to skid / leave skid marks	*déraper / laisser des traces de dérapage*
to slow down	*ralentir*
to start	*démarrer*
to steer	*diriger*
to take on the inside	*passer à droite*
to win	*gagner*

ATHLETICS
L'ATHLETISME (m)

THE KIT		*LES AFFAIRES*	
a track suit	*un jogging*	a leotard	*un collant*
a sweat shirt	*un sweatshirt*	trainers	*des tennis*
shorts	*un short*	spikes	*des chaussures à pointe (f)*
a shirt	*un maillot*	a towel	*une serviette*
a skirt	*une jupe*	a sports bag	*un sac de sport*

THE ATHLETES	*LES ATHLETES*
a jogger / to jog	*un joggeur / faire du jogging*
I go jogging.	*Je fais du jogging.*
to keep fit	*être en bonne forme physique*
a sprinter / to sprint / to run	*un sprinteur / sprinter / courir*
to race against	*faire la course avec*
a middle distance runner	*un(e) coureur(se) de demi-fond*
a marathon runner	*un(e) coureur(se) de Marathon*

JUMPERS	*LES SAUTEURS(EUSES)*
to jump	*sauter*
a hurdler	*un(e) coureur(se) d'obstacles*
to hurdle / a hurdle	*faire de la course d'obstacles / une haie*
a high jumper	*un(e) sauteur(se) en hauteur*
a long jumper	*un(e) sauteur(se) en longueur*
a pole vaulter	*un(e) sauteur(se) à la perche*
to vault	*sauter*

THROWERS	*LES LANCEURS(EUSES)*
a discus thrower	*un(e) lanceur(se) de disques (m)*
to throw	*lancer*
a javelin thrower	*un(e) lanceur(se) de javelots (m)*
a shot putter	*un(e) lanceur(se) de poids (m)*

ATHLETICS cont.

L'ATHLETISME suite

OTHER SPORTSMEN AND WOMEN	*AUTRES SPORTIFS ET SPORTIVES*
a gymnast	*un(e) gymnaste*
a decathlete	*un(e) coureur(se) de décathlon*
a heptathlete	*un(e) coureur(se) d'heptathlon*
an amateur	*un(e) amateur(rice)*
a professional	*un(e) professionnel(le)*
a coach	*un(e) entraîneur(euse)*

RECORD HOLDERS	*LES DETENEURS DE RECORD*
to break the record	*battre le record*
a record breaker	*un nouveau record (man) / une nouvelle record (woman)*
Well inside the record time.	*En temps tout à fait record.*
Just inside the record time.	*Juste en temps record.*
a world record holder	*un détenteur / une détentrice du record mondial*
a champion	*un(e) champion(ne)*
to run one's personal best	*faire son meilleur temps*

EVENTS	*LES EVENEMENTS*
a meeting	*une course / une rencontre*
warm-up exercises	*exercices (m) d'échauffement (m)*
to warm up	*s'échauffer*
track events / field events	*épreuves (f) sur piste / concours*
runs / walks	*courses (f) / courses à pied*
jumps / throws	*sauts (m) / lancers (m)*
short races / sprints	*les courtes distances (f) / sprints(m)*
one hundred metres	*le cent mètres*
middle distance races	*les courses de demi-fond*
one thousand five hundred metres	*le mille-cinq-cents mètres*
long distance races	*les courses de fond*
the half marathon / the marathon	*le semi-marathon / le Marathon*
a steady pace / a final spurt	*un rythme régulier / le sprint final*

ATHLETICS cont.   *L'ATHLETISME suite*

RELAY RACES	*LES COURSES DE RELAI*
the baton	*le témoin / le relais*
a leg	*une distance / un relais*
the first / last leg	*la première distance / la dernière distance*
a hand over	*une passe de relais*

HURDLING	*COURSE DE HAIES*
hurdles / to hurdle	*les haies (f) / les obstacles (m) / faire une course de haies*
to clear	*dégager*

THE LONG JUMP	*LE SAUT EN LONGEUR*
distance	*distance*
the take off	*l'envol (m)*
the landing	*la réception*

HIGH JUMP	*LE SAUT EN HAUTEUR*
the cross bar	*la barre transversale*
the height	*la hauteur*
to raise	*relever*
to attempt	*tenter*
to clear	*dégager*
three attempts	*trois essais (m)*
the first / second / third attempt	*le premier / deuxième / troisième essai*
the final attempt	*l'essai final (m)*
to be disqualified	*être disqualifié(e)*

TRIPLE JUMP	*LE TRIPLE SAUT*
a hop / a skip / a jump	*un saut*

ATHLETICS cont.   L'ATHLETISME suite

POLE VAULTING	LE SAUT A LA PERCHE
the pole	la perche
the cross bar	la barre transversale
a height increase	une élévation
to dislodge the bar	faire tombé la barre
three misses	trois essais manqués
to disqualify	disqualifier

SHOT PUT	LE LANCER DE POIDS
the longest throw	le plus long lancer
the discus throw	le lancer de disques
the javelin throw	le lancer de javelots

GYMNASTICS   GYMNASTIQUE

Qualities needed (abc)		Les qualités requises	
agility	agilité (f)	grace	grâce (f)
balance	équilibre (m)	rhythm	rythme (m)
flexibility	souplesse (f)	strength	force (f)

The moves (abc)		Les mouvements	
a balance	un équilibre	a jump	un saut
a cartwheel	une roue	a landing	une réception
a drop	une sortie	a leap	un bond
(a back drop)	une sortie arrière	a skip	un petit saut
(a front drop)	une sortie de face	a turn	un tour
(a tuck)	un saut périlleux	(a half turn)	un demi-tour
the floor exercises	les exercices (m) au sol	(a full turn)	un tour entier
the grip changes	les changements (m) de prise	a vault	un saut
a handstand	un appui renversé		

ATHLETICS cont.   *L'ATHLETISME suite*

THE APPARATUS	*L'EQUIPEMENT (m)*
a horizontal bar	*la barre horizontale*
a horse vault	*un cheval d'arçons*
the parallel bars	*les barres parallèles*
the rings	*les anneaux*
the side horse / a springboard	*le cheval / un tremplin*
a trampoline	*un trampoline*
the uneven bars	*les barres asymétriques (f)*

THE STADIUM	*LE STADE*
the arena	*l'arène (f)*
the track / the lanes	*le vélodrome / les couloirs (m)*
the inside / the outside lane	*le couloir de droite / de gauche*
the middle lane	*le couloir du milieu*
the starting line	*la ligne de départ*
the starting block	*les starting-blocks (m)*
the starting pistol	*le pistolet de starter*
a false start	*un faux-départ*
On your marks, get ready, go!	*A vos marques, prêts, partez?*

MEDALS	*LES MEDAILLES*
a Gold medal	*une médaille d'or*
a Silver / Bronze medal	*une médaille d'argent / de bronze*
to be awarded	*recevoir*
to win / to be presented	*gagner/ être présenté*

THE OLYMPICS	*LES JEUX OLYMPIQUES*
an Olympic medal	*la médaille olympique*
the Olympic games / torch	*les Jeux Olympiques / la torche*
to light / to carry / to burn	*allumer / porter / brûler*
an Olympic Champion	*un Champion Olympique*
the next Olympics	*les prochains Jeux Olympiques*
the last Olympics	*les derniers Jeux Olympiques*

CRICKET
LE CRICKET

Although cricket is not generally played on the Continent, this section may be useful to help your foreign exchange to understand the game when he/she visits England.

Bien que ce jeu ne soit pas joué sur le continent, ce chapitre peut être utile aux étrangers pour comprendre le jeu quand ils séjourneront en Angleterre.

CLOTHES	*LA TENUE*
cricket whites	*les pantalons de cricket (m)*
leg pads	*des genouillères (f)*
a pullover	*un pullover*
trousers	*un pantalon*
a shirt	*une chemise*
gloves	*des gants (m)*

EQUIPMENT	*L'EQUIPEMENT*
a cricket bat	*une batte de cricket*
a cricket ball	*une balle de cricket*
the wickets	*les guichets (m)*
the stumps	*les piquets (m)*
the grooves	*les siffons (m)*
the bails	*les témoins (m)*

THE CRICKET FIELD	*LE TERRAIN DE CRICKET*
the pitch	*le terrain*
the wickets	*les trois piquets (m)*
the boundary	*la limite*
the bowling crease	*la ligne qui rejoint les piquets*
the popping crease	*la ligne du lanceur*

CRICKET cont.

LE CRICKET suite

THE FIELDERS' POSITIONS		*LES POSITIONS DES JOUEURS DE CHAMP*	
slip	*slip*	long on	*long on*
second slip	*deuxième slip*	mid on	*mid on*
gully	*gully*	mid wicket	*mid wicket*
point	*point*	square leg	*square leg*
cover point	*cover point*	legside	*côté leg*
mid off	*mid off*	offside	*côté off*
long off	*long off*		

THE PLAYERS	*LES JOUEURS*
the captain	*le capitaine*
the umpires	*les arbitres*
the teams	*les équipes (f)*
the batsman	*le batteur*
the bowler	*le lanceur*
the wicket keeper	*le gardien de guichet*
the fielders	*les joueurs de champ*

PLAYING CRICKET	*JOUER AU CRICKET*
to toss a coin	*tirer à pile ou face*
to win / lose the toss	*gagner / perdre le pile ou face*
to bat first	*battre d'abords*
to position the fielders	*positionner les joueurs de champ*

CRICKET cont.

LE CRICKET suite

BOWLING	*LE LANCER*
to bowl	*lancer*
overarm	*par en dessus*
underarm	*par en dessous*
to bowl out	*éliminer sur lancer*
to be bowled out	*être éliminé sur lancer*
to throw	*lancer*
a bye / a leg bye	*un bye / un leg bye*
a wide	*un wide*
no ball	*une balle fausse / un no ball*
a full-pitch ball	*une balle directe*
a shooter	*un shooteur*
a yorker	*un yorker*
to spin the ball	*faire tourner la balle*
an over	*un over / une série*
(= six balls)	*(=six balles)*
a maiden over	*(une série sans points marqués)*
(an over with no score)	*(une série sans points marqués)*
a fast bowler / a spin bowler	*un lanceur rapide / un spinneur*

BATTING	*LES COUPS*
to bat / to hit	*battre / frapper*
to cut	*couper*
He is batting now.	*Il est à la batte maintenant.*
She is a good batter.	*Elle est une bonne batteuse.*
They have just gone into bat.	*Ils viennent d'entrer sur le terrain.*
to be out	*sortir*
to be bowled out	*être éliminé sur lancer*
leg before wicket (L.B.W.)	*obstruction*
to hit the wicket	*toucher les guichets*
to be stumped out	*être éliminé sur zone*
to be run out	*être éliminé sur course*
to be caught out	*être catché*

CRICKET cont.

BATTING cont.

LE CRICKET suite

LES COUPS suite

to be out for a duck	*être canard*
(= to score no runs)	*(=ne rien marquer)*
to score	*marquer*
a run	*une course*
a four (=hit the ball to the boundary)	*un quatre points (frapper la balle hors de la zone)*
a six (=as a four but without the ball bouncing)	*un six (=comme un quatre points mais sans que la balle ne rebondisse)*
a century (=one hundred runs)	*un centurion*

FIELDING	*FIELDER / ETRE DANS LE CHAMP*
to field	*fielder*
to catch	*catcher*
to drop a catch	*lâcher*
a good catch	*un bon catch*

AN INNINGS	*UNE MANCHE*
the first innings	*la première manche*
the second innings	*la seconde manche*
to retire	*se retirer*

TYPE OF GAME	*TYPES DE JEUX*
a test match	*un match-essai*
one day cricket	*match d'une journée*
a friendly match	*un match amical*

SWIMMING
LA NATATION

DO YOU LIKE SWIMMING?	*VOUS AIMEZ / TU AIMES NAGER?*
Yes, I love swimming.	*Oui, j'adore nager.*
No, I'm sorry, but I can't swim.	*Non, je regrette mais je ne sais pas nager.*
Would you like to go swimming?	*Vous voulez / tu veux aller nager?*
I don't really like swimming.	*Je n'aime pas vraiment nager.*

TYPES OF POOL	*LES TYPES DE PISCINE*
a public swimming pool	*une piscine municipale*
a private pool	*une piscine privée*
an indoor / outdoor pool	*une piscine intérieure / extérieure*
a heated / unheated pool	*une piscine chauffée / non chauffée*
an aquatic park	*un parc aquatique*

CLOTHES AND EQUIPMENT	*LA TENUE*
a swimming costume	*un maillot de bain*
a bikini	*un bikini*
trunks	*un slip de bain / maillot de bain*
shorts	*un short*
a swimming hat	*un bonnet de bain*
a towel	*une serviette*
goggles	*les lunettes de plongée (f)*
a snorkel	*un tuba*
flippers	*palmes (f)*
a rubber ring	*une lanière de plastique*
armbands	*des brassards (m)*
a lilo	*un matelas pneumatique*
a float	*un flotteur*

SWIMMING cont.

LA NATATION suite

BUYING TICKETS	*ACHETER LES BILLETS*
an adult's ticket	*un billet adulte*
a child's ticket	*un billet enfant*
a swimmer's ticket	*un billet nageur*
a spectator's ticket	*un billet spectateur*
Could I have tickets for two children, please?	*Je peux avoir des billets pour deux enfants, s'il vous plaît?*
Could I have two adult spectator tickets, please?	*Je peux avoir deux billets adulte-spectateur, s'il vous plaît?*
Are there tubes at this swimming pool?	*Y a-t-il des toboggans dans cette piscine?*
Could we have tickets to go down the tubes, please?	*On peut avoir des billets pour les toboggans s'il vous plaît?*

TIMES OF SESSIONS	*LES HEURES DES SEANCES*
When does this session start?	*Quand commence cette séance?*
When does this session end?	*Quand termine cette séance?*
When does our session end?	*Quand finit notre séance?*
They blow a whistle at the end of the session.	*Ils sifflent à la fin de chaque séance.*
When does the next session start?	*Quand commence la prochaine séance?*
What time does the pool open on Saturday?	*A quelle heure la piscine oeuvre-t-elle le samedi?*
What time does the pool close?	*A quelle heure ferme la piscine?*

SWIMMING cont.	*LA NATATION suite*
THE PARTS OF THE POOL	*LES PARTIES DE LA PISCINE*

NON-SWIMMING AREAS	*LES PARTIES AUTRES QUE LA PISCINE*
The Spectator Area	*Le Coin des Spectateurs*
I think I will sit and watch, if you don't mind.	*Je crois que je vais m'asseoir et regarder, si cela ne vous dérange pas.*
The Café	*Le Café*
I shall go and get something to eat and drink.	*Je vais chercher quelque chose à manger et à boire.*
The Drinks Machine	*Les Distributeurs de Boisson*
What change does the drinks machine take?	*Quelles pièces la machine prend-elle?*

THE CHANGING ROOMS	*LES VESTIAIRES*
Where are the changing rooms?	*Où sont les vestiaires?*
Is there a family changing room?	*Y a-t-il un vestiaire familial?*
They are all individual cubicles.	*Ce sont tous des vestiaires individuels.*
There are separate changing rooms for men and women.	*Il y a des vestiaires séparés pour hommes et femmes.*
The changing rooms are for both sexes.	*Les vestiaires sont mixtes.*

SWIMMING cont.

LA NATATION suite

GETTING CHANGED

SE CHANGER

Shall we get changed together?	*On se change ensemble?*
I'll use this cubicle.	*Je vais dans ce vestiaire-ci.*
to get undressed / to get dressed	*se déshabiller / s'habiller*
to dry oneself	*se sécher*
to use talcum powder	*utiliser du talc*
to dry one's hair	*se sécher le cheveux*
a coin operated hair dryer	*un séchoir payant*
a hair brush / to brush	*une brosse à cheveux / brosser*
a comb / to comb	*un peigne / peigner*
a mirror / to look in	*un miroir / se regarder*

THE LOCKERS

LES CASIERS (m)

What coins do you need for the lockers?	*Quelles pièces faut-il pour les casiers?*
How do the lockers work?	*Comment marchent les casiers?*
Don't forget the number of your locker.	*N'oubliez pas / n'oublie pas le numéro de votre / ton casier.*
Can you remember our locker number?	*Vous vous souvenez / tu te souviens de notre numéro de casier?*
I have forgotten the number of my locker.	*J'ai oublié le numéro de mon casier.*
My locker was somewhere here.	*Mon casier était quelque part par là.*
to lock / unlock the door	*fermer / ouvrir le casier*
Don't lose your key.	*Ne perdez pas votre / ne perds pas ta clé.*
Put your clothes in here.	*Mettez vos / mets tes vêtements là-dedans.*

THE FOOTBATH AND SHOWERS

LE BAIN DE PIED ET LES DOUCHES

You have to walk through the footbath.	*Il faut traverser le bain de pieds.*
You are supposed to shower before getting into the pool.	*Vous êtes / tu es censé(e)(s) prendre une douche d'abord aller dans la piscine.*

SWIMMING cont.   *LA NATATION suite*

THE POOLS	*LES PISCINES (f)*
the paddling pool	*la pataugeoire*
the children's pool	*le petit bassin*
the main pool	*le grand bassin*

PARTS OF THE POOL	*LES PARTIES DE LA PISCINE*
the deep end	*le fond profond*
the shallow end	*le fond peu profond*
a length / a width	*une longueur / une largeur*
How long is the pool?	*Quelle est la longueur de la piscine?*
How wide is it?	*Quelle est sa largeur?*
the depth	*la profondeur*
How deep is it at the deep / shallow end?	*Quelle est la profondeur du côté profond / du côté peu profond?*
the diving board	*le plongeoir*
the slide	*le toboggan*

WAVE MACHINES	*LES MACHINES A VAGUES*
Does this pool have a wave machine?	*Est-ce que cette piscine a une machine à vagues?*
They put the wave machine on at intervals.	*Ils mettent la machine à vagues en marche en alternance.*
The waves are just starting.	*Les vagues (f) commencent tout de suite.*
They usually have the waves on for five minutes.	*Ils mettent généralement les vagues pendant cinq minutes.*
There's also a water spout.	*Il y a aussi un jet d'eau.*

SWIMMING cont.   *LA NATATION suite*

TUBES	*LES TOBOGGANS (m)*
Pick up a mat.	*Prenez / prends un matelas.*
This session is using blue / red / yellow mats.	*Cette session propose des tapis, bleus / rouges / jaunes.*
You sit on a mat.	*Vous vous asseyez / tu t'assois sur un tapis.*
Wait till the tube is clear.	*Attendez / attends que le toboggan se libère.*
You can go down now.	*Vous pouvez / tu peux descendre maintenant.*
What is this tube like?	*Comment est ce toboggan?*
It's steep. / It has a gentle slope.	*Il est raide./ Il a une pente douce.*
It bends a lot.	*Il a plein de tournants.*
There's a corkscrew.	*Il y a un tire-bouchon.*
That one is really fast.	*Celui-là est vraiment rapide.*
It's like a water chute.	*C'est comme une chute d'eau.*
Which tube do you like best?	*Quel toboggan préférez-vous / préfères-tu?*
I like this one / that one best.	*Je préfère celui-ci / celui-là.*
Have you been down all the tubes?	*Vous avez / tu as fait tous les toboggans?*
I didn't like that one.	*Je n'ai pas aimé celui-là.*
That one was brilliant.	*Celui-là était génial.*

SWIMMING STROKES	*LES NAGES*
to swim / to go for a swim	*nager / aller nager*
to float on your back / front	*faire la planche sur le dos / sur le ventre*
to swim breast stroke / side stroke	*nager la brasse / la brasse indienne*
back stroke / crawl	*le dos crawlé / crawl*
butterfly stroke	*brasse papillon*
Can you swim back stroke?	*Vous savez / tu sais nager le dos crawlé?*
I can't do butterfly.	*Je ne sais pas faire la brasse papillon.*

SWIMMING cont.	*LA NATATION suite*

UNDERWATER SWIMMING	*LA NAGE SOUS-MARINE*
Can you swim under water?	*Vous savez / tu sais nager sous l'eau?*
I only like swimming under water with goggles on.	*Je n'aime nager sous l'eau qu'avec des lunettes.*
How far can you swim under water?	*Jusqu'où pouvez-vous / peux-tu nager sous l'eau?*
to swim between someone's legs	*nager entre les jambes de quelqu'un*

RACING	*LES COURSES (f)*
to race	*courir*
Let's have a race.	*Faisons une course.*
I'll race you to the far end.	*On fait une course jusqu'au bout.*
I won / you won.	*J'ai gagné / vous avez / tu as gagné.*
It was a draw.	*C'était un ex-aequo.*
Let's see who can swim furthest?	*On regarde qui nage le plus loin?*
How many lengths can you swim?	*Vous pouvez / tu peux faire combien de longueurs?*

DIVING	*PLONGER*
to dive	*plonger*
Is it deep enough for diving?	*C'est assez profond pour plonger?*
I can dive but I'm not very good.	*Je sais plonger mais je ne suis pas très bon(ne)?*
Did I splash a lot then?	*J'ai fait un plat, alors?*
What did that dive look like.	*Comment était ce plongeon?*

SWIMMING cont.   *LA NATATION suite*

DIVING FOR COINS

Should we dive for coins?

Have you any coins?
Will you throw some coins in for us to find?

PLONGER POUR RAMASSER LES PIECES (f)

On plonge pour des pièces de monnaie?

Vous avez / tu as des pièces?
Vous pouvez / tu peux jeter des pièces pour qu'on aille les ramasser?

SAFETY
a lifeguard / the First Aid post
Can you life save?

Don't go out of your depth.
Stay in the children's pool.
Don't run in case you slip.

You shouldn't swim just after eating.

I sometimes get cramp.
I have got cramp in my right / left leg.

LA SECURITE
un maître-nageur / le poste de secours
Vous avez / tu as des notions de secourisme?
N'allez pas / ne va pas trop profond.
Restez / reste dans le petit bassin.
Ne courez pas / ne cours pas au cas où vous glisseriez / tu glisserais.
Vous ne devriez pas / tu ne devrais pas nager après avoir mangé.
Quelquefois, j'ai des crampes.
J'ai des crampes dans ma jambe droite / gauche.

GETTING OUT OF THE POOL
They just blew the whistle to get out.
It's the end of our session now.
Shall we get out just before the end of our session so the changing rooms won't be so busy?
My mother said we have to get out now.
You're looking cold.
You're shivering.
I think we should get out now.

Can't we have five more minutes?

SORTIR DE LA PISCINE
Ils viennent de siffler pour la sortie.
C'est la fin de la séance maintenant.
On sort avant la fin de la séance pour que les vestiaires ne soient pas trop pleins?
Ma maman a dit qu'il fallait sortir maintenant.
Vous avez / tu as l'air d'avoir froid.
Vous tremblez / tu trembles.
Je pense qu'on devrait sortir maintenant.
On ne peut pas avoir cinq minutes de plus?

THE BEACH
LA PLAGE

THE SEA		*LA MER*	
the tide	*la marée*	to go out	*baisser*
high tide	*marée haute*	a wave	*une vague*
low tide	*marée basse*	to break	*se briser*
to come in	*avancer*	spray	*embruns (m.pl)*

THE BEACH	*LA PLAGE*
the sand	*le sable*
a rock	*un rocher*
a rock pool	*une mare entre des rochers (m)*
a starfish	*une étoile de mer*
a pebble / shingle	*un cailloux / galet (m)*
the cliffs / a sand dune	*les falaises (f) / une dune*
a jellyfish / seaweed	*une méduse / algues (f)*

CLOTHES AND EQUIPMENT	*LA TENUE ET L'EQUIPEMENT*
a swimming costume	*un maillot de bain*
a bikini	*un bikini*
trunks	*un slip de bain*
to get changed / to get dressed	*se changer / s'habiller*
to dry oneself / a towel	*se sécher / une serviette*
a rubber ring / armbands	*une bouée / des brassards (m)*
a surfboard	*une planche de surf*
an inflatable	*un (matelas) gonflable*
a lilo / to float	*un matelas pneumatique / flotter*
to have a turn on / with	*prendre son tour sur / avec*
a deckchair / a beach mat	*un transat / un tapis de plage*
a wind break / a parasol	*un pare-vent / un parasol*

THE BEACH cont.   *LA PLAGE suite*

SWIMMING AND SNORKELLING	*NAGER AVEC ET SANS TUBA (m)*
Swimming - see pages 301-308	*Nager*
to float	*flotter*
to ride on the waves	*voguer*
Snorkelling	*Nager avec un tuba*
to snorkel	*nager avec un tuba*
a mask	*un masque*
a snorkel	*un tuba*
a mouthpiece	*une embouchure*
a tube	*un tube*
flippers	*des palmes (f)*
goggles	*des lunettes de plongée (f)*

BUILDING SANDCASTLES	*CONSTRUIRE DES CHATEAUX DE SABLE (m)*
a bucket / a spade	*un seau / une pelle*
a sandcastle	*un château de sable*
battlements / a drawbridge	*créneaux (m) / un pont-levis*
a flag	*un drapeau*
a moat / a mound	*un douve / un remblai*
a tunnel / a tower	*un tunnel / une tour*
to build / to collect pebbles	*construire / ramasser des cailloux*
to decorate with shells	*décorer avec coquillage blancs*
to dig / to fill	*creuser / remplir*
to jump on / to knock down	*sauter dessus / détruire*
to make	*faire*
to pat / to smooth	*aplatir / aplanir*
to tunnel	*creuser des tunnels*
to turn out	*retourner*
to wait for the tide to come in	*attendre que la mer monte*

THE BEACH cont. *LA PLAGE suite*

WALKING ON THE BEACH	*MARCHER SUR LA PLAGE*
to go for a walk	*aller se promener*
along the beach	*le long de la plage*
on the cliffs	*sur les falaises (f)*
over the rocks	*par dessus les rochers (m)*
at the edge of the sea	*au bord (m) de l'eau (f)*

COLLECTING SHELLS	*RAMASSER DES COQUILLAGES (m)*
an unusual one	*un original*
a different type	*une espèce différente*
a pretty one	*un joli*
broken	*cassé*
to wash the sand off	*enlever le sable*
to put in a bucket	*mettre dans un seau*

SHRIMPING	*LA PECHE A LA CREVETTE*
a fishing net / to catch	*un filet / attraper*
to look at the rock pools	*regarder dans les mares / les crevasses*
a crab / a shrimp	*un crabe / une crevette*

CRICKET AND FRENCH CRICKET	*LE CRIQUET ANGLAIS ET FRANCAIS*
Cricket - see 297-300	***Cricket Anglais***
French Cricket	***Cricket Français***
a bat / a ball	*une batte / une balle*
to bat / to bowl / to field	*battre / lancer*
to throw / to catch / to drop	*lancer / attraper / lâcher*
to get hit by the ball below the knee	*recevoir la balle sous le genou*
to swivel round	*pivoter*

THE BEACH cont.

FRENCH CRICKET cont.

LA PLAGE suite

CRICKET FRANCAIS suite

to stand still	*se tenir immobile*
You're not allowed to move your feet.	*Vous n'avez pas / tu n'a pas le droit de bouger les pieds.*
to hit the ball into the sea	*frapper la balle dans la mer*
to hit the ball a long way	*frapper la balle très loin*
to be out	*être faute*
It's your turn to bat now.	*C'est à vous / toi de battre maintenant.*
Well caught! / Out!	*Bien reçu! / Faute!*

DONKEY RIDES	**PROMENADES A DOS D'ANE**
to have a ride on a donkey	*faire une promenade à dos d'âne*
to put your feet in the stirrups	*mettre ses pieds dans les éperons*
to hold on to the reins	*tenir les rênes (f)*
to sit in the saddle	*s'asseoir sur la selle*
to walk / to trot / to pat	*marcher / trotter / caresser*

OTHER ACTIVITIES	**AUTRES ACTIVITES**
to paddle	*barboter*
to get wet	*se mouiller*
to play boules	*jouer aux boules*
to play catch	*jouer au chat*
to play pig in the middle	*jeu où deux enfants se lancent un ballon tandis qu'un troisième placé au milieu, essaie de l'intercepter*
to play with a beach ball	*jouer au beach volley*
to ride	*monter*
to run into the water	*courir dans l'eau*
to stay at the edge	*rester au bord*
to swim a long way out	*nager*
to surf	*surfer*

THE BEACH cont.   *LA PLAGE suite*

EATING ON THE BEACH	*MANGER A LA PLAGE*
to have something to eat	*manger quelque chose*
a stick of rock	*un bâton de sucre d'orge*
an ice cream	*une glace*
an iced lolly	*une sucette glacée*
a cold drink	*une boisson fraîche*
a picnic - see 235-236	*un pique-nique*
a sandwich	*un sandwich*
a barbecue - see 184-185	*un barbecue*
a disposable barbecue	*un barbecue jetable*
to gather firewood	*ramasser du bois*
driftwood	*bois flotté*
to build a wind shield	*construire un paravent*

WATER SKIING	*LE SKI NAUTIQUE*
to have a water skiing lesson	*prendre un cours de ski nautique*
a motorboat	*un bateau à moteur*
to tow / to be towed	*remorquer / être remorqué*
a towrope	*une corde à remorque*
a handle	*une poignée*
skis / bindings	*des skis / les fixations*
a life-jacket	*un gilet de sauvetage*
to crouch	*se recroqueviller*
to hold the towrope	*tenir la corde*
to accelerate	*accélérer*
to stand upright	*se tenir droit*
the surface of the water	*la surface de l'eau*
to skim	*raser la surface de l'eau*
to zigzag	*faire des zigzags (m)*
to cross the wake	*traverser le sillage*
to fall	*tomber*
to get back up again	*se rétablir*

WINDSURFING	**LA PLANCHE A VOILE**
to windsurf	*faire de la planche à voile*
to surfboard / a surfboard	*faire du surf / une planche de surf*
the crest of a wave	*la crête de la vague*
a big / small wave	*une grosse / petite vague*
There's a huge wave coming.	*Une énorme vague arrive.*

PROBLEMS	**LES PROBLEMES (m)**
Take care, there is…	*Attention, il y a…*
• broken glass	• *un bout de verre*
• a jellyfish	• *une méduse*
• sewage	• *eaux usées*
• a steeply shelving beach	• *une plage en pente raide*
• a strong current	• *un courant fort*

WARNING AND SAFETY SIGNS	**LES SIGNAUX D'ALERTE ET DE SECURITE**
Bathing Forbidden	*Baignade interdite*
Unsupervised Bathing	*Baignade non-surveillée*
First Aid Post / Lifeguard	*Poste de secours / Maître-nageur*
Lifebuoy	*Bouée de sauvetage*

BOATS	**LES BATEAUX**
a speed boat / to have a ride on	*un zodiac / monter sur*
a rowing boat / an oar	*un canot (à rames) / un aviron*
to row	*ramer*
a yacht	*un yacht*
to sail / a sail	*faire de la voile / une voile*
the crew	*l'équipage (m)*
to go yachting	*se promener en yacht*
to race / to win / to lose	*faire la course / gagner / perdre*
a canoe / a paddle	*un canoë / une pagaie / pagayer*
a pedal-boat	*un pédalo*
to pedal	*pédaler*
to hire	*louer*

CRUISES	LES CROISIERES
to go for a cruise	*faire une croisière*
to pay the fare	*payer*
a short / long cruise	*une croisière courte / longue*
a two hour cruise	*une croisière de deux heures*
the captain / the crew	*le capitaine / l'équipage*
a sailor	*un marin*
to go aboard	*monter à bord*
to go on deck	*aller sur le pont*
to get soaked by the spray	*se faire mouiller par les embruns*
to go back inside	*retourner à l'intérieur*
to get out of the wind	*se protéger du vent*
to have a drink in the bar	*prendre un verre au bar*
to feel seasick	*avoir le mal de mer*

THE HARBOUR	LE PORT
the quay	*le quai*
the lighthouse	*le phare*
a flashing light	*un clignotant*
a warning siren	*une sirène*
the fishing boats	*les bateaux de pêche (f)*
the nets	*les filets (m)*
the catch	*la prise / la pêche*
the fishes	*les poissons (f)*
to anchor	*ancrer*
an anchor	*l'ancre (f)*

SUNBATHING
LES BAINS DE SOLEIL

SUNBATHING EQUIPMENT		L'EQUIPEMENT POUR BRONZER	
a sunbed	*un lit pliant*	suntan lotion	*lait solaire (m)*
a deckchair	*un transat*	suntan oil	*huile solaire (f)*
a mat	*un tapis de plage*	coconut	*noix de coco (m)*
a rug	*un tapis*	water resistant	*résiste à l'eau*
a cushion	*un coussin*	after sun lotion	*lait après-soleil*
a sunshade	*une ombre*	a sun bed	*un lit solaire*
suntan cream	*crème solaire*	a sun lamp	*une lampe solaire*

USEFUL EXPRESSIONS	EXPRESSIONS UTILES
Can you put some cream on my back, please?	*Vous pouvez / tu peux mettre de la crème sur le dos, s'il vous / te plaît?*
May I borrow some suntan cream, please?	*Je peux emprunter de la crème solaire, s'il vous / te plaît?*
What factor is your cream?	*Quel est l'indice de la crème?*
It's too hot for me.	*Il fait trop chaud pour moi.*
I am going to move into the shade for a bit.	*Je vais me mettre à l'ombre pendant un moment.*
I am going to cool off in the swimming pool / sea.	*Je vais me rafraîchir dans la piscine / mer.*
I don't like to sunbathe in the middle of the day.	*Je n'aime pas prendre des bains de soleil au milieu de la journée.*

SUNBATHING cont.   *LES BAINS DE SOLEIL suite.*

USEFUL EXPRESSIONS cont.   *EXPRESSIONS UTILES suite*

Can you see the mark where my strap was?	*Vous voyez / tu vois les marques de ma bretelle?*
Is my back looking brown?	*Est-ce que mon dos est bronzé?*
I have got sunburnt.	*J'ai des coups de soleil.*
My skin is peeling.	*Ma peau pèle.*
I am sore.	*J'ai mal.*
Have you any calamine lotion?	*Vous avez / tu as de la lotion à la calamine?*
Insects keep biting me.	*Les insectes n'arrêtent pas de me piquer.*
I don't want skin cancer.	*Je ne veux pas avoir le cancer.*
You are looking rather red.	*Vous avez / tu as l'air plutôt rouge.*

THE WEATHER	*LE TEMPS*
The sun has gone in.	*Le soleil a disparu.*
I wish the sun would come out again.	*J'aimerais que le soleil revienne.*
The sun is about to go behind that cloud.	*Le soleil va bientôt disparaître derrière ce nuage.*
There's not a cloud in the sky.	*Il n'y a pas un nuage dans le ciel.*

FAMILY AND FRIENDS
LA FAMILLE ET LES AMIS

IMMEDIATE FAMILY	*LA FAMILLE IMMEDIATE*
mother / Mum / Mummy	*mère / maman*
father / Dad / Daddy	*père / papa*
a sister	*une soeur*
an older sister	*une soeur aînée*
the oldest sister	*la soeur aînée*
a younger sister	*une soeur cadette / petite sœur*
the youngest sister	*la plus jeune soeur / petite sœur*
a brother	*un frère*
an older brother	*un frère aîné / grand frère*
the oldest brother	*le frère aîné / grand frère*
a younger brother	*le frère cadet / petit frère*
the youngest brother	*le plus jeune frère / petit frère*
a twin	*un jumeau*
identical twins	*des vrais jumeaux*
non-identical twins	*des faux jumeaux*
a daughter	*une fille*
a son	*un fils*

COMMON QUESTIONS	*LES QUESTIONS USUELLES*
How many brothers and sisters have you?	*Combien de frères et soeurs avez-vous / as-tu?*
I have one of each.	*J'ai un frère et une soeur.*
I have two sisters and one brother.	*J'ai deux soeurs et un frère.*
Are you the eldest / the youngest?	*Etes-vous / es-tu l'aîné(e) / le(la) plus jeune?*

FAMILY AND FRIENDS cont.　　*LA FAMILLE ET LES AMIS suite*

COMMON QUESTIONS cont.　　*LES QUESTIONS USUELLES suite.*

How old is your sister / brother?	*Quel âge a votre / ta soeur / votre / ton frère?*
What are your brothers and sisters called?	*Comment s'appellent vos / tes frères et soeurs?*
The oldest / youngest is called..	*L'aîné(e) / le(la) plus jeune s'appelle…*
The next one is thirteen and is called..	*L'autre a treize ans et s'appelle…*

THE GENERATIONS　　*LES GENERATIONS*
the older generation　　*la génération précédente*
the younger generation　　*la génération suivante*
my / our / your generation　　*ma / nôtre / vôtre / ta génération*
the generation gap　　*le fossé entre les générations*

CLOSE RELATIVES　　*LA FAMILLE PROCHE*
a grandmother / granny / grandma　　*une grand-mère / mamie / mémé*
a great-grandmother　　*une arrière grand-mère*
a grandfather / granddad /grandpa　　*un grand-père / papy / pépé*
a great-grandfather　　*un arrière grand-père*
a granddaughter / a grandson　　*une petite-fille / un petit-fils*
a great-granddaughter　　*une arrière-petite-fille*
a great-grandson　　*un arrière petit-fils*
an aunt / aunty　　*une tante / tata*
a great-aunt　　*une grand-tante*
an uncle / a great-uncle　　*un oncle / un grand-oncle*
a niece / a nephew　　*une nièce / un neveu*
a cousin　　*un cousin*
a first / second cousin　　*un cousin germain / cousin au deuxième degré*
a cousin once / twice removed　　*un cousin éloigné*

FAMILY AND FRIENDS cont.   *LA FAMILLE ET LES AMIS*
suite

RELATIVES BY MARRIAGE	*LA FAMILLE PAR ALLIANCE*
a wife	*une femme*
a husband	*un mari*
a mother-in-law	*une belle-mère*
a father-in-law	*un beau-père*
a daughter-in-law	*une belle-fille*
a son-in-law	*un beau-fils / gendre*
a sister-in-law	*une belle-soeur*
a brother-in-law	*un beau-frère*

SEPARATION AND DIVORCE	*SEPARATION ET DIVORCES*
to decide to separate	*décider de se séparer*
to have a trial separation	*se séparer à l'essai*
My parents are separated.	*Mes parents sont séparés.*
to divorce	*divorcer*
a divorce	*un divorce*
My parents are divorced.	*Mes parents sont divorcés.*
to decide where the children will live	*décider où les enfants vont vivre*
I live with my father in the holidays.	*J'habite avec mon père pendant les vacances.*
I live with my mother in term time.	*J'habite avec ma mère en dehors des vacances.*
I spend alternate weekends with each parent.	*Je passe un week-end sur deux avec chacun de mes parents.*
a one parent family	*une famille monoparentale*
to have access to the children	*avoir la garde des enfants*
to pay maintenance	*payer une pension*
to spend the holidays with	*passer les vacances avec*

FAMILY AND FRIENDS cont.	*LA FAMILLE ET LES AMIS suite*

SEPARATION AND DIVORCE cont.	*SEPARATION ET DIVORCES suite*

My father / mother has re-married.	*Mon père / ma mère s'est remarié(e).*
My father and mother have both re-married.	*Mon père et ma mère se sont tous les deux remariés.*
a stepmother / a stepfather	*une belle-mère / un beau-père*
a stepdaughter / a stepson	*une belle-fille / un beau - fils*
a stepsister / a stepbrother	*une demi-soeurs / un demi - frère*

FRIENDS	*LES AMIS*
an acquaintance	*une connaissance*
a friend of the family	*un ami de la famille*
a god parent	*un parrain / une marraine*
to become friends	*devenir amis*
a good friend / a best friend	*un(e) bon ami(e) / un(e) meilleur(e) ami(e)*
a friend of mine	*un(e) de mes ami(e)(s)*
a boyfriend / a girlfriend	*un petit ami / une petite amie (Use petit/petite only if you love them.)*
a group of friends	*un groupe d'amis*
I go around with a group of people.	*Je me balade avec un groupe d'amis.*
I don't have one particular boyfriend / girlfriend.	*Je n'ai pas de petit(e) ami(e) attitré(e).*
I have a boyfriend. His name is..	*J'ai un petit ami. Il s'appelle...*
My girlfriend is called..	*Ma petite amie s'appelle...*
a fiancée	*une fiancée*
a lover	*un(e) amoureux(se)*
to live with	*vivre avec*

FAMILY AND FRIENDS cont.　　*LA FAMILLE ET LES AMIS suite*

LIKING / NOT LIKING PEOPLE　　*AIMER / NE PAS AIMER LES GENS*

LIKING	AIMER
to like	aimer / apprécier
to get on well with	bien s'entendre avec
to make friends with	faire la connaissance de
to fancy	bien aimer
to chat up	draguer
to get off with	sortir avec
to have a date with	avoir un rendez-vous avec
to go out with	sortir avec
to flirt with	flirter avec
to fall for	tomber amoureux de
to fall in love	tomber amoureux
to love	aimer
to adore	adorer

NOT LIKING	NE PAS AIMER
not to get on well together	ne pas s'entendre
to fall out	se brouiller
to have a row	se disputer
to dislike / to get fed up with	ne pas aimer / avoir assez de
to hate	détester / haïr
to break up with	rompre avec
to finish a relationship	mettre fin à une relation

FAMILY AND FRIENDS cont.

LA FAMILLE ET LES AMIS suite

PHYSICAL RELATIONSHIPS	*RELATIONS PHYSIQUES*
to hold hands	*se tenir la main*
to put your arm round someone	*mettre le bras sur l'épaule de quelqu'un*
to cuddle	*enlacer, caresser*
to kiss / to snog	*embrasser*
to go to bed together	*coucher ensemble*
to make love	*faire l'amour*
to have sex	*coucher avec*
to be faithful / unfaithful	*être fidèle / infidèle*
to live with	*vivre avec*
to use contraception	*utiliser un contraceptif*
to have safe sex	*avoir des relations protégées*
to use a condom	*utiliser un préservatif*
to be on the pill	*prendre la pilule*
to sleep around	*coucher à droite à gauche*
the morning after pill	*la pilule du lendemain*
AIDS	*SIDA*
VD	*Maladie vénérienne*
a late period	*des règles en retard*
a missed period	*un cycle de retard*
to do a pregnancy test	*faire un test de grossesse*
to be pregnant	*être enceinte*
a urine sample	*un échantillon d'urine*
to see the doctor	*voir un médecin*
to go to the family planning clinic	*aller au planning familial*
to get advice	*demander conseil*
to decide on a termination	*décider d'avorter*
to have a baby	*avoir un enfant*

FAMILY AND FRIENDS cont.

LA FAMILLE ET LES AMIS
suite

BABIES	*LES ENFANTS OU BEBES*
birth / a baby	*naissance / un bébé / un enfant*
to be born	*être né*
What time were you born?	*Quand êtes-vous / es-tu né(e)?*
Where were you born?	*Où êtes-vous / es-tu né(e)?*
a baby / twins / triplets / quads	*un enfant / jumeaux / triplés / quadruplés*
When is your birthday?	*Quand est votre / ton anniversaire?*
My birthday is..	*Mon anniversaire est...*
I am adopted.	*Je suis adopté(e).*

BABIES' PROBLEMS	*LES PROBLEMES*
to cry	*pleurer*
to need the nappy changed	*avoir besoin de changer la couche*
disposable nappies	*couches jetables*
towelling nappies	*couches en éponge*
a safety pin	*une épingle à nourrice*
plastic pants	*une culotte en plastique*
to be tired	*être fatigué(e)*
to sleep	*dormir*
to be hungry	*avoir faim*
to have wind	*avoir des gaz*

FEEDING BABIES	*NOURRIR LES BEBES*
to need a feed	*avoir besoin de manger*
to have a feed / to feed	*manger / nourrir*
breast fed / bottle fed	*nourri au sein / au biberon*
to sterilize the bottles	*stériliser les biberons*
to warm a bottle	*réchauffer un biberon*
demand feeding	*réclamer son biberon*
to be fed four hourly	*être nourri quatre fois par jour*
milk / solid food	*lait (m) / nourriture solide (f)*

FAMILY AND FRIENDS cont.   *LA FAMILLE ET LES AMIS*
suite

BABY EQUIPMENT	*L'EQUIPEMENT (m) POUR BEBES*
a carry cot / a cot	*un porte-bébé / un lit bébé*
a pram	*un landau*
a baby sling	*un porte-bébé (à la bretelle)*
a baby seat for the car	*un siège*
a high chair	*une chaise haute*
a play pen	*un parc*
a changing mat	*un matelas à langer*
a bib	*un bavoir*
toys / a musical box / a mobile	*jouets / une boîte à musique / un mobile*

YOUNG CHILDREN	*LES ENFANTS*
to learn to roll over / to crawl	*apprendre à se retourner / ramper*
to stand up / to walk	*se lever / marcher*
for the first time	*pour la première fois*
to say his / her first words	*dire ses premiers mots*
to go to nursery school	*aller à la maternelle*
to play	*jouer*
to draw / to colour / to paint	*dessiner / colorier / peindre*
to do jigsaws	*faire des puzzles*
to learn the alphabet	*apprendre l'alphabet*
to learn to count	*apprendre à compter*
to learn to read and write	*apprendre à lire et écrire*

ADOLESCENCE	*L'ADOLESCENCE*
to be a teenager	*être adolescent(e)*
to be independent	*être indépendant(e)*
to grow up	*grandir*
a social life	*une vie sociale*
to go out with friends	*sortir avec des amis*

FAMILY AND FRIENDS cont.

LA FAMILLE ET LES AMIS suite

ADOLESCENCE cont

L'ADOLESCENCE suite

to go to parties	*aller à des soirées*
to go to bed late	*se coucher tard*
to lie in	*faire la grasse matinée*
to come of age	*être majeur*
to have the right to vote	*avoir le droit de vote*
to be old enough to drink	*être en âge de boire*
to learn to drive - see 397-398	*apprendre à conduire*
to be adult	*être adulte*

MARITAL STATUS

LE STATUT MARITAL

unmarried	*célibataire*
a spinster	*une célibataire*
a bachelor	*un célibataire*
to get engaged	*se fiancer*
a fiancé / fiancée	*un fiancé / une fiancée*
an engagement ring	*une bague de fiançailles*
to announce the engagement	*annoncer les fiançailles*

WEDDINGS

MARIAGES (m)

to decide on a wedding day	*fixer la date de mariage*
to send out invitations	*envoyer les invitations (f)*
to look at a wedding present list	*regarder une liste de mariage*
to get married in church / in a registry office	*se marier religieusement / civilement*
the bride / bridegroom	*la mariée / le marié*
the best man	*le témoin*
a bridesmaid / a pageboy	*une demoiselle d'honneur /un garçon d'honneur*
the vicar / the registrar	*le prêtre / l'officier de mairie*
the organist / the choir	*l'organiste / le choeur*

FAMILY AND FRIENDS cont.

WEDDINGS cont

LA FAMILLE ET LES AMIS suite

MARIAGES suite

the photographer	le photographe
to pose for photos / to have photos taken	poser pour les photos / faire prendre en photo
the guests	les invités (m/f)
the wedding dress / the veil / the train / the wedding ring	la robe de mariée / le voile / la traîne / l'alliance (f)
a bouquet / to carry	un bouquet / porter
to throw / to catch	lancer / attraper
a buttonhole	une boutonnière
the wedding service	la célébration du mariage
to walk down the aisle	sortir de l'église (f)
the father of the bride	le père de la mariée
to kneel	s'agenouiller
to sing hymns / to pray	chanter des cantiques (m) / prier
to throw confetti / rice	jeter des confettis / du riz

THE WEDDING RECEPTION

LA RECEPTION DU MARIAGE

to shake hands	serrer les mains
to welcome guests	accueillir les invités
to make a speech	faire un discours
the best man's speech	le discours du témoin
to make a joke	faire une plaisanterie
to make a toast	faire un toast
to raise your glasses	lever son verre

THE HONEYMOON

LA LUNE DE MIEL

to leave the reception	quitter la réception
to get changed	se changer
to go on honeymoon	partir en lune de miel
to decorate the car	décorer la voiture
newly married	jeunes mariés
to throw confetti	jeter des confettis
to wave goodbye	faire un signe de la main

FAMILY AND FRIENDS cont.   *LA FAMILLE ET LES AMIS suite*

WEDDING ANNIVERSARIES	*LES ANNIVERSAIRES DE MARIAGE*
a silver wedding	*les noces (f.pl) d'argent*
a golden wedding	*les noces d'or*
a diamond wedding	*les noces de diamant*
to celebrate a wedding anniversary	*fêter un anniversaire de mariage*

MIDDLE AGE	*LA CINQUANTAINE*
to be middle aged	*avoir la cinquantaine*
to have grown up children	*avoir de grands enfants*
to become a grandparent	*devenir grand-parent*
to go through the menopause	*être ménopausée*
middle age spread	*l'embonpoint (pris avec l'âge)*
hormone replacement therapy	*un traitement hormonal*
to feel depressed	*être déprimé*
to start getting wrinkles	*commencer à avoir des rides*
to have more free time	*avoir plus de temps libre*
to take up new interests	*avoir de nouveaux centres d'intérêt*

OLD AGE	*LA VIEILLESSE*
to retire	*prendre sa retraite*
to take partial / early retirement	*prendre une retraite anticipée*
to enjoy retirement	*aimer la retraite*
a pension / a senior citizen	*une retraite / un retraité*
to get discounts	*avoir des réductions (f)*
to live on one's own	*vivre seul(e)*
to live with one's family	*vivre avec sa famille*
to go into sheltered housing	*aller dans un foyer-logement*
a retirement home	*une maison de retraite*
to be looked after / to be nursed	*être pris en charge / soigné*

DEATH	*LA MORT*
to die	*mourir*
to have a heart attack	*avoir une crise cardiaque / une attaque*
to have a stroke	*avoir un infarctus / un attaque*
to have cancer	*avoir le cancer*
to be unconscious	*être inconscient*
to be unable to talk properly	*être incapable de parler correctement*
to forget things	*oublier les choses*
to be in pain	*souffrir*
to take painkillers	*prendre des analgésiques*
to die in one's sleep	*mourir dans son sommeil*
to die peacefully	*mourir en paix*
to call the doctor	*appeler le médecin*
to sign the death certificate	*signer la certificat de décès*
to call the mortuary	*appeler les pompes funèbres*
the funeral	*l'enterrement (m)*
a church / a crematorium	*une église / une crématoire*
the coffin / a grave	*un cercueil / une tombe*
a wreath / flowers	*une couronne / des fleurs (f)*
to mourn / to weep	*être en deuil / pleurer*
to pray	*prier*
to comfort	*réconforter*
a widow / a widower	*une veuve / un veuf*

CONTACTING PEOPLE BY POST & TELEPHONE

CONTACTER LES GENS PAR COURRIER ET TELEPHONE

BY POST   *PAR COURRIER*

STATIONERY   *PAPETERIE (f)*

Notepaper		*Du papier à lettre*	
headed	*à en-tête*	cream	*crème*
lined	*réglé*	azure	*azure*
unlined	*uni*	blue	*bleu*
white	*blanc*	a line guide	*une ligne*

Postcards	*Les cartes postales (f)*
a picture postcard	*une carte postale*
a funny postcard	*une carte amusante*
a scenic postcard	*une carte panoramique*
a photograph	*une photographie*
an art reproduction	*une reproduction*

| CONTACTING PEOPLE BY POST cont. | *CONTACTER LES GENS PAR COURRIER suite* |

STATIONERY cont.   *PAPETERIE (f) suite*

Envelopes	*Les enveloppes*
an envelope	*une enveloppe*
to seal	*seller*
to lick	*lécher*
to slit open	*ouvrir*
to address	*adresser*
a padded envelope	*une enveloppe rembourrée*
to enclose a stamped addressed envelope (an SAE)	*joindre une enveloppe timbrée*

Stamps	*Les Timbres*
a stamp	*un timbre*
to lick	*lécher*
to stick on	*coller sur*
to buy	*acheter*
a book of stamps	*un carnet de timbres*
a first class stamp	*un timbre à tarif normal*
a second class stamp	*un timbre à tarif réduit*

USEFUL EXPRESSIONS	*EXPRESSIONS UTILES*
What stamp do I need for ..?	*J'ai besoin de quel timbre pour...?*
How much does it cost to send a letter to America?	*Combien ça coûte d'envoyer une lettre en Amérique?*
by the cheapest means possible	*au moyen le moins cher possible*
as fast as possible	*aussi vite que possible*
How long will it take to get there?	*Combien de temps cela prendra pour arriver?*
How much does it weigh?	*Cela pèse combien?*
Put it on the scales.	*Mettez-la / mets-la sur la balance.*

CONTACTING PEOPLE BY POST cont.

CONTACTER LES GENS PAR COURRIER suite

USEFUL EXPRESSIONS cont.

EXPRESSIONS UTILES suite

Guaranteed next day delivery	*Délivré(e) en vingt-quatre chrono*
to send by recorded delivery	*envoyer avec avis de réception*
by air mail	*par avion*
an international reply coupon	*un coupon international*
to fill in details on a form	*remplir des détails sur une fiche*
the sender / the recipient	*l'expéditeur / le receveur*
Surname	*Nom (m) de famille (f)*
Christian names	*Prénoms (m)*
address and postcode	*adresse (f) et code postal (m)*
date	*date (f)*
contents	*contenu (m)*
value	*valeur (f)*

PARCELS

LES COLIS (m)

to wrap up a parcel	*envelopper un colis*
wrapping paper / gift wrap	*du papier d'emballage / cadeaux*
brown paper / tissue paper	*du papier marron / de soie*
corrugated paper / bubble wrap	*du papier ondulé / emballage à bulles*
sellotape / to sellotape	*de scotch ® / scotcher*
string / to tie a knot	*une cordelette / faire un noeud*
to put your finger on the knot	*mettre son doigt sur le noeud*
scissors	*des ciseaux (m)*
a knife / to cut	*un couteau / couper*
tape / to stick	*bolduc / coller*
to undo	*défaire*
Fragile! Handle with Care!	*Fragile!*
This way up!	*Haut-Bas!*

CONTACTING PEOPLE BY POST cont.

CONTACTER LES GENS PAR COURRIER suite

POST BOXES	*LES BOÎTES A LETTRES*
Is there a post box near here?	*Y a-t-il une boîte à lettre près d'ici?*
to take a letter to the post	*poster une lettre*
What are the collection times?	*Quelles sont les heures de levées?*
the first post / the next post	*la première levée / la prochaine levée*
to catch the last post	*saisir la dernière levée*
to miss the post	*manquer la levée*
Local Mail Only	*Courrier local*
Other Desinations	*Autres destinations*
Working Days	*Jours ouvrers*
Public Holidays	*Jours fériés*

THE POST OFFICE	*LA POSTE*
to queue up	*faire la queue*
to wait to be served	*attendre d'être servi(e)(s)*
to go to the counter	*aller au comptoir*

POSTAL DELIVERIES	*LES LIVRAISONS POSTALES (f)*
a postman / a post van	*un facteur / une camionnette de la poste*
a postal round	*la tournée du facteur*
What time does the post usually arrive?	*A quelle heure passe le courrier d'habitude?*
Has the post been delivered yet?	*Le courrier est déjà passé?*
Is there a letter for me?	*Y a-t-il une lettre pour moi?*

CONTACTING PEOPLE BY POST cont.	*CONTACTER LES GENS PAR COURRIER suite*
WRITING LETTERS	*ECRIRE DES LETTRES (f)*

Formal letters	*Lettres formelles*
Dear Sir.......Yours faithfully,..	*Monsieur.............Je vous prie, Monsieur, d'agréer mes salutations distinguées,....*
Dear Mr. / Mrs./ Miss....	*Cher Monsieur / Madame / Mademoiselle*
.....Yours sincerely	*Veuillez agréer l'expression de mes sentiments respectueux*
Informal letters	*Lettres amicales*
Dear James, ...	*Cher James...*
With best wishes / Affectionately / Love / Lots of love / All my love..	*Affectueusement / je t'embrasse / je t'embrasse bien fort...*

BY TELEPHONE	*AU TELEPHONE*

To telephone England from France dial 00 (the international code), followed by 44 (the U.K. code), followed by your area code minus the first zero and finally the rest of the telephone number.	*Pour téléphoner en Angleterre de la France, faire le 00 (code international) suivi du 44 (code de l'Angleterre), suivi du code de la région, sans le premier zéro et enfin le reste du numéro.*

To telephone to France from England note that there are no French area codes. For Paris City and Greater Paris dial 00 33(1) + 8 digits. For the rest of France dial 00 33(code) + 8 digits.	*Pour téléphoner en France de l'Angleterre, noter qu'il y a des code régional. Pour Paris et la région parisienne, faire le 00 33(1) + 8 chiffres. Pour le reste de la France, faire le 00 33 (code de la region) + 8 chiffres.*

CONTACTING PEOPLE BY TELEPHONE cont.

CONTACTER LES GENS AU TELEPHONE suite

British Directory Enquiries = 192	*Renseignements Généraux en Angleterre = 192*
International Directory Enquiries = 153	*Renseignements Généraux Internationaux = 153*
French Directory Enquiries = 12	*Renseignements en France = 12*
French International Directory Enquiries = 00 33 13 + national prefix	*Renseignements à l'étranger = 00 33 12 + indicatif national / + national prefix*

France's ringing tone consists of long equal on/off tones (slower than the U.K.'s engaged tone). France's engaged tone is similar to the U.K.'s engaged tone.	*La sonnerie française consiste en de longues tonalités clairement distinctes les unes des autres. Quand la ligne est occupée, la tonalité est la même qu'en Angleterre.*

THE TELEPHONE

LE TELEPHONE

the receiver	*le combiné*
to pick up / to listen	*décrocher / écouter*
The telephone is ringing.	*Le téléphone sonne.*
Shall I answer it? I'll get it.	*Je réponds? Je vais répondre.*
I'll take it in the kitchen.	*Je le prends dans la cuisine.*
the dial / to dial a number	*le cadran / composer un numéro*

**CONTACTING PEOPLE
BY TELEPHONE cont.**

*CONTACTER LES GENS AU
TELEPHONE suite*

THE TONES	*LES TONALITES (f)*
the dialling tone	*la tonalité de sonnerie*
to get the engaged tone	*entendre la sonnerie: occupé*
It's engaged / It's ringing.	*C'est occupé / Ca sonne.*
It's out of order.	*Ca ne marche pas.*
It's unobtainable.	*C'est inaccessible.*
There isn't any dialling tone.	*Il n'y a pas de tonalité.*
Can you help me, please?	*Pouvez-vous / peux-tu m'aider, s'il vous / te plaît?*
I was cut off.	*J'ai été coupé(e).*

ANSWERING THE PHONE	*REPONDRE AU TELEPHONE*
Hello, is that Peter?	*Allô, c'est Peter?*
Could I speak to your mother?	*Pourrais-je parler à votre / ta mère?*
Is Julia there please?	*Est-ce que Julia est là, s'il vous plaît?*
Who is that speaking?	*Qui est à l'appareil?*
Who do you want to talk to?	*A qui voulez-vous / veux-tu parler?*
To whom do you want to speak?	*A qui voulez-vous / veux-tu parler?*
Hang on.	*Un instant.*
I'll just get him / her for you.	*Je vais le / la chercher.*
He / she won't be a minute.	*Il / elle en a pour une seconde.*
I am sorry he / she isn't in at the moment.	*Je regrette il / elle n'est pas là en ce moment.*
When will he / she be back?	*Il / elle sera de retour à quelle heure?*
Can you say I rang?	*Pouvez-vous / peux-tu dire que j'ai appelé?*
Could you give him / her a message, please?	*Pouvez-vous / peux-tu lui laisser un message, s'il vous / te plaît?*
I will ring again another time.	*Je rappellerai une autre fois.*
We are just about to eat. Can we ring you later?	*On va juste se mettre à table. On peut vous appeler / t'appeler plus tard?*
What is your number?	*Quel est votre / ton numéro?*
Can I take a message?	*Je peux prendre un message?*
Whom shall I say called?	*De la part de qui?*

CONTACTING PEOPLE BY TELEPHONE cont.

CONTACTER LES GENS AU TELEPHONE suite

FINDING TELEPHONE NUMBERS	*TROUVER LES NUMEROS DE TELEPHONE*
a telephone directory	*un annuaire téléphonique*
an address book	*un carnet d'adresses*
to look up a number	*chercher un numéro*
What is their name?	*Quel est leur nom?*
How do you spell it?	*Comment s'écrit-il?*
What is their initial?	*Quelles sont leurs initiales?*
What is their address?	*Quelle est leur adresse?*
Yellow Pages	*Pages Jaunes*
Directory Enquiries	*Renseignements*

USING A PUBLIC CALL BOX	*UTILISER UNE CABINE TELEPHONIQUE*
I need some change.	*J'ai besoin de monnaie.*
What coins does it take?	*Quelles pièces prend-il / elle?*
a telephone token	*un jeton téléphonique*
Does it take a 'phone card?	*Est-ce qu'elle prend une carte téléphonique?*
a twenty five unit card	*une carte à vingt-cinq unités*
Could I reverse the charge, please?	*Je peux appeler en P.C.V., s'il vous / te plaît?*
out of order	*en panne*
How do you use this telephone?	*Comment on utilise ce téléphone?*
Can you use a chargecard?	*On peut utiliser une carte privative?*

CONTACTING PEOPLE BY TELEPHONE cont.

CONTACTER LES GENS AU TELEPHONE suite

ANSWERPHONES	*LES REPONDEURS TELEPHONIQUES (m)*
to switch on / off	*mettre en marche / arrêter*
Is the answerphone on?	*Le répondeur est-il en marche?*
There is a message on the answerphone for you.	*Il y a un message sur le répondeur pour vous / toi.*
The answerphone is flashing / beeping.	*Le répondeur clignote / sonne.*
to play back the tape	*rembobiner la cassette*
to listen to the messages	*écouter les messages (m)*
to record a message	*enregistrer un message*
to rewind	*rembobiner*
to reset	*remettre à zéro*

SCHOOL AND COLLEGE
L'ECOLE, LE COLLEGE ET L'UNIVERSITE

TYPES OF SCHOOL	*LES TYPES (m)D'ECOLES (f)*
I go to..	*Je vais à*
• a nursery school	• *la maternelle*
• a primary school	• *l'école primaire*
• a secondary school	• *le collège*
• a private school	• *une école privée*
• a state school	• *une école public*
• a coeducational school	• *une école mixte*
• a sixth form college	• *un lycée*

SCHOOL BUILDINGS AND ROOMS	*LE BATIMENT ET LES SALLES (f)*
the school office	*le bureau du directeur*
the staff room	*la salle du personnel*

The assembly hall	*La salle de réunion*
the platform	*la chaire*
a microphone	*un micro*
chairs / to stack	*les chaises (f) / empiler*
to put out in rows	*mettre en rang*

The classroom	*La salle de classe*
a desk / a desk lid	*un pupitre / un couvercle de pupitre*
to open / to close	*ouvrir / fermer*
a chair / to sit down	*une chaise / s'asseoir*
the blackboard / to write on	*le tableau / écrire sur*
chalk / a blackboard duster	*craie (f) / un chiffon à effacer*
to wipe the blackboard	*essuyer le tableau*
the notice board	*le tableau d'annonce*
to pin up a notice	*accrocher une annonce*

SCHOOL BUILDINGS & ROOMS cont.

LE BATIMENT ET LES SALLES suite

The dining room	*La réfectoire*
the canteen	*la cantine*
to queue up	*faire la queue*
to take a tray	*prendre un plateau*
to ask for	*demander*
to help yourself	*se servir*
self-service	*le self-service*
Could I have a little…, please?	*Pourrais-je avoir un petit peu de…s'il vous plaît?*
Could I have a lot of…,please?	*Pourrais-je avoir beaucoup de…s'il vous plaît?*
to clear the table	*débarrasser la table*
to wipe the table	*nettoyer la table*

The gymnasium	*La salle de gym*
the wall bars	*les espaliers (m)*
a vault / to vault	*un saut / sauter*
a horse / a box	*un cheval d'arçons / une caisse*
a monkey bar	*une cage à poules*
to balance	*être en équilibre*
a rope / to climb	*une corde / grimper*
to climb	*grimper*
to swing	*se balancer*
a rope ladder	*une échelle de corde*
a spring board	*un tremplin*
a trampoline	*une trampoline*
a mat	*un tapis*
the showers	*les douches (f)*
a changing room	*un vestiaire*

SCHOOL BUILDINGS &
ROOMS cont.

LE BATIMENT ET LES
SALLES suite

The music rooms	*La salle de musique*
a practice room	*une salle d'exercice*
a piano	*un piano*
a music stand	*un pupitre à musique*
lockers	*un casier de consigne*
soundproofed	*insonorisé(e)*

(See pages 157-158 for music lessons)

The art room	*La salle de dessin*
an easel	*un chevalet*
paints	*de la peinture*
paintbrushes	*des pinceaux (m)*
paper	*du papier*
to have a painting on the wall	*peindre sur le mur*
to be on display	*être exposé*
an exhibition of work	*une exposition*

(See page 230 for details of art equipment)

The science block	*Les salles de Science*
a laboratory	*un laboratoire*
an overall	*une blouse*
safety glasses	*des lunettes (f)*
a work bench	*une paillasse*
a sink	*un évier*
acid / alkali / litmus paper	*acide / alcalin(e) / papier de tournesol*
the Periodic Table	*la classification périodique des éléments*

SCHOOL BUILDINGS & ROOMS cont.	*LE BATIMENT ET LES SALLES suite*
THE SCIENCE BLOCK cont.	*LES SALLES DE SCIENCE suite.*

Apparatus	*Le matériel*
a beaker	*un vase à bec*
a Bunsen burner	*un bec-Bunsen*
a tripod	*un trépied*
gauze	*gaze*
a burette	*une éprouvette*
a condenser	*un condensateur*
a crucible	*un creuset*
a crystallizing dish	*un récipient de cristallisation*
a delivery tube	*un catalyseur*
an evaporating basin	*un évaporateur*
filter paper	*un papier filtre*
a flask	*un ballon*
conical	*conique*
round / flat bottomed	*à fond rond / à fond plat*
a fractionating column	*une colonne de fractionnement*
a funnel	*un entonnoir*
a gas jar	*une bombonne de gaz*
a measuring cylinder	*une éprouvette graduée*
a pair of tongs	*des pincettes*
a pipette	*une pipette*
scales	*des balances*
a spatula	*une spatule*
a stand / a clamp	*un pupitre / un clamp*
a syringe	*une seringue*
a test tube	*un tube à essai*
a test tube holder	*un support*
a test tube rack	*un portoir*
a thermometer	*un thermomètre*

SCHOOL BUILDINGS & ROOMS cont.

LE BATIMENT ET LES SALLES suite

The library	*La bibliothèque*
the librarian	*le(la) bibliothécaire*
to take a book out	*prendre un livre*
to return a book	*rendre un livre*
to be overdue	*être en retard*
to reserve	*réserver*
to read	*lire*
a reference book	*un ouvrage de référence*
a catalogue	*un catalogue*
a list of authors	*une liste d'auteurs*
a list of titles	*une liste de titres*
alphabetical	*alphabétique*
to look up	*regarder*

The cloakroom	*Les vestiaires*
a peg / to hang up	*un porte-manteau / accrocher*
a locker / to lock / to unlock	*un casier / fermer à clef / ouvrir*
to put away / to get out	*mettre de côté / sortir*
the toilets / engaged / vacant	*les toilettes / occupé / libre*
the washbasin	*le lavabo*
to wash one's hands	*se laver les mains*
to dry one's hands	*se sécher les mains*
a towel	*une serviette*
a mirror / to look in	*un miroir / se regarder dans*
to brush one's hair	*se brosser les cheveux*

| SCHOOL BUILDINGS & ROOMS cont. | LE BATIMENT ET LES SALLES suite |

For details of illnesses see pages 406-417

The medical room	*L'infirmerie (f)*
the nurse	*l'infirmière*
to feel ill / to lie down	*se sentir malade / s'allonger*
to have a headache	*avoir mal à la tête*
to feel sick	*avoir envie de vomir*
to take your temperature	*prendre sa température*
to have an accident	*avoir un accident*
to go to hospital / to go home	*aller à l'hôpital (m)/ aller à la maison*
to ring your family	*appeler sa famille*

THE SCHOOL GROUNDS	*LE DOMAINE DE L'ECOLE*
the playground	*la cour de récréation*
the netball courts	*les terrains (m) de netball*
the tennis courts (See pages 255-261 for vocabulary for playing tennis)	*les courts de tennis*
the sportsfield	*le terrain de sport*
the hockey / lacrosse pitch	*le terrain de hockey / de lacrosse*
the swimming pool (See pages 301-308 for vocabulary for swimming)	*la piscine*

THE STAFF	*LE PERSONNEL*
the headmaster / headmistress	*le directeur / la directrice*
the deputy headmaster/mistress	*le sous-directeur/ directrice*
the head of year (There is no equivalent position in France.)	*le professeur responsable de toutes les classes de même niveau. N'a pas d'équivalent en France.*
a head of department	*le chef du département*
the form teacher	*un professeur principal*
a subject teacher	*un professeur de...(matière)*
the cooks / the caretaker	*les cuisiniers / le (la) concierge*
the cleaners	*le personnel de nettoyage*

SCHOOL AND COLLEGE cont. *L'ECOLE ET LE COLLEGE suite*

THE PUPILS	LES ELEVES
head boy / head girl	*un délégué de classe / une déléguée de classe*
a prefect / a monitor	*un élève des classes supérieures chargé de la discipline / un chef de classe*
a pupil	*un élève*
a day pupil / a boarding pupil	*un externe / un interne*
a weekly boarder	*un pensionnaire à la semaine*
a new girl / a new boy	*une nouvelle / un nouveau*
a first year	*un sixième*
a sixth former	*un lycéen*

For detailed stationery vocabulary see pages 359-362.

CLOTHES AND EQUIPMENT	LES TENUES (f) ET AFFAIRES (f) DE CLASSE
school uniform	*un uniforme scolaire*
an overall	*une blouse*
Do you have to wear school uniform?	*Vous devez / tu dois porter un uniforme?*
What colour is your school uniform?	*De quelle couleur est votre / ton uniforme?*
Do you like your uniform?	*Vous aimez votre / tu aimes ton uniforme?*

SCHOOL AND COLLEGE cont.

L'ECOLE ET LE COLLEGE suite

A briefcase	***Une serviette***
a holdall / a satchel	*un fourre-tout / un cartable*
a school bag / a duffle bag	*un cartable / un sac de paquetage*
a text book / an exercise book	*un manuel / un cahier d'exercice*
a notebook	*un cahier*
a file / a folder	*un classeur / une chemise*
filepaper	*une feuille de classeur*
a pencil case / a pencil	*une trousse / un crayon à papier*
a felt tip pen / a fountain pen	*un feutre / un crayon à plume*
a rubber / a pencil sharpener	*une gomme / un taille-crayon*
a calculator	*une machine à calculer*

A sports bag	***Un sac de sport***
sports kit	*des affaires (f) de sport*
sports shoes	*des chaussures (f) de sport*
a towel	*une serviette*

THE SCHOOL DAY

LA JOURNEE SCOLAIRE

Registration	***L'appel (m)***
to take the register	*faire l'appel*
to be present / absent	*être présent / absent*
to give out notices	*communiquer les notifications (f)*

SCHOOL ASSEMBLY	***LA REUNION DE TOUS LES ELEVES***
to sing a hymn	*chanter un cantique*
to pray	*prier*
to march in / out	*entrer / sortir d'un pas énergique*
to walk in single file	*marcher en file indienne*

SCHOOL AND COLLEGE cont.

L'ECOLE ET LE COLLEGE suite

THE LESSONS (abc)	LES COURS		
Art	*Art (m)*	(English)	*Anglais (m)*
Biology	*Biologie (f)*	(French)	*Français (m)*
Business Studies	*Commerce (m)*	(German)	*Allemand (m)*
Chemistry	*Chimie (f)*	(Italian)	*Italien (m)*
Design	*Stylisme (m)*	(Russian)	*Russe (m)*
Domestic Science	*Arts ménagers(m)*	(French)	*Espagnol (m)*
General Studies	*Culture générale-f*	(Literature)	*Littérature (f)*
Geography	*Géographie (f)*	(Language)	*Langue (f)*
Greek	*Grec (m)*	(Vocabulary)	*Vocabulaire (m)*
Gymnastics	*Gymnastique (f)*	(Grammar)	*Grammaire (f)*
History	*Histoire (f)*	(to translate)	*traduire*
Information Technology	*Education manuelle et technique (f)*	Music	*Musique (f)*
Latin	*Latin (m)*	Needlework	*Couture (f)*
Mathematics	*Mathématiques - f*	Physical Education	*Education Physique*
(Algebra)	*Algèbre (f)*	Physics	*Sciences-Physiques*
(Geometry)	*Géométrie (f)*	Religious Studies	*Science religieuse (f)*
Metalwork	*Ferronnerie (f)*	Technical Drawing	*Dessin technique (m)*
Modern Languages	*Langues (f)*	Woodwork	*Menuiserie (f)*

THE TIMETABLE	L'EMPLOI DU TEMPS (m)
a free period	*une heure libre*
the mid-morning break	*la pause du matin*
playtime	*la récréation*
lunchtime	*le déjeuner*
afternoon break	*la pause de l'après-midi*
a bell / to ring	*une cloche / sonner*
the end of the school day	*la fin de l'école*
homework	*les devoirs*

SCHOOL AND COLLEGE cont.

L'ECOLE ET LE COLLEGE suite

STUDYING	*LE TRAVAIL*
to study	*étudier*
to work	*travailler*
to concentrate	*se concentrer*
to do homework	*faire ses devoirs*
to read	*lire*
to write	*écrire*
to take notes	*prendre des notes*
headings	*des titres (m)*
a synopsis	*un résumé*
an abbreviation	*une abréviation*
shorthand	*écriture (f)*

WRITING AN ESSAY	*REDIGER UNE DISSERTATION*
the title	*le titre*
to plan an essay	*faire un plan de dissertation*
an introduction	*une introduction*
a new paragraph	*un nouveau paragraphe*
a conclusion / to sum up	*une conclusion / conclure*
a quotation	*une citation*
a bibliography	*une bibliographie*
to argue / an argument	*argumenter / un argument*
to discuss / a discussion	*discuter / une discussion*
to describe / a description	*décrire / une description*
to look at both sides	*regarder les deux côtés*
to examine	*examiner*
to include facts / dates	*inclure des faits (m) / dates (f)*

SCHOOL AND COLLEGE cont.

L'ECOLE ET LE COLLEGE suite

LEARNING	APPRENDRE
to learn	apprendre
to memorize	mémoriser
facts	faits (m)
dates	dates (f)
a poem	un poème
to revise	réviser
to be tested on	être interrogé sur
to test yourself	s'interroger

EXAMS	LES EXAMENS
to take an exam	passer un examen
to pass exams	être reçu à un examen
to fail exams	échouer à un examen
to re-take exams	repasser des examens
to take a course in	suivre des cours de
to wait for the results	attendre les résultats
When do you hear your results?	Quand avez-vous vos / as-tu tes résultats?
The results come on Wednesday.	Les résultats sont Mercredi.
How do you get your results?	Comment allez-vous /vas-tu connaître vos / tes résultats?
We have to go into school for them.	Il faut aller dans l'école pour les connaître.
The results come by post.	Les résultats sont envoyés par la poste.

SCHOOL AND COLLEGE cont.

L'ECOLE ET LE COLLEGE suite

ASSESSMENTS	*L'APPRECIATION DES PROFESSEURS*
a school report	*un bulletin*
a mark / a percentage / a grade	*une note / un pourcentage / un grade, une note*
an A grade / a B grade etc.	*un grade A / un grade B...*
to be graded	*être noté*
a distinction	*une distinction*
to come top	*être premier*
to be about average	*être dans les moyens*
to be near the bottom	*être dans les derniers*
to do one's corrections	*faire ses corrections (f)*
to do better / worse than one had thought	*faire mieux / moins bien qu'on ne pensait*
to be upset	*être triste / ennuyé(e)*
to be disappointed	*être déçu(e)*
to be relieved	*être soulagé(e)*
to be delighted	*être ravi(e)*

THE SCHOOL YEAR	*L'ANNEE SCOLAIRE (f)*
the terms	*les trimestres (m)*
the Autumn Term	*le premier trimestre*
the Spring Term	*le troisième trimestre*
the Summer Term	*le trimestre d'été*
the holidays	*les vacances (f.pl)*
a half-term holiday	*les vacances de milieu de trimestre*
the Christmas holidays	*les vacances de Noël*
the Easter holidays	*les vacances de Pâques*
the Summer holidays	*les grandes vacances*
Speech Day	*distribution (f) des prix (m)*
Founder's Day - no French equivalent	*la journée des fondateurs (m/f) (n'existe pas en France)*
a Bank Holiday	*un pont*
a public holiday	*un jour férié*

SCHOOL AND COLLEGE cont.

L'ECOLE ET LE COLLEGE suite

USEFUL EXPRESSIONS

EXPRESSION UTILES

My school is:-

Mon collège est:

- co-educational
- a girls' school
- a boys' school
- selective
- mixed ability
- streamed
- large / small
- boarding / day

- *mixte*
- *un collège de filles*
- *un collège de garçons*
- *sélectif*
- *non-sélectif*
- *réparti en niveaux*
- *grand / petit*
- *interne / externe*

My school starts at nine o'clock.

Mon collège commence à neuf heures.

My lessons last forty minutes.

Mes cours durent quarante-cinq minutes.

We have / don't have school on Saturdays.

On a / n'a pas cours le samedi.

We have four French lessons a week.

On a quatre cours de français par semaine.

What's your favourite subject?

Quelle est votre / ta matière préférée?

I like Maths. best.

Je préfère les maths. (f)

I hate Latin.

Je déteste le latin.

I think History is really interesting.

Je trouve que l'histoire est vraiment intéressante.

SCHOOL AND COLLEGE
cont.

L'ECOLE ET LE COLLEGE
suite

WHAT IS YOUR TEACHER LIKE?

I think my teacher is..

- boring
- excellent
- quite good
- strict
- can't keep order
- funny
- eccentric

My teacher is...

- old / young
- male / female

COMMENT EST VOTRE / TON / TA PROFESSEUR?

Je trouve que mon / ma professeur est:

- *ennuyeux(se)*
- *excellent(e)*
- *assez bon(ne)*
- *stricte*
- *n'a pas d'autorité*
- *drôle*
- *excentrique*

Mon / ma professeur est...

- *vieux / vieille / jeune*
- *un homme / une femme*

WHAT ARE YOU GOING TO DO WHEN YOU LEAVE SCHOOL?

I am planning to..
I have a place at…
I don't know yet.

QUE ALLEZ-VOUS / VAS-TU FAIRE APRES L'ECOLE?

J'ai l'intention (f) de…
J'ai une place à…
Je ne sais pas encore.

HIGHER EDUCATION

to apply for a place at..

an interview
to be called for an interview
to do an exam
to get the examination results
the grade
A levels

L'UNIVERSITE (f)

poser sa candidature pour une place à…
une entrevue
être appelé(e) pour une entrevue
passer un examen
obtenir les résultats d'examen
le grade, la note
les épreuves (f) du baccalauréat

SCHOOL AND COLLEGE cont.	***L'ECOLE ET LE COLLEGE*** ***suite***
HIGHER EDUCATION cont	***L'UNIVERSITE suite***

University entrance	*L'entrée à l'université*
to go to college	*aller à la faculté*
to go to secretarial college	*aller à une Ecole de Secrétariat*
technical college	*un I.U.T (Institut universitaire technique)*
a former polytechnic / a new university	** See end note (i) on next page*
to get a place at	*obtenir une place à*
to read for a degree in	*poursuivre des études de...*

LIVING AT COLLEGE	***LA VIE A L'UNIVERSITE***
to be in your first / second year	*être en première / deuxième année*
to be a fresher	*être un bizut*
to be in your third / last year	*être en troisième / quatrième année*
to be an undergraduate / a student	*être étudiant:* See end note (ii) on page 357*
to have a place in the hall of residence	*avoir une chambre en cité universitaire*
self-catering	*indépendant avec cuisine*
to live in digs	*vivre dans une "piaule"*
to rent a flat	*louer un appartement*
to live with some friends	*habiter avec des amis*
the student union	*l'union des étudiants*
a faculty building	*un bâtiment (de faculté)*
the library	*la bibliothèque*

HIGHER EDUCATION cont   *L'UNIVERSITE suite*

UNIVERSITY DEGREES	*LES DIPLÔMES UNIVERSITAIRES*
a first degree	*une licence / une maîtrise*
a further degree	*un diplôme de troisième cycle*
a doctorate	*un doctorat*
a degree in	*un diplôme de*
a graduate	*un diplômé*
What class of degree did you get?	*Quelle mention avez-vous / as-tu en?*
What class are you hoping for?	*Quelle mention espérez-vous / espères-tu avoir?*
a first class degree	*une mention très bien avec félicitations du jury*
an upper second	*une mention très bien*
a lower second	*une mention bien*
a third	*une mention assez bien*
a pass degree	*une mention passable*
an honours degree	*avec mention*

* *(i)*

There is no equivalent to polytechnics in France. These institutes of further education used to provide mainly scientific or technical diplomas but changed status in the nineties and became fully fledged universities.

Les "Polytechnics" n'ont pas d'équivalent en France. Ces instituts universitaires proposaient des diplômes professionnels essentiellement scientifiques ou techniques et furent abolis dans les années quatre-vingt-dix pour devenir des universités à part entière.

HIGHER EDUCATION cont   *L'UNIVERSITE suite*

DEGREE COURSES	*LES MATIERES*		
accountancy	*comptabilité*	librarianship	*documentalisme*
architecture	*architecture*	literature	*littérature*
the Arts	*les beaux-arts*	mathematics	*mathématique*
biochemistry	*biochimie*	mechanical engineering	*génie mécanique*
botany	*botanique*	media studies	*journalisme*
business studies	*commerce*	medicine	*médecine*
classics	*lettres classiques*	modern languages	*langues vivantes*
computer sciences	*informatique*	philosophy	*philosophie*
dentistry	*dentaire*	politics	*sciences-politiques*
Divinity	*théologie*	psychology	*psychologie*
economics	*économie*	sociology	*sociologie*
electrical engineering	*génie électrique*	social sciences	*sciences sociales*
engineering	*études d'ingénieur*	statistics	*statistiques*
film production	*production cinémato-graphique*	theatre production	*production théâtrale*
geography	*géographie*	theology	*théologie*
geology	*géologie*	veterinary science	*vétérinaire*
history	*histoire*	zoology	*zoologie*
law	*droit*		

*(ii)
The French equivalent to being an undergraduate is to be taking one's DEUG (the Diploma of General University Studies) which is a three year course.*

être en DEUG ou licence - le DEUG (Diplôme d'Etudes Universitaires Général) est obtenu à l'issue des examens de deuxième année et sanctionne les deux premières années du cycle. La licence est la troisième année d'étude.

STATIONERY
PAPETERIE

PAPER	*DU PAPIER*
coloured paper	*du papier de couleur*
file paper / ring reinforcers	*feuille(f) de classeur(m) / œillets(m)*
graph paper	*du papier à graphique*
headed notepaper	*du papier à lettre à en-têtes*
lined / unlined paper	*du papier réglé / uni*
squared paper	*du papier à carreaux*
tracing paper	*du papier-calque*
writing paper	*du papier à lettre*

BOOKS	*LES LIVRES ET CAHIERS (m)*
an exercise book	*un cahier d'exercice*
a rough book	*un cahier de brouillon*
a note book	*un cahier*
a text book	*un manuel*

FILES	*LES CLASSEURS (m)*
to file	*classer*
a ringbinder file	*un classeur à anneaux*
an envelope file	*une serviette*
a folder	*une chemise*
a file divider	*un intercalaire*

WRITING EQUIPMENT   *LE MATERIEL D'ECRITURE*

A pencil case	*Une trousse*
to open / to close	*ouvrir / fermer*
to zip up / to unzip / a zip	*ouvrir / fermer / la fermeture éclair*

STATIONERY cont.   *PAPETERIE suite*

Pens	Les crayons
a ball point pen	un crayon à bille
a biro	un bic
a felt-tip pen	un feutre
a fine tip	un crayon à pointe fine
a thicker tip	un crayon à grosse pointe
a fountain pen	un crayon à plume
a fine nib	une plume fine
a medium nib	une plume normale
a thick nib	une grosse plume
a cartridge pen	un crayon à encre

Ink	L'encre (f)
a bottle of ink	une bouteille d'encre
to fill the pen	remplir le crayon
to run out of ink	manquer d'encre
a cartridge	une cartouche
to need a new cartridge	avoir besoin d'une nouvelle cartouche
to put a cartridge in	mettre une cartouche dans
a full / half-full / empty cartridge	une cartouche pleine / à moitié pleine / vide
What type of cartridge does it take?	Quel genre de cartouche doit-on mettre?
an ink eradicator	un effaceur d'encre
a mistake	une erreur
blotting paper / to blot	un buvard / tâcher
an ink blot	une tâche d'encre
to spill the ink	renverser l'encre

STATIONERY cont.   *PAPETERIE suite*

Pencils	*Les crayons à papier*
a lead pencil	*un crayon*
a colouring pencil	*un crayon de couleur*
hard / soft	*dur(e) / mou (molle)*
the point / blunt / sharp	*la pointe / émoussée / pointue*
to break the lead	*casser la mine*
a pencil sharpener	*un taille-crayon*
to sharpen	*tailler*
to throw away the shavings	*jeter les copeaux*

Rubbers	*Les gommes (f)*
to make a mistake	*faire une faute*
to rub out	*gommer*
an ink rubber	*un gommeur d'encre*

Rulers	*Les règles (f)*
metric / imperial	*métrique / britannique*
to measure	*mesurer*
to draw a straight line	*tirer un trait droit*
to underline / double underline	*souligner / souligner deux fois*

GEOMETRY EQUIPMENT	*LE MATERIEL GEOMETRIQUE*
a compass	*un compas*
a protractor	*un rapporteur*
a set square	*une équerre*
to draw an angle	*dessiner un angle*
to measure an angle	*mesurer un angle*

STATIONERY cont.   *PAPETERIE suite*

OTHER EQUIPMENT   *AUTRE MATERIEL*

Scissors	*Des ciseaux (m.pl)*
to cut	*couper*
sharp / blunt	*pointus / émoussés*
to cut along a line	*couper le long d'une ligne*
to cut out	*couper*

Fastening things together	*Attacher les choses (f)*
glue	*colle (f)*
sellotape	*scotch® / ruban adhésif*
double sided sticky tape	*du scotch ® double faces*
a stapler / a staple	*une agrafeuse / une agrafe*
to staple	*agrafer*
to run out of staples	*manquer d'agrafe*
Have you any more staples?	*Avez-vous / as-tu d'autres agrafes?*
How do you load the staples.	*Comment change-t-on les agrafes?*

Hole punchers	*Une perforeuse*
to punch holes	*perforer*
to use ring reinforcers	*utiliser des œillets (m)*

Stencils	*Pochoirs (m)*
to stencil / a stencil	*marquer au pochoir / un pochoir*
an alphabet stencil	*un pochoir alphabétique*
capital letters / lower case letters	*lettres majuscules (f) / lettres de bas de case*

CURRENT EVENTS
L'ACTUALITE

POLITICS

LA POLITIQUE

ELECTIONS	*LES ELECTIONS (f)*
to call an election	*appeler aux urnes*
to hold an election	*organiser une élection*
to hold a referendum	*organiser un référendum*
a general election	*une élection présidentielle*
to nominate / a nomination	*nommer / une nomination*
to choose a candidate	*choisir un candidat*
to stand at an election	*se présenter à une élection*
to canvass opinion	*faire des sondages(m) d'opinion(f)*
to campaign	*faire campagne*
to give a speech	*faire un discours*
the election day	*le jour de l'élection*
a polling station / a ballot paper	*un bureau de vote*
a ballot paper / to put a cross	*un bulletin de vote / mettre une croix*
to vote for / against	*voter pour / contre*
to vote by secret ballot	*voter à bulletin secret*
a postal vote	*une vote par procuration*
the results of an election	*les résultats d'une élection*
to announce the result	*annoncer les résultats*
to win an election	*gagner une élection*
by a narrow margin	*à une courte majorité*
by a large majority	*à une large majorité*
to be elected / to be defeated	*être élu / être battu*
to lose an election	*perdre une élection*
to demand a re-count	*demander un re-comptage*
How would you vote?	*Comment voteriez-vous / voterais-tu?*
I don't bother to vote.	*Je m'en fiche de voter.*
I voted for…	*J'ai voté pour…*
private versus public life	*vie public contre vie privée*
media attention	*l'attention des médias*

CURRENT EVENTS cont.   *L'ACTUALITE cont.*

THE ECONOMY	*L'ECONOMIE (f)*
to pay taxes	*payer des impôts (m)*
high / low taxation	*forte / légère imposition (f)*
V.A.T.	*T.V.A.*
income tax	*impôt sur le revenu*
exempt from tax	*exempté d'impôt*
the Budget	*le Budget*
the recession	*la récession*
inflation	*l'inflation (f)*
the depression	*la depression*
unemployment	*le chômage*
the Welfare State	*l'Etat-Providence (m)*

THE WORKERS	*LES TRAVAILLEURS*
a Trades Union	*un syndicat*
to call a strike	*lancer un ordre de grève*
to go on strike	*faire la grève*
to go out in sympathy	*faire la grève de solidarité*
to demand	*exiger*
• a pay rise	• *une augmentation de salaire*
• better hours	• *des horaires meilleurs (m)*
• better conditions	• *des conditions meilleurs (f)*
• equality	• *l'égalité (f)*
• a minimum wage	• *un salaire minimum*
to wave a banner	*agiter une banderole*
to picket	*faire un piquet de grève*
a peaceful / violent demonstration	*une manifestation paisible / violente*

CURRENT EVENTS cont.   *L'ACTUALITE cont.*

EMERGENCIES   *LES URGENCES (f)*

to declare a state of emergency	*déclarer un état d'urgence*
a riot	*une émeute*
the riot police	*les C.R.S*
shields / truncheons / tear gas	*boucliers (m) / matraques (f) / bombe lacrymogène (f)*
a bomb scare / a car bomb	*une alerte à la bombe / une voiture piégée*
terrorists	*des terroristes*
to evacuate the area	*évacuer le territoire*
the bomb disposal squad	*l'équipe de déminage*

WAR   *LA GUERRE*

to declare war on	*déclarer la guerre à*
to be at war with	*être en conflit avec*
to fight / to wound	*se battre / blesser*
casualties / the wounded	*victimes / les blessés*
the number of dead	*le nombre de morts*
guerrilla warfare	*une guérilla*
nuclear war / a nuclear explosion	*la guerre nucléaire / une explosion nucléaire*
radiation / fall out	*radiation (f) / retombées (f)*
an anti-nuclear protest	*une manifestation antinucléaire*
to be a pacifist	*être pacifiste*
to campaign for	*faire campagne pour*
a protest march	*une marche de protestation*
a peaceful demonstration	*une manifestation silencieuse*
unilateral disarmament	*désarmement unilatéral*
multilateral disarmament	*désarmement multilatéral*
to declare a truce	*faire une trêve*
to cease fighting	*arrêter le combat*

CURRENT EVENTS cont.   *L'ACTUALITE cont.*

LAW AND ORDER   *L'ORDRE PUBLIC (m)*

the police	*la police*
a policeman / a policewoman	*un policier / une femme policier*
a police car / a siren	*une voiture de police / une sirène*
to break the law	*enfreindre la loi*
to break the speed limit	*dépasser la limite de vitesse*
speed cameras	*les radars (m.pl)*
to be over the breathalyser limit	*dépasser la limite de l'Alcootest*
to be disqualified from driving	*se faire retirer son permis de conduire*
to take illegal drugs	*consommer des drogues illicites (f)*
to be under age	*être mineur*
to caution / to arrest / to imprison	*avertir / arrêter / emprisonner*
to witness / to give evidence	*attester / témoigner*
to sign a statement	*signer une déclaration*
to telephone your home	*téléphoner à la maison*
to ask for a solicitor	*demander un avocat*
to remain silent	*rester silencieux*

LAW COURTS   *LES TRIBUNAUX (m.pl)*

the judge / the jury	*le juge / le jury*
to try	*faire un procès*
the case for the prosecution	*les arguments du Ministère Public*
to prosecute	*poursuivre en justice*
the case for the defence	*les arguments de la défense*
to defend	*défendre*
a solicitor (The distinction between solicitors and barristers does not exist in France.)	*un avocat (La distinction "solicitor" / "barrister" n'existe pas en France.)*
a barrister	*un avocat / un plaidant*

CURRENT EVENTS cont.　　*L'ACTUALITE cont.*

LAW AND ORDER cont.　　*L'ORDRE PUBLIC cont.*

a summons	*une assignation*
a criminal	*un accusé*
to acquit	*acquitter*
to get let off	*obtenir la grâce*
to find guilty	*trouver coupable*
a sentence / a fine / to fine	*une peine / une amende / infliger une amende*
to be put on probation	*être mis en liberté surveillée*
a term of imprisonment	*une peine de prison*
censorship / freedom of speech	*la censure / la liberté de parole*

SEXUALITY	***LA SEXUALITE***
heterosexual	*hétérosexuel*
homosexual	*homosexuel*
lesbian / gay	*lesbienne / gay*
sexually transmitted disease	*maladie sexuellement transmissible*
HIV positive	*séro positif*
AIDS	*SIDA*
a blood test	*une analyse sanguine*
a clinic	*une clinique*
confidential	*confidentiel(le)*
pornography	*pornographique (f)*
prostitution	*prostitution (f)*
equal opportunities	*l'égalité des chances*
sexual discrimination	*la discrimination sexuelle*

CURRENT EVENTS cont.   *L'ACTUALITE cont.*

THE MONARCHY	*LA MONARCHIE*
the King / the Queen	*le Roi / la Reine*
the Prince / the Princess	*le Prince / la Princesse*
the heir to the throne	*l'héritier du trône*
the Queen Mother	*la Reine-Mère*
to be a member of the royalty	*être un membre de la royauté*
What do you think of the future of the monarchy?	*Que pensez-vous / penses-tu de l'avenir de la royauté?*
Do you think we should become a republic?	*Pensez-vous / pense-tu qu'on devrait devenir une république?*
Are you glad you have a royal family?	*Etes-vous / es-tu content d'avoir une famille royale?*
Do you wish you had a royal family?	*Vous aimeriez / tu aimerais avoir une famille royale?*
Have you ever met any of the royal family?	*Avez-vous / as-tu déjà rencontré un membre de la famille royale?*
I saw the Queen once.	*J'ai vu la Reine une fois.*

CURRENT EVENTS cont.   *L'ACTUALITE suite*

THE NATIONAL LOTTERY	*LA LOTERIE NATIONALE / LE LOTO*
to buy a lottery ticket	*acheter un billet de loto*
to buy an instant lottery ticket	*acheter un billet à gratter*
to choose your numbers	*choisir ses numéros (m)*
a bonus number	*le numéro complémentaire*
to watch the lottery draw	*regarder le tirage du loto*
The first ball / the final ball is...	*la première boule / la dernière boule est...*
The results of the lottery were..	*les résultats du loto étaient...*
The jackpot is..	*la cagnotte est...*
a roll-over week	*une semaine de cumul*
No-one won the lottery.	*Personne n'a gagné au loto*
a ten pound prize	*un lot de dix livres*
a syndicate	*un consortium*
to share the winnings	*partager le gain*
How much is the lottery jackpot this week?	*A combien s'élève la cagnotte cette semaine?*
Do you approve of the lottery?	*Que pensez-vous / penses-tu du loto?*
The charities are suffering because of the lotteries.	*Les oeuvres de charité souffrent du loto.*
It gives people an interest.	*Cela donne un intérêt aux gens.*
It's just good fun.	*C'est juste pour s'amuser.*
Some people get addicted to it.	*Certaines personnes en deviennent dépendantes.*
What would you do if you won the lottery?	*Que feriez-vous / ferais-tu si vous gagniez / tu gagnais au loto?*
I only got two numbers right.	*J'ai seulement deux bons numéros.*

TRAVEL
LES VOYAGES

SIGNS   *LES INDICATIONS*

TOILETS	***TOILETTES***
Ladies / Gentlemen	*Femmes / Hommes*
vacant / engaged	*libre / occupé*
out of order	*hors-service*
hot water / cold water	*eau chaude / eau froide*

ENTRANCES	***ENTREES***
push / pull / no entry	*pousser / tirer / entrée interdite*

EXITS	***SORTIES***
Fire Exit	*Sortie de secours*
Fire Escape	*Sortie de secours*

LIFTS	***ASCENSEURS***
up / down	*en haut / en bas*
It's coming	*Il arrive.*
Push the button.	*Appuyer sur le bouton.*
Which floor do you want?	*Quel étage voulez-vous / veux-tu?*
I want the third floor.	*Je vais au troisième étage.*
Which floor is it for..?	*A quel étage est...?*
the top floor / the ground floor	*le dernier étage / le rez-de-chaussée*
the basement	*le sous-sol*
Excuse me, I want to get out here.	*Pardon, je voudrais sortir ici.*

| **TRAVEL - SIGNS cont** | ***LES VOYAGES -*** |
| | ***LES INDICATIONS suite*** |

ESCALATORS	***LES ESCALATEURS (m)***
the up escalator	*l'escalator montant*
the down escalator	*l'escalator descendant*
Hold on to the hand rail.	*Tenir la rampe.*
Stand in the middle.	*Rester au milieu.*
Take care.	*Attention*
Mind your feet.	*Faites attention à vos pieds.*

OPEN	***OUVERT***
When do you open?	*Quand ouvrez-vous?*
We open at..	*Nous ouvrons à...*
Opening hours	*Heures d'ouverture*
Open from.../ Open until...	*Ouvert de.../ Ouvert jusqu'à*

CLOSED	***FERME***
When do you close?	*Quand fermez-vous?*
We shut at..	*On ferme à...*
We are just about to close.	*On va fermer tout de suite.*

SALE	***LES SOLDES (m)***
Great reductions!	*Grosses réductions?*
10% off everything.	*10% de réduction sur tous les articles.*
One third off.	*Réduction d'un-tiers*
Half price.	*Moitié-prix.*
a bargain	*une aubaine*
Closing down sale.	*Les soldes de liquidation.*
Sale ends on...	*Les soldes se terminent le...*

PRIVATE	***PRIVE***
No Admittance	*Entrée interdite*
Strictly Private	*Privé*
Staff Only	*Personnel autorisé*
Trespassers Will Be Prosecuted.	*Défense d'entrée sous peine de poursuites.*

TRAVEL - SIGNS cont   *LES VOYAGES -*
LES INDICATIONS suite

NO SMOKING	*NE PAS FUMER*
BEWARE OF THE DOG.	*ATTENTION! CHIEN MECHANT.*

TRAVELLING BY TRAIN

VOYAGER EN TRAIN

AT THE STATION	*A LA GARE*
the entrance	*l'entrée*
the main concourse	*le hall principal*
Shall we meet by the..	*On se donne rendez-vous près de...*
the book stall	*le bouquiniste*
the newspaper kiosk	*le Kiosque à journaux*
the big clock	*la grosse horloge*

THE BUFFET	*LE BUFFET*
to buy	*acheter*
a sandwich	*un sandwich*
a coffee / a cup of tea	*un café / une tasse de thé*
a bottle of water	*une bouteille d'eau*

THE WAITING ROOM	*LA SALLE D'ATTENTE*
Toilets - see page 61 for using the loo & page 371 for public toilets.	*les toilettes (f)*

TRAVELLING BY TRAIN cont.   *VOYAGER EN TRAIN suite*

THE LEFT LUGGAGE OFFICE	*LE BUREAU DES OBJETS TROUVES (m)*
I have lost my..	*J'ai perdu mon / ma...*
Has my wallet been handed in?	*Est-ce que mon portefeuille a été déposé?*
Can I leave my suitcase here?	*Je peux laisser ma valise ici?*
Do you have lockers?	*Avez-vous des consignes? (f)*
How much are they?	*Combien coûtent-elles?*
What coins do they take?	*Elles prennent quelles pièces?*
Do you have any change?	*Avez-vous de la monnaie?*
How do they work?	*Comment marchent-elles?*

THE TAXI RANK	*LA RANGEE DE TAXI*
Shall we take a taxi?	*On prend un taxi?*
There is a very long queue.	*Il y a une très grande queue.*
to give a tip	*donner un pourboire*
How much would it cost for a taxi to…?	*Combien coûterait un taxi pour…?*

THE ENQUIRY OFFICE	*LE BUREAU DE RENSEIGNEMENTS*
Could I have a timetable for..?	*Je peux avoir les horaires (m) de…*
What time is the next train for..?	*A quelle heure est le prochain train pour…?*
Is it a through train?	*C'est un train direct?*
Do I have to change?	*Je dois changer?*
Where do I have to change?	*Où dois-je changer?*
Is there a good connection?	*Y a-t-il une bonne correspondance?*

TRAVELLING BY TRAIN cont.   *VOYAGER EN TRAIN suite*

THE ENQUIRY OFFICE cont.   *LE BUREAU DE RENSEIGNEMENTS suite*

What time is the connection?	*A quelle heure est la correspondance?*
What time does it arrive at..?	*A quelle heure arrive-t-il à...?*
What time is the one after that?	*A quelle heure est le prochain?*
How long does it take?	*Cela prend combien de temps?*
What platform does it leave from?	*De quel quai part-il?*

THE TICKET OFFICE   *LE GUICHET*

May I have..?	*Puis-je...?*
How much is..?	*Combien coûte...?*

- a return ticket — *un aller-retour*
- a day return ticket — *un aller-retour dans la journée*
- returning tomorrow — *retour demain*
- returning next week — *retour la semaine prochaine*
- returning next month — *retour dans un mois*
- a single ticket — *un aller simple*
- first class — *première classe*
- second class — *deuxième classe*
- a child rate ticket — *un billet à tarif enfant*
- a student rate ticket — *un billet à tarif étudiant*
- a season ticket — *une carte d'abonnement*
- for a week — *pour une semaine*
- for a month — *pour un mois*
- a book of tickets — *un carnet de tickets*

May I reserve a seat on..?	*Je peux réserver une place sur...?*
Is there a reduction for students?	*Vous faites des réduction-étudiants?*
Do you have a student card?	*Avez-vous une carte d'étudiant?*
Do you have proof of your age?	*Avez-vous une preuve de votre âge?*

TRAVELLING BY TRAIN cont.　　*VOYAGER EN TRAIN suite*

THE ARRIVALS / DEPARTURES BOARD	*LE TABLEAU DES ARRIVEES / DES DEPARTS*
due to arrive / depart at..	*devrait arriver / partir à*
delayed by ten minutes	*retardé de dix minutes*
on time	*à l'heure*
early	*en avance*
just arrived	*vient d'arriver*
leaving from Platform Nine	*quitte le quai numéro neuf*
now boarding	*embarquement*

ANNOUNCEMENTS	*LES ANNONCES (f)*
What was that announcement?	*Que disait cette annonce?*
I didn't hear what he / she said.	*Je n'ai pas entendu ce qu'il / elle a dit.*
The next train to depart from Platform One is the three forty five for Paddington, calling at all stations.	*Le prochain train partira du quai numéro un est celui de trois heures quarante-cinq pour Paddington, faisant toutes les escales.*
The train just arriving at Platform Four is the two thirty from Edinburgh.	*Le train qui vient d'arriver en gare quai numéro quatre est celui de deux heures trente en provenance d'Edimbourg.*
We apologize for the delay.	*Nous vous prions de bien vouloir nous excuser pour ce retard.*

THE TICKET PUNCHING MACHINE	*LA MACHINE A COMPOSTER*
to punch your ticket	*composter son billet*
You have to punch your ticket before boarding the train.	*Il faut composter son billet avant d'embarquer dans le train.*

TRAVELLING BY TRAIN cont. *VOYAGER EN TRAIN suite*

THE PLATFORM	*LE QUAI*
a barrier	*une barrière*
a ticket inspector	*un contrôleur*
to catch / miss the train	*prendre / rater le train*
a seat	*un siège / une place*
to sit down	*s'asseoir*
a luggage trolley / a porter	*un chariot à bagages / un porteur*

TYPES OF TRAIN	*LES TYPES DE TRAIN*
an intercity	*un rapide*
an express train	*un train express*
a local train	*un micheline*
a sleeper	*un train-couchette*
Trans Europe Express (T.E.E.)	*Trans-Europe Express*
French Railway System (S.N.C.F.)	*la Société Nationale des Chemins de Fer Français*
British Railway system (B.R.)	*la Société Nationale des Chemins de Fer Anglais*

THE CHANNEL TUNNEL TRAIN	*LE TUNNEL SOUS LA MANCHE*
to drive on	*embarquer (une voiture)*
to drive off	*débarquer (une voiture)*
to sit in your car	*rester dans sa voiture*

BOARDING A TRAIN

EMBARQUER DANS UN TRAIN

THE CARRIAGES	LES VOITURES
the front / rear carriage	*la voiture avant / arrière*
a compartment	*un compartiment*
No Smoking / Smoking	*non fumeurs / fumeurs*
First Class / Second Class	*Première classe / deuxième classe*
the buffet	*le buffet*
the dining car	*la voiture / le wagon-restaurant*
the bar	*le bar*
a snacks trollet	*un chariot de sandwiches*
the sleeping compartment	*un compartiment-lit*
the Guard's van	*le fourgon du chef de train*

The door	*La porte*
to open / to close	*ouvrir / fermer*
Press the button to open the door.	*Appuyer sur le bouton pour ouvrir la porte*

The windows	*Les fenêtres*
Do you mind if I open / shut the window?	*Ca ne vous dérange pas si j'ouvre / ferme la fenêtre?*

The corridor	*Le couloir*
to walk along / to look for a seat	*marcher le long / chercher une place*

The communication cord	*La sonnette d'alarme*
to pull	*tirer*
an emergency	*une urgence*
to stop the train	*arrêter le train*

TRAVELLING BY TRAIN cont.   *VOYAGER EN TRAIN suite*

TRAVELLING BY TRAIN cont.	*VOYAGER EN TRAIN suite*
The seats	***Les sièges / les places***
Is this seat taken?	*Est-ce que cette place est prise?*
May I sit here?	*Puis-je m'asseoir ici?*
I'm sorry, someone is sitting here.	*Je regrette, quelqu'un est assis là.*
That is a reserved seat.	*Cette place est réservée.*
Would you like to sit by the window?	*Vous voulez vous / tu veux t' asseoir près de la fenêtre?*
Do you prefer to face the way we are going?	*Vous préférez / tu préfères être assis(e) dans le sens de la marche?*
Shall we sit together?	*On s'assoit l'un à côté de l'autre / ensemble?*

The luggage rack	***La soute à bagages***
Can I help you to put your case up?	*Puis-je vous aider à mettre votre valise en haut?*
Can you manage to get your coat down?	*Vous arrivez / tu arrives à descendre votre / ton manteau?*

THE PASSENGERS AND RAILWAY STAFF	*LES PASSAGERS ET LE PERSONNEL DES CHEMINS DE FER*
a commuter	*un banlieusard*
the driver / the guard	*le conducteur / le chef de gare*
The ticket inspector	***Le contrôleur***
Tickets please.	*Billets, s'il vous plaît.*
Could I see your ticket, please?	*Pourrais-je voir votre billet, s'il vous plaît?*
I didn't have time to buy one, I'm afraid.	*Je n'ai pas eu le temps d'acheter malheureusement.*
Can I pay now, please?	*Je peux payer maintenant, s'il vous plaît?*
The ticket office was shut.	*Le guichet était fermé.*
I can't find my ticket.	*Je ne trouve pas mon ticket.*
to be fined	*avoir une amende*
to be surcharged / to pay extra	*payer une surcharge / un supplément*

TRAVELLING BY UNDERGROUND

VOYAGER EN METRO

COMMON EXPRESSIONS	*EXPRESSIONS USUELLES*
Shall we go by tube?	*On prend le métro?*
Which lines is this station on?	*Sur quelles lignes est cette station?*
Which line do we need to take?	*Quelle ligne devons-nous prendre?*
What is this line called?	*Comment s'appelle cette ligne?*
What is this line number?	*Quel est le numéro de cette ligne?*
Let's look at a plan of the underground.	*Regardons un plan de métro.*
We are here.	*On est ici.*
We need to go there.	*On doit aller là.*
Which line do I take for the Louvre?	*Quelle ligne dois-je prendre pour le Louvre?*
Take the Pont Neuilly line.	*Prenez / prends la ligne Port-de-Neuilly.*
Where do I get off for ..?	*Où dois-je descendre?*

CHANGING TRAINS	*CHANGER DE TRAIN*
You need to change at Euston.	*Il faut changer à Euston.*
We will have to change here.	*Il faudra changer ici.*
a connecting station	*une station correspondante*

ZONES	*LES ZONES*
the central zone	*la zone centrale*
an outer zone	*la zone suburbaine*
zone one / two / three	*zone un / deux / trois*

TRAVELLING BY UNDERGROUND cont.

VOYAGER EN METRO suite

BUYING TICKETS AT THE TICKET OFFICE

ACHETER LES TICKETS AU GUICHET

Please could I have two tickets for...

Pourrais-je avoir deux tickets pour... s'il vous plaît?

to buy...

acheter...

- a single / a return
- a child's ticket
- an adult's ticket
- a student's ticket
- a daily pass
- a weekly pass

- a book of ten tickets

un aller simple / un aller-retour

- *un ticket-enfant*
- *un ticket-adulte*
- *un ticket-étudiant*
- *un abonnement à*
- *un abonnement pour la semaine*

- *un carnet de dix tickets*

Can you use the passes on the buses too?

Peut-on utiliser son ticket dans les bus aussi?

Is it more expensive at certain times of the day?

Est-ce que c'est plus cher à certaines heures de la journée?

When does the cheap rate start?

Quand commencent les tarifs réduits?

There is a flat rate fare.

Il y a un tarif forfaitaire.

AT THE TICKET BARRIER

AUX BARRIERES (f)

Put your ticket in here.

Mettez son ticket ici.

Take your ticket out there.

Prenez son ticket là-bas.

You have to show your ticket.

Il faut montrer son ticket.

The barrier isn't working.

La barrière ne marche pas.

ESCALATORS

LES ESCALATORS (m)

a down / up escalator

un escalator descendant / montant

to read the advertisements

lire les publicités (f)

to stand on the right

tenir la droite

TRAVELLING BY BUS

VOYAGER EN BUS

BUS STOPS	**LES ARRETS DE BUS**
Which buses stop here?	*Quels bus s'arrêtent ici?*
Is this the right bus stop for..?	*C'est le bon arrêt de bus pour...?*
How often do the buses run?	*Quelle est la fréquence des bus?*
Have I just missed a bus?	*Est-ce que je viens de manquer un bus?*
How long have you been waiting?	*Vous attendez depuis combien de temps?*
to look at the timetable	*regarder les horaires (m)*
a request stop	*un arrêt sur demande*
the next stop	*le prochain arrêt*
You have to put your arm out to stop the bus.	*Il faut étendre le bras pour arrêter le bus.*
This is the bus you want.	*C'est ton bus.*
to get on / off the bus	*monter dans le / descendre du bus*

TYPES OF BUS	**LES TYPES DE BUS**
a single / double decker	*un autobus sans / à impériale*
a coach	*un car*

GETTING ON THE BUS	**MONTER DANS LE BUS**
Do you want to sit upstairs or downstairs?	*Vous voulez vous / tu veux t'asseoir en haut ou en bas?*
Shall we go upstairs?	*On va en haut?*
Press the button to stop the bus.	*Appuyez / appuie sur le bouton pour arrêter le bus.*
You pay the driver / conductor.	*On paie le conducteur.*

TRAVELLING BY BUS cont.   *VOYAGER EN BUS suite*

TICKETS	LES TICKETS
Could I have a single ticket to..?	*Pourrais-je avoir un aller simple pour...?*
a return ticket to..	*un aller-retour pour...*
I have a bus pass.	*J'ai une carte de bus.*

TRAVELLING BY AIR

VOYAGER PAR AVION

AIRPORTS

LES AEROPORTS

THE TERMINAL	LE TERMINAL
Which terminal does Air France use?	*Quel terminal utilise Air France?*
British Airways flights use Terminal...	*Les vols de British Airways utilisent le terminal....*
Which airline are you flying with?	*Avec quelle compagnie aérienne partez-vous / pars-tu?*

THE CAR PARK	LE PARKING
a short stay car park	*un parking à stationnement de courte durée*
a long stay car park	*un parking à stationnement longue durée*
to get a ticket	*prendre un ticket*
You pay before leaving.	*On paie avant de partir.*
How much is the ticket?	*Combien coûte le ticket?*
Can we take a bus to the terminal?	*On peut prendre un bus jusqu'au terminal?*

TRAVELLING BY AIR cont.   *VOYAGER PAR AVION suite*

LUGGAGE TROLLEYS	*LES CHARIOTS A BAGAGES*
Can you find a luggage trolley?	*Tu trouves / vous trouvez un chariot?*
to push / to pull	*pousser / tirer*
to steer / to brake	*diriger / freiner*

AT THE TERMINAL	*AU TERMINAL*
automatic doors	*portes automatiques (f)*
an escalator	*un escalator*
a moving floor	*un tapis roulant*
a lift	*un ascenseur*
the shops	*les boutiques (f)*
the toilets	*les toilettes (f)*
a restaurant / a bar	*un restaurant / un bar*

THE ARRIVALS / DEPARTURES BOARD	*LE TABLEAU DES ARRIVEES / DES DEPARTS*
destination	*destination (f)*
due to arrive at	*arrivée à*
just arrived	*vient d'atterrir*
delayed	*retardé*
about to depart	*décollage immédiat (m)*
last call	*dernier appel (m)*
now boarding	*embarquement immédiat*

THE INFORMATION DESK	*LE BUREAU DE RENSEIGNEMENTS*
Can you tell me..?	*Pouvez-vous me dire…?*
Has flight number .. arrived yet?	*Est-ce que le vol numéro… arrivé?*
Is the flight delayed?	*Est-ce que le vol est retardé?*
How late is it likely to be?	*Il est retardé de combien de temps?*
Why is it so late?	*Pourquoi est-il si en retard?*
Is there a problem?	*Y a-t-il un problème?*

TRAVELLING BY AIR cont.

VOYAGER PAR AVION suite

THE INFORMATION DESK cont.

LE BUREAU DE RENSEIGNEMENTS suite

Where is the meeting point?	*Où est le point de rendez-vous?*
I am supposed to meet a passenger called....but I can't find him / her.	*Je suis censé(e) retrouver un passager qui s'appelle...mais je le / la trouve pas.*
Have there been any messages left for me?	*Y a-t-il en des messages (m) pour moi?*
My name is...	*Je m'appelle...*
Can you put a message out on the tannoy for me, please?	*Pouvez-vous passer une annonce au haut-parleur pour moi?*

THE CHECK-IN DESK

LE COMPTOIR D'EMBARQUEMENT

to queue	*faire la queue*
Can you put your luggage on the scales, please?	*Pouvez-vous mettre vos bagages (m) sur le tapis, s'il vous plaît?*
to lift a suitcase up	*soulever un valise*
How many suitcases do you have?	*Combien de valises avez-vous?*
Is this one yours?	*Est-ce que celle-ci est à vous?*
the baggage allowance	*la limite des bagages*
excess baggage	*l'excédent (m) de bagages (m)*
to pay a surcharge	*payer un supplément*
hand luggage	*les bagages à main*
Did you pack your suitcase yourself?	*Vous avez fait votre valise vous-même?*
Are there any prohibited articles in your luggage?	*Contient-elle des articles interdit?*
Your hand luggage is too large.	*Votre bagage à main est trop gros.*
It will have to be put in the hold.	*Il faudra le mettre en soute.*
Could I see your ticket, please?	*Puis-je voir votre billet, s'il vous plaît?*

TRAVELLING BY AIR cont. *VOYAGER PAR AVION suite*

THE CHECK-IN DESK cont. *LE COMPTOIR D'EMBARQUEMENT suite*

Do you prefer smoking or non-smoking?	*Vous préférez fumeurs ou non-fumeurs?*
This child is travelling alone and needs looking after.	*Cet enfant voyage tout seul et a besoin d'être surveillé.*
Could I have a seat with extra leg room, please?	*Pourrais-je avoir un siège avec suffisamment de place pour mettre mes jambes, s'il vous plaît?*
Could I possibly have an aisle / a window seat?	*Pourrais-je avoir une place côté fenêtre / couloir?*
Here is your boarding card.	*Voici votre carte d'embarquement.*
Go to passport control when you are ready.	*Allez au contrôle des passeports quand vous serez prêt(e).*

PASSPORT CONTROL *LE CONTRÔLE DES PASSEPORTS*

to show your passport	*montrer son passeport*
to put your hand luggage on the conveyor belt	*mettre son bagage à main sur le convoyeur*
to walk through the detector	*traverser le détecteur*
to be stopped / to be searched	*être arrêté / être fouillé*
to have your bag searched	*se faire fouiller son sac*

THE DEPARTURE LOUNGE *LE HALL DES DEPARTS*

the duty free shop	*les boutiques détaxées*
your duty free allowance	*votre / ta réduction dans les magasins détaxés*
to buy	*acheter*
• perfume	• *du parfum*
• cigarettes	• *des cigarettes (f)*
• alcohol	• *de l'alcool (m)*

TRAVELLING BY AIR cont.   *VOYAGER PAR AVION suite*

THE BOARDING GATE	**LA PORTE D'EMBARQUEMENT**
Our flight has been called.	*Notre vol a été annoncé.*
Now boarding.	*Embarquement immédiat.*
Last call.	*Dernier appel.*
They are boarding at gate..	*Ils embarquent à la porte…*
to show your boarding pass	*montrer sa carte d'embarquement*
Seats numbered…. board first / next.	*Les places numérotées ...... embarquent d'abord / à la fin.*
Please board from the front / rear of the aircraft.	*Veuillez embarquer à l'avant / à l'arrière de l'appareil.*
Excuse me, could I get to my seat, please.	*Pardon, je peux rejoindre ma place, s'il vous plaît?*

THE SATELLITE	**LE SATELLITE**
Our flight is leaving from the satellite.	*Notre vol part du satellite.*
We have to take the monorail / a bus.	*Il faut prendre la navette / un bus.*

THE FLIGHT   *LE VOL*

THE CREW	**L'EQUIPAGE (m)**
the Captain	*le Commandant de bord*
the steward	*le steward*
the stewardess	*l'hôtesse*
an air hostess	*une hôtesse de l'air*

TRAVELLING BY AIR cont.   *VOYAGER PAR AVION suite*

SAFETY   *SECURITE (f)*

to fasten your seatbelt	*attacher sa ceinture*
to keep your seatbelt fastened	*maintenir sa ceinture attachée*
to remain seated	*rester assis*
to call the stewardess	*appeler l'hôtesse*
to undo your seatbelt	*défaire sa ceinture*
to extinguish cigarettes	*éteindre les cigarettes (f)*
to put on a life jacket	*mettre un gilet de sauvetage*
to fasten the strap	*attacher la lanière*
to inflate	*gonfler*
a whistle / to blow	*un sifflet / souffler*
oxygen masks	*masques (m) à oxygène*
an emergency	*une urgence*
emergency lighting	*allumage (m) de sécurité (f)*
escape routes	*les sorties de secours*

THE TAKE OFF   *LE DECOLLAGE*

the runway	*la piste d'atterrissage*
to taxi / to accelerate	*rouler au sol / accélérer*
to take off / to lift off / to climb	*décoller*
My ears hurt.	*Mes oreilles me font mal.*
Would you like to suck a sweet?	*Vous voulez / tu veux sucer un bonbon?*
the altitude / the speed	*l'altitude / la vitesse*
to look out of the window	*regarder par la fenêtre*
to get a good view	*avoir une bonne vue*
the clouds / turbulence	*les nuages (m) / les turbulences (f)*

THE DESCENT   *LA DESCENTE*

the touch down	*toucher terre*
to land / a good landing	*atterrir / un bon atterrissage*
to remain in your seats until the plane has stopped	*rester assis jusqu'à l'arrêt complet du moteur*
to disembark	*désembarquer*

TRAVELLING BY AIR cont.   *VOYAGER PAR AVION suite*

BAGGAGE RECLAIM	*LA LIVRAISON DES BAGAGES*
to collect your luggage	*prendre ses bagages (m)*
a carousel	*un carrousel*
Can you see your suitcase?	*Vous voyez votre / tu vois ta valise?*
There's mine.	*Voilà la mienne.*
How many cases do you have?	*Combien de valises avez-vous / as-tu?*
Is that everything?	*C'est tout?*
a trolley	*un chariot*
to push / to steer / to brake	*pousser / diriger / freiner*

CUSTOMS	*LA DOUANE*
to go through customs	*passer la douane*
the green / red channel	*le couloir vert / rouge*
to have nothing to declare	*n'avoir rien à déclarer*
to have something to declare	*avoir quelque chose à déclarer*
Have you anything to declare?	*Avez-vous quelque chose à déclarer?*
to have your baggage searched	*se faire fouiller ses bagages (m)*

TRAVELLING BY FERRY

VOYAGER EN FERRY

to go by ferry	*prendre le ferry*
to take the Cross Channel ferry	*prendre le ferry qui traverse la Manche*

THE PARTS OF THE FERRY

LES PARTIES DU FERRY

THE RAMP

LA PASSERELLE

to queue	*faire la queue*
to wait	*attendre*
to drive up the ramp	*monter la passerelle (en conduisant)*
to drive down	*descendre la passerelle*
to embark	*embarquer*
to disembark	*désembarquer*

THE VEHICLE DECK

LE PARKING

to follow the car in front	*suivre la voiture devant*
to go right up to the bumper	*aller directement au pare-chocs*
to park	*garer*
to take important things with you	*prendre le nécessaire avec soi*
to lock the car	*fermer la voiture à clef*
to leave the car	*quitter la voiture*
to remember where the car is parked	*se rappeler où la voiture est garée*

THE PASSENGER DECKS

LE PONT

the restaurant / the bar	*le restaurant / le bar*
the toilets	*les toilettes (f)*
the lounge / the shops / the cinema	*le salon / les boutiques / le cinéma*
the telephone	*le téléphone*
to stay inside	*rester à l'intérieur (m)*
to go outside for some air	*sortir pour prendre l'air (m)*

TRAVELLING BY FERRY cont.   *VOYAGER EN FERRY suite*

THE SLEEPING AREA	*LE COUCHAGE*
to sit up all night	*rester debout toute la nuit*
to have a cabin booked	*avoir une cabine réservée*
a sleeping berth	*une couchette*

A ROUGH CROSSING	*UNE TRAVERSEE DIFFICILE*
Do you feel seasick?	*Vous avez / tu as le mal de mer?*
I feel dreadful.	*Je me sens très mal.*
I am going to be sick.	*Je vais vomir.*
Would you like to take a tablet?	*Vous voulez / tu veux un comprimé?*
I can't walk straight.	*Je ne peux pas marcher droit.*
Hold on to the handrail.	*Tenez-vous / tiens-toi à la rampe.*
Would you like to go outside for some fresh air?	*Vous voulez / tu veux aller dehors prendre l'air?*
I feel cold. Can we go back inside now?	*J'ai froid. On peut retourner à l'intérieur maintenant?*
I have got wet by the spray.	*J'ai été éclaboussé(e) par les embruns.*

SAFETY EQUIPMENT	*LE MATERIEL DE SECURITE*
a life belt	*une ceinture de sécurité*
a life jacket	*un gilet de sauvetage*
the safety drill	*la sonnerie d'urgence*
a siren	*une sirène*

TRAVELLING BY CAR

VOYAGER EN VOITURE

TYPES OF CAR	*LES TYPES DE VOITURE*
a saloon	*un coupé*
an estate car	*un break*
a hatchback	*coupé avec hayon à l'arrière*
a sportscar	*une voiture de sport*
an open car	*une voiture à toit ouvrant*
a four wheel drive	*un quatre-quatre*
a two door car	*une voiture deux portes*
a four door car	*une voiture quatre portes*
a five door car	*une voiture cinq portes*
an automatic	*une automatique*
a hire car	*une voiture de location*
a racing car	*une voiture de course*

THE PARTS OF THE CAR

LES PARTIES DE LA VOITURE

THE ROOF	*LE TOIT*
a roof rack	*une galerie*
to load / unload	*charger / décharger*
to lift up	*soulever*
to tie / to secure	*attacher / protéger*

THE DOORS	*LES PORTES (f)*
to lock / to unlock	*fermer / ouvrir (à clef)*
central locking	*verrouillage central (m)*
to open / to shut	*ouvrir / fermer*
the driver's door	*la porte du conducteur*
the passengers' doors	*la porte des passagers*
the front / rear doors	*les portes-avant / arrière*

TRAVELLING BY CAR cont.   *VOYAGER EN VOITURE suite*

THE PARTS OF THE CAR cont.   *LES PARTIES DE LA VOITURE suite*

THE BOOT	*LE COFFRE*
to open / to shut	*ouvrir / fermer*
to put something in the boot	*mettre quelque chose dans le coffre*
to get something out of the boot	*sortir quelque chose du coffre*

THE SEATS	*LES SIEGES*
to adjust the seat	*régler le siège*
to alter the height	*changer la hauteur*
to move the seat backwards / forwards	*reculer / avancer le siège*
to fold the seat forwards	*replier le siège en avant*
to put the seat back	*remettre le siège*
the headrest	*le repose-tête*
the ashtray	*le cendrier*

THE SEATBELTS	*LES CEINTURES DE SECURITE*
to fasten / to unfasten	*attacher / détacher*
Fasten your seatbelt, please.	*Attachez votre / ta ceinture, s'il vous plaît / s'il te plaît.*
How do you fasten the seatbelt?	*Comment on attache la ceinture?*
Can you help me to fasten the seatbelt?	*Pouvez-vous / peux-tu m'aider à attacher la ceinture?*
I think the seatbelt is stuck under the seat.	*Je crois que la ceinture est coincée sous le siège.*

TRAVELLING BY CAR cont.   *VOYAGER EN VOITURE suite*

THE WINDOWS	*LES FENETRES*
to open / to shut	*ouvrir / fermer*
May I open the window a little?	*Je peux ouvrir un peu la fenêtre?*
Could you shut the window now, please?	*Pouvez-vous / peux-tu fermer la fenêtre, s'il vous plaît / s'il te plaît?*
automatic windows	*fenêtres automatiques*
Press this button to open / close the windows.	*Appuyer sur ce bouton pour ouvrir / fermer les fenêtres.*
the sun roof	*le toit ouvrant*

THE MAIN CONTROLS   *LES PRINCIPALES COMMANDES*

The ignition	*L'allumage (m)*
to start the car	*démarrer la voiture*

The gears	*Les vitesses (f)*
the gear lever	*le levier de vitesse*
the reverse gear	*la marche arrière*
to reverse	*faire marche arrière*
the clutch	*l'embrayage (m)*

The brakes	*Les freins (m)*
to brake	*freiner*
to put the handbrake on	*mettre le frein à main*
to take the handbrake off	*enlever le frein à main*

The accelerator	*L'accélérateur (m)*
to accelerate	*accélérer*

The steering wheel	*Le volant*
to steer / to turn	*diriger / tourner*

TRAVELLING BY CAR cont.   *VOYAGER EN VOITURE suite*

The indicators	***Les clignotants (m)***
to indicate right / left	*mettre le clignotant à droite / gauche*
to turn on the hazard lights	*mettre les feux de détresse / les warnings*

The horn	***Le klaxon***
to blow the horn	*klaxonner*

The headlights	***Les phares (m)***
to turn on / off	*allumer / éteindre*
to flash your lights	*faire un appel de phares*
full beam	*plein phare*
to dip / dipped headlights	*se mettre en code*
sidelights / fog lights	*feux de position / antibrouillard*

The windscreen	***Le pare-brise***
dirty / to clean	*sale / nettoyer*
windscreen wipers	*les essuies-glace (m)*
to turn on / off	*mettre en marche / arrêter*
to wash the screen	*laver le pare-brise*
the rear windscreen heater	*le chauffage de la lunette arrière*
to get fogged up / to wipe	*avoir de la buée / essuyer*
a duster	*un chiffon*

BASIC CAR MAINTENANCE   *L'ENTRETIEN (m) DE BASE D'UNE VOITURE*

Needing some petrol	***Avoir besoin d'essence (f)***
to put in petrol	*mettre de l'essence*
to undo the filler cap	*enlever le bouchon du réservoir*
to serve yourself / to fill it up	*se servir / remplir*
lead free / leaded / diesel	*sans plomb / au plomb / diesel*
two / three / four star	*ordinaire / super*

TRAVELLING BY CAR cont.

BASIC CAR MAINTENANCE cont.

VOYAGER EN VOITURE suite

L'ENTRETIEN DE BASE D'UNE VOITURE suite

Oil and water	Huile (f) et eau (f)
to check the oil / the water	vérifier l'huile / l'eau
Where is the dipstick?	Où est la jauge?
It needs more oil / water.	Il faut ajouter de l'huile / l'eau
to pour the oil / water in	verser l'huile / l'eau dans

Tyres	Les pneus (m)
to check the tyre pressures	vérifier la pression des pneus
The tyres look a bit flat.	Les pneus ont l'air un peu à plats.
to pump up	gonfler
to have a puncture	avoir une crevaison
to change the wheel	changer la roue
to fit the spare wheel	mettre la roue de secours

LEARNING TO DRIVE
APPRENDRE A CONDUIRE

DRIVING LESSONS — *LES LEÇONS DE CONDUITE*

I am having driving lessons.	*J'ai une leçon de conduite.*
My sister / brother is learning to drive.	*Ma soeur / mon frère apprend à conduire.*
I have had six lessons.	*J'ai eu six leçons.*
My parents are teaching me.	*Mes parents m'apprennent.*
I am having lessons with a driving school.	*Je prends des leçons dans une école de conduite.*
a dual control car	*une voiture à double commande*
a driving instructor	*un moniteur de conduite*

THE DRIVING TEST — *L'EXAMEN DE CONDUITE*

I am about to take my driving test.	*Je vais bientôt passer mon examen de conduite.*
I have passed my test.	*J'ai réussi mon examen.*
I passed my test..	*J'ai réussi mon examen...*
• at the first attempt	• *du premier coup*
• at the second / third attempt	• *du deuxième / troisième coup*
I failed my test.	*J'ai échoué à mon examen.*

LEARNING HOW TO.. — *APPRENDRE A...*

to do a hill start	*démarrer en côte*
to reverse	*faire marche arrière*
to park	*se garer*
to do a three point turn	*un demi-tour en trois manoeuvres*
to do an emergency stop	*faire un arrêt d'urgence*
to overtake	*doubler*

LEARNING TO DRIVE cont.

APPRENDRE A CONDUIRE suite

REMEMBERING ..	NE PAS OUBLIER...
to look over your shoulder	de regarder par dessus son épaule
to look in your rear view mirror	de regarder dans le rétroviseur
to look both ways	de regarder des deux côtés (m)
to indicate	de mettre son clignotant

PROBLEMS ON THE ROAD	PROBLEMES SUR LA ROUTE
to break down	tomber en panne
to have an accident	avoir un accident
to have a puncture	avoir un pneu crevé
to be delayed / long queues	être retardé / embouteillages (m)
roadworks	travaux routiers (m.pl)
a diversion	une déviation
to run out of petrol	manquer d'essence (f)

TYPES OF ROAD	LES TYPES DE ROUTES
a motorway	une autoroute
a dual carriageway	une route à quatre voies
a ring road	une rocade
a main road	une grand-route
a minor road	une départementale

JUNCTIONS	LES JONCTIONS (f)
a roundabout	un rond-point
Give way to the right	priorité à droite
a cross roads	un carrefour
traffic lights	les feux (m) de circulation (f)
a pedestrian crossing	un passage pour piétons
a level crossing	un passage à niveau

TRAVELLING BY BIKE

VOYAGER EN DEUX-ROUES

TYPES OF BIKE	*LES TYPES DE BICYCLETTES (f)*
a motorbike	*une moto*
a bicycle	*un vélo*
a mountain bike / a BMX	*un V.T.T / une BMX*
a tricycle	*un tricycle*
a tandem	*un tandem*

PARTS OF THE BIKE   *LES PARTIES DES DEUX-ROUES*

The handlebars	*Les guidons (m)*
drop / raised handlebars	*guidons de course / de ville*
straight handlebars	*guidons droits*

The brakes	*Les freins (m)*
front / back	*avant / arrière*
to apply / to brake / to slow down	*actionner / freiner / ralentir*

The gears	*Les vitesses (f)*
a gear lever	*un levier de vitesse*
to change gear	*changer les vitesses*
to go up a gear / down a gear	*monter / descendre une vitesse*
low / middle / top gear	*en première / seconde / troisième / quatrième vitesse*
three / six / twelve gears	*trois / six / douze vitesses*
fifteen / eighteen / twenty one speed	*vitesse de quinze / dix-huit / vingt-et-un*

The frame	*Le cadre*
a kickstand	*la béquille*

TRAVELLING BY BIKE cont.

VOYAGER EN DEUX-ROUES suite

The chain	*La chaîne*
the chainguard	*le carter*
to adjust the tension	*régler la tension*
too loose	*trop lâche*

The pedals	*Les pédales (f)*
to pedal	*pédaler*
to back pedal	*rétro-pédaler*
to free wheel	*être en roue libre*

The seat	*La selle*
to raise / to lower	*lever / baisser*
too high / too low	*trop haute / trop basse*
the height adjustment	*le réglage de la hauteur*
to screw / to unscrew	*visser / dévisser*
a release lever	*un levier de desserrement*
to pull / to push	*tirer / pousser*

The wheels	*Les roues (f)*
a mudguard	*un garde-boue*
the spokes	*les rayons (m)*

The tyres	*Les pneus (m)*
Your tyres are flat.	*Vos / tes pneus sont à plats.*
Have you got a pump?	*Avez-vous / as-tu une pompe?*
to unscrew / replace the dust cap	*dévisser / remplacer le bouchon*
to pump up / to inflate	*pomper / gonfler*
the tyre pressure	*la pression des pneus*
I think I have a puncture.	*Je crois que j'ai crevé.*
a puncture repair kit	*une trousse de réparation*

TRAVELLING BY BIKE cont.   *VOYAGER EN DEUX-ROUES suite*

The lights	*Les feux (m)*
a dynamo	*une dynamo*
to turn on / off	*mettre / arrêter*
a headlamp	*un phare-avant*
a rear lamp	*un phare-arrière*
a bulb	*une ampoule*
to replace	*remplacer*
The bulb has gone.	*L'ampoule est cassé.*
a battery	*une pile*
a reflector	*un réflecteur*

EQUIPMENT	*L'EQUIPEMENT*
a bicycle lock / a key	*un antivol / une clef*
to lock / to unlock	*fermer / ouvrir (à clef)*
to padlock / a padlock	*cadenasser / cadenas (m)*
a crash helmet	*un casque*
a fluorescent strip	*une bande fluorescente*
cycling shorts	*un short de cycliste*
gloves	*des gants (m)*
sunglasses	*des lunettes (f) de soleil*
a pump	*une pompe*
a basket	*un panier*
a water bottle	*une bouteille d'eau*
a child seat	*une siège-bébé*
a seat belt	*une ceinture de sécurité*

TRAVELLING BY BIKE cont.   *VOYAGER EN DEUX-ROUES suite*

USEFUL VERBS (abc)	*VERBES UTILES*
to accelerate	*accélérer*
to borrow	*emprunter*
to brake	*freiner*
to fall off	*tomber*
to get off	*descendre*
to hire	*louer*
to lend	*prêter*
to lock	*fermer à clef*
to lose your balance	*perdre son équilibre*
to mount	*monter*
to pedal	*pédaler*
to push	*pousser*
to ride	*monter*
to signal	*signaler*
to steer	*diriger*
to wobble	*chanceler*

EMERGENCIES
LES URGENCES

ACCIDENTS	*LES ACCIDENTS*

TELEPHONING EMERGENCY SERVICES	*LES SERVICES D'URGENCE TELEPHONIQUES*

IN ENGLAND	*EN ANGLETERRE*
Police - 999	*Police - 999*
Ambulance - 999	*Ambulance - 999*
Fire Brigade - 999	*Pompiers - 999*

IN FRANCE	*EN FRANCE*
Police - 17	*Police - 17*
Ambulance - 15	*Ambulance - 15*
Fire Brigade - 18	*Pompiers - 18*

CALLING OUT FOR HELP	*DEMANDER DE L'AIDE*
Help!	*Au secours!*
Come quickly!	*Venez vite!*
Fire!	*Au feu!*
Bomb scare!	*Alerte à la bombe!*
Everybody out!	*Tout le monde dehors!*
Call the ...	*Appeler...*
• fire brigade	• *les pompiers (m)*
• an ambulance	• *une ambulance*
• the police	• *la police*
• a doctor	• *un docteur*

EMERGENCIES cont.

URGENCES suite

THERE HAS BEEN AN ACCIDENT	*IL Y A EU UN ACCIDENT*
a traffic accident	*un accident de la route*
a pile-up	*un carambolage*
to warn	*avertir*
a warning triangle / hazard lights	*triangle (m) de présignalisation / les feux (m) de détresse*

SOMEONE HAS BEEN RUN OVER	*QUELQU'UN A ETE RENVERSE*
They are injured.	*Ils sont blessés.*
They are conscious / unconscious.	*Ils sont conscients / inconscients*
a broken bone	*une fracture*
He / she is bleeding.	*Il / elle saigne.*
to give mouth to mouth resuscitation	*faire du bouche-à-bouche*
to administer first aid	*administrer les premiers soins*

FIRE	*INCENDIES (m)*
Press the fire alarm button!	*Appuyez sur le bouton d'incendie!*
That's the fire bell.	*C'est l'alarme-incendie.*
an alarm / to go off	*une alarme / déclencher*
a smoke detector	*un détecteur de fumée*
a fire door	*une porte coupe-feu*
a fire exit	*une sortie de secours*
a fire blanket	*une couverture coupe-feu*
a fire extinguisher	*un extincteur*
smoke	*fumée (f)*
flames	*flammes (f)*
to be on fire	*être en feu*
to burn	*brûler*
to put out	*enlever*
water	*eau (f)*
sand	*sable (m)*

EMERGENCIES cont.   *LES URGENCES suite*

A BOMB SCARE	UNE ALERTE A LA BOMBE
to clear the area	*évacuer le secteur*
to evacuate the building	*évacuer le bâtiment*
to call the bomb squad	*appeler l'équipe de déminage*
a sniffer dog	*un chien*
to cordon off the area	*fermer le secteur*
to detonate	*détoner*
to explode / to go off	*exploser*
a false alarm	*une fausse alerte*
a suspicious package	*un bagage suspect*
an abandoned package	*un paquet abandonné*
to report a package to the police	*signaler un paquet à la police*

ILLNESS

MALADIE (f)

INITIAL SYMPTOMS	*PREMIERS SYMPTOMES (m)*
to feel off colour	*être mal en point*
to feel ill	*se sentir mal*
to look ill	*avoir mauvaise mine*
to be taken ill	*tomber malade*

GENERAL SYMPTOMS	*SYMPTOMES GENERAUX*
I am hot / cold	*J'ai chaud / froid.*
I feel hot and cold.	*J'ai chaud et froid.*
I feel shivery.	*J'ai des frissons.*
I feel faint.	*Je me sens faible.*
I am thirsty.	*J'ai soif.*
I am not hungry	*Je n'ai pas faim.*
I have no appetite.	*Je n'ai pas d'appétit.*
I couldn't eat a thing.	*Je ne pourrais rien manger.*
I have a slight / a high temperature	*J'ai une légère / forte température.*

I HAVE A HEADACHE	*J'AI MAL A LA TETE*
I have a migraine.	*J'ai une migraine.*
The light hurts my head.	*La lumière me donne mal à la tête.*
Do you have any pain killers?	*Avez-vous / as-tu des calmants?*

FAINTING	*MALAISES (m)*
I feel dizzy.	*J'ai la tête qui tourne.*
I think I am going to faint.	*Je crois que je vais m'évanouir.*
Put your head between your knees.	*Mettez votre / mets ta tête entre vos / tes genoux.*
Can I lie down, please?	*Puis-je m'allonger, s'il vous plaît?*
to pass out	*perdre connaissance*

ILLNESS cont.　　　　　　　　*MALADIES suite*

STOMACH UPSETS	*LES MAUX DE VENTRE*
I have indigestion.	*J'ai une indigestion.*
I have heartburn.	*J'ai mal au coeur.*
I feel sick.	*Je suis barbouillée.*
I am going to be sick.	*Je vais vomir.*
I have been sick.	*Je viens de vomir.*
My stomach hurts.	*J'ai mal au ventre.*
I have diarrhoea.	*J'ai de la diarrhée.*
I think it's food poisoning.	*Je crois que c'est une intoxication alimentaire.*
Could I have a drink of water, please?	*Puis-je avoir un verre d'eau, s'il vous plaît?*
Could I have a bowl by my bed, please?	*Pourrais-je avoir une bassine près de mon lit, s'il vous plaît?*

MY THROAT IS VERY SORE.	*J'AI TRES MAL A LA GORGE*
I have tonsillitis.	*J'ai une amygdalite.*
My throat is dry.	*Ma gorge est sèche.*
It hurts to swallow.	*Cela fait mal d'avaler.*
My glands are swollen.	*Mes glandes sont enflées.*
to gargle	*faire des gargarismes*
to have a hot drink	*prendre une boisson chaude*
Have you any throat sweets?	*Avez-vous / as-tu des pastilles pour la gorge?*
I like lemon ones / honey / menthol / eucalyptus / blackcurrant / T.C.P.®	*J'aime bien celles au citron / miel / menthol / eucalyptus / cassis. T.C.P.® n'existe pas en France.*

ILLNESS cont.   *MALADIES*

I HAVE CAUGHT A COLD	*J'AI ATTRAPE UN RHUME*
to sneeze / Bless you!	*éternuer / A tes souhaits!*
to blow your nose	*se moucher*
a handkerchief	*un mouchoir*
paper handkerchiefs	*un mouchoir en papier*
to find it difficult to breathe	*avoir des difficultés à respirer*
a decongestant	*un décongestionnant*
a cold remedy	*une remède contre le rhume*

I HAVE A BAD COUGH	*J'AI UNE MAUVAISE TOUX*
a tickly cough	*une toux irritante*
a dry cough	*une toux sèche*
a productive cough	*une toux grasse*
a spasm of coughing	*un spasme*
to take cough medicine	*prendre des médicaments contre le toux*
to need antibiotics	*avoir besoin d'antibiotiques*

ASTHMA	*L'ASTHME*
to suffer from asthma	*souffrir d'asthme*
to be asthmatic	*être asthmatique*
to wheeze	*respirer bruyamment*
to cough a lot	*tousser beaucoup*
to control one's asthma	*contrôler son asthme*
to be allergic to..	*être allergique ...*
• dust	• *à la poussière*
• animals	• *aux animaux*
• chest infections	• *aux infections de poitrine*
to use an inhaler	*utiliser un inhalateur*
• to inhale	• *inhaler*
• Ventolin ®	• *Ventoline (f) ®*
• Becotide ®	• *Becotide (f) ®*
• steroids	• *stéroïdes (m)*
• a nebuliser	• *un nébuliseur*

ILLNESS cont.   *MALADIES suite*

SKIN PROBLEMS   *LES PROBLEMES DE PEAU*

SUNBURN	*COUPS DE SOLEIL (m)*
to be burnt	*être brûlé*
to be sore	*avoir mal*
to peel	*peler*
to apply after-sun lotion	*appliquer un lait après-soleil*
calamine	*calamine (f)*
to rub on	*passer*

A RASH	*ERUPTIONS CUTANEES (f)*
an allergy	*une allergie*
to be allergic to	*être allergique à*
nettle rash	*urticaire (f)*
prickly heat	*fièvre miliaire (f)*
to itch / to scratch	*démanger / gratter*
to feel sore	*avoir mal*
antihistamine cream	*crème antihistaminique (f)*

SPLINTERS	*LES ECHARDES (f)*
I have a splinter in my foot / hand.	*J'ai une écharde dans le pied / la main*
to get it out	*l'enlever*
a needle / tweezers	*une aiguille / une pince à épiler*
surgical spirit / disinfectant	*alcool à 90 degrés / désinfectant*

MINOR INJURIES	*BLESSURES MINEURES (f)*
a spot	*un bouton*
acne	*acné (f)*
a scratch	*une éraflure*
a graze	*une écorchure*
a cut	*une coupure*

ILLNESS cont.   *MALADIES suite*

SERIOUS CUTS	*COUPURES PLUS GRAVES*
to need stitches	*nécessiter des points de suture*
butterfly stitches	*un pansement de suture*
local anaesthetic	*anesthésie locale (f)*
a bandage	*un bandage*
an elastoplast	*un elastoplast*
a sticking plaster	*un pansement adhésif*
a blister	*une ampoule*

STINGS	*PIQURES (f)*
a wasp / bee sting	*une piqûre de guêpe / d'abeille*
a mosquito bite	*une piqûre de moustique*
I have been stung by something.	*J'ai été piqué(e) par quelque chose*
a jelly fish sting	*une piqûre de méduse*
insect repellent	*un anti-moustiques*
antihistamine cream / tablets	*des comprimés (m) / de la crème antihistaminique(s)*

TOILET PROBLEMS	*LES PROBLEMES INTIMES*
to have cystitis	*avoir une cystite*
to have diarrhoea	*avoir la diarrhée*
to take kaolin and morphine	*prendre du Kaolin et de la morphine*
to be constipated	*être constipé*
a laxative	*un laxatif*
to eat more roughage	*manger davantage d'aliments de lest*
to drink more water	*boire plus d'eau*

ILLNESS cont.

PERIOD PROBLEMS	*LES PROBLEMES (m) DE REGLES (f)*
to have period pains	*avoir des règles douloureuses*
to take pain killers	*prendre des analgésiques (m)*
My period is..	*Mes règles sont*
• late	• *en retard*
• heavy	• *abondantes*
• painful	• *douloureuses*
• prolongued	• *longues*

INJURIES	*BLESSURES (f)*
I hurt here.	*J'ai mal ici.*
I have bruised my..	*Je me suis fait un bleu à...*
I have cut my..	*Je me suis coupé...*
I have sprained my..	*Je me suis tordu...*
I have broken my..	*Je me suis cassé...*
I have dislocated my..	*Je me suis démis...*
I have burnt my..	*Je me suis brûlé...*
I can't move my..	*Je ne peux pas bouger...*

PARTS OF THE BODY

LES PARTIES DU CORPS

THE SKIN	*LA PEAU*		
dry	*sèche*	cracked	*craquelée*
sore	*irritée*	wrinkled	*ridée*
burnt	*brûlé*	soft / hard	*fine / épaisse*

ILLNESS cont.   *MALADIES suite*

PARTS OF THE BODY cont.   *LES PARTIES DU CORPS suite*

THE HAIR		*LES CHEVEUX*	
straight	*raides*	short / long	*courts / longs*
wavy	*ondulés*	to wear it up	*les relever*
curly	*bouclés*	to wear it loose	*les détacher*
blonde	*blonds*	shoulder length	*aux épaules*
auburn	*auburn*	balding	*calvitie*
brown	*châtains*	to be bald	*être chauve*
red	*roux*	dandruff	*pellicules*
black	*bruns*	oily / dry	*gras / secs*
grey	*gris*	dyed / streaked	*teints / méchés*
white	*blancs*	permed	*permanentés*

THE HEAD	*LA TETE*
the brain	*le cerveau*
the skull	*le crâne*
the scalp	*le cuir chevelu*

THE FACE	*LE VISAGE*
the cheeks	*les joues (f)*
the cheekbones	*les pommettes (f)*
to blush	*rougir*

THE EYES		*LES YEUX*	
an eye	*un oeil*	an eyelash	*un cil*
the eyebrows	*les sourcils (m)*	the pupil	*la pupille*
the eyelid	*la paupière*	the iris	*l'iris (m)*

ILLNESS - PARTS OF THE BODY cont.

MALADIES - LES PARTIES DU CORPS suite

THE EYESIGHT	*LA VUE*
to wear glasses	*porter des lunettes (f)*
to wear contact lenses	*porter des lentilles de contact (f)*
to be short / long sighted	*être myope / être astigmate*
to have good eyesight	*avoir une bonne vue*
to have an eye test	*passer un examen oculaire*
to wear sunglasses	*porter des lunettes de soleil*
to be partially sighted	*être malvoyant*
to be blind	*être aveugle*
a white stick	*une canne blanche*
a guide dog	*un chien-guide*

THE NOSE	*LE NEZ*
a nostril	*une narine*
to blow the nose	*se moucher*

THE MOUTH	*LA BOUCHE*
the lips	*les lèvres (f)*
the tongue	*la langue*
the jaw	*la mâchoire*
the throat	*la gorge*
the tonsils	*les amygdales (f)*

THE TEETH	*LES DENTS (f)*
a molar / a canine	*une molaire / une canine*
an incisor / a wisdom tooth	*une incisive / une dent de sagesse*
the gums	*les gencives*
to clean one's teeth	*se laver les dents*
a toothbrush / to brush	*une brosse à dent / brosser*
toothpaste / to squeeze the tube	*un dentifrice / presser le tube*
to floss	*nettoyer avec un fil dentaire*
to use mouthwash	*utiliser une eau-dentifrice*
to gargle	*faire des gargarismes*

ILLNESS cont.

PARTS OF THE BODY cont.

MALADIES suite

LES PARTIES DU CORPS suite

THE EARS	*LES OREILLES (f)*
the ear lobe	*le lobe de l'oreille*
the outer ear / the middle ear	*l'oreille externe / l'oreille moyenne*
the ear drum	*le tympan*
earwax	*cérumen (m)*
an ear infection	*une infection*
to be unable to hear properly	*être malentendant*
to be deaf	*être sourd*
a hearing aid	*un appareil*

THE BEARD	*LA BARBE*
clean shaven	*rasée de près*
to grow a beard	*faire pousser sa barbe*
to shave (See page 60)	*se raser*
a moustache	*une moustache*
sideburns	*des pattes (f)*
a chin	*un menton*

THE BODY		*LE CORPS*	
the neck	*le cou*	a rib	*une côte*
the shoulder	*l'épaule (f)*	the rib cage	*la cage thoracique*
the back	*le dos*		
the spine	*la colonne vertébrale*	the waist	*la taille*
		the hip	*la hanche*
the bottom	*les fesses (f)*	the stomach	*l'estomac (m)*
the chest	*la poitrine*	the abdomen	*l'abdomen*

ILLNESS cont.   *MALADIES suite*

PARTS OF THE BODY cont.   *LES PARTIES DU CORPS suite*

THE ARMS	*LES BRAS*
the upper arm	*le bras*
the forearm	*l'avant-bras*
the elbow	*le coude*
the funny bone	*le petit bicot*
the wrist	*le poignet*

THE HANDS	*LES MAINS*
the palm / the back of the hand	*la paume /*
the knuckles	*les articulations (f)*
the fingers / the thumbs	*les doigts (m) / les pouces (m)*
left / right	*gauche / droite*
a fingernail	*un ongle*
a cuticle / cuticle remover	*une petite peau / un cuticule / un repousse-peau*
a manicure / to manicure	*une manicure / manicurer*
an emery board / a nail file	*une lime à ongle*
nail varnish / nail varnish remover	*du vernis à ongle / un dissolvant*

THE LEGS	*LES JAMBES (f)*
the thigh	*la cuisse*
the knee	*le genou*
the calf	*le mollet*
the shin	*le tibia*
the ankle	*la cheville*

ILLNESS cont.   *MALADIES suite*

PARTS OF THE BODY cont.   *LES PARTIES DU CORPS suite*

THE FEET	*LES PIEDS*
a foot	*un pied*
the heel / the sole	*le talon / la plante*
the toes / the big toe / the little toe	*les orteils / le gros orteil / le petit orteil*
a toenail	*un ongle de pied*
to cut the toenails	*couper les ongles de pied*
nail scissors / nail clippers	*des ciseaux à ongle / un coupe-ongles*
hard skin / bunions	*peau dure (f)/ des oignons (m)*
a pumice stone	*une pierre ponce*

THE MAIN INTERNAL ORGANS		*LES PRINCIPAUX ORGANES INTERNES*	
the lungs	*les poumons (m)*	the intestines	*les intestins (m)*
the heart	*le coeur*	the bowel	*le côlon*
the liver	*le foie*	the bladder	*la vessie*
the kidney	*les reins (m)*	the digestive system	*le système digestif*

THE CIRCULATION	*LA CIRCULATION*
the blood	*le sang*
to be anaemic	*être anémique*
an artery / a vein	*une artère / une veine*
to bleed	*saigner*
to haemorrhage	*une hémorragie*
to bruise	*contusionner*
to clot / to form a scab	*coaguler / former une croûte*

ILLNESS cont.

MALADIES suite

PARTS OF THE BODY cont.

LES PARTIES DU CORPS suite

THE MAIN MUSCLES	*LES MUSCLES PRINCIPAUX (m)*
the biceps / the triceps	*les biceps / les triceps*
the pectorals	*les pectoraux (m.pl)*
the ham string	*le tendon du jarret*
the Achilles tendon	*le tendon d'Achille*

THE MAIN BONES		**LES PRINCIPAUX OS (m)**	
the skeleton	*le squelette*	the shoulder blade	*l'omoplate (f)*
the skull	*le crâne*	the ribs	*les côtes (f)*
the collar bone	*la clavicule*	the hip bone	*l'os iliaque*
the spine	*la colonne vertébrale*	the thigh bone	*le fémur*
the vertebrae	*les vertèbres (f)*	the shin bone	*le tibia*
the coccyx	*le coccyx*	the knee cap	*la rotule*

THE CENTRAL NERVOUS SYSTEM	*LE SYSTEME NERVEUX CENTRAL*
the cerebellum	*le cervelet*
the spinal chord	*la moelle épinière*
the nerves	*les nerfs (m)*

MALE / FEMALE CHARACTERISTICS		*LES CARACTERISTIQUES MASCULINES / FEMININES*	
the penis	*le pénis*	the breasts	*les seins (m)*
the testicles	*les testicules (m)*	the nipples	*les mamelons (m)*
a broken voice	*une voix qui mue*	the womb	*l'utérus (m)*
		the vagina	*le vagin (m)*

THE BODY cont.

LE CORPS suite

PREGNANCY	*LA GROSSESSE*
to do a pregnancy test	*faire un test de grossesse*
positive / negative	*positif / négatif*
to be pregnant	*être enceinte*
to be three months pregnant	*être enceinte de trois mois*
to be at full term	*être en fin de grossesse*
to go into labour	*commencer à avoir des contractions*
to have a baby	*avoir un enfant*
the embryo / the foetus	*l'embryon (m) / le foetus*

THE FIVE SENSES

LES CINQ SENS (m)

TOUCH		*LE TOUCHER*	
to touch	*toucher*	rough	*dur*
hot	*chaud*	smooth	*doux*
cold	*froid*	painful	*douloureux*

TASTE		*LE GOUT*	
to taste	*goûter*	sour	*aigre*
bitter	*amer*	savoury	*salé*
sweet	*doux / sucré*		

SMELL		*L'ODORAT (m)*	
to smell	*sentir*	unpleasant	*désagréable*
pleasant	*agréable*	to stink	*puer*

HEARING		*L'OUÏE (f)*	
to hear	*entendre*	noisy	*bruyant*
loud	*fort*	quiet	*silencieux*

SIGHT		*LA VUE*	
to see	*voir*	blurred	*brouillé(e)*
to focus	*fixer*	clear	*clair(e)*

ILLNESS cont.

MALADIES suite

GETTING TREATMENT
Shall I call..?
Can I make an appointment to see ..?
- the doctor / the nurse
- the dentist
- the hospital

RECEVOIR UN TRAITEMENT
Est-ce que j'appelle…?
Je peux prendre rendez-vous avec…?
- *le médecin / l'infirmière*
- *le dentiste*
- *l'hôpital (m)*

THE DOCTOR'S SURGERY
the waiting room
to sit down / to wait
to read a magazine
I have an appointment to see..

LE CABINET MEDICAL
la salle d'attente
s'asseoir / attendre
lire un magazine
J'ai un rendez-vous avec…

THE CONSULTATION
I am going to ..
- to take your blood pressure.
- to take your pulse.
- to take a blood sample.
- to do a urine test.
- to listen to your heart / chest.
- to look down your throat.
- to look in your ear.
- to test your reflexes.

LA CONSULTATION
Je vais…
- *prendre votre / ta tension*
- *prendre votre / ton pouls*
- *faire une prise de sang*
- *faire une analyse d'urine*
- *écouter votre / ton coeur*
- *regarder votre / ta gorge*
- *regarder votre / ton oreille*
- *tester vos / tes réflexes*

ILLNESS cont.   *MALADIES suite*

COULD YOU..	POUVEZ-VOUS...

COULD YOU..
- roll up your sleeve.
- undo your jacket.
- lift up your shirt.
- take off your clothes.
- take everything off except your pants.
- put this gown on.
- climb on the bed.
- put this blanket over you
- open your mouth wide
- do a urine / stool sample

POUVEZ-VOUS...
- *relever votre / ta manche*
- *défaire votre / ta veste*
- *relever votre / ta chemise*
- *vous / te déshabiller*
- *enlever tout sauf votre / ton slip*
- *mettre ce peignoir*
- *monter sur la banquette*
- *mettre cette couverture sur vous / toi*
- *ouvrir grand votre / ta bouche*
- *faire une analyse d'urine / des selles*

SAYING WHERE YOU HURT   *DIRE OÙ CELA FAIT MAL*

Where does it hurt?
Où avez-vous / as-tu mal?

Show me where it hurts.
Montre moi où vous avez / tu as mal.

Does it hurt...
Est-ce que ça fait...
- badly?
- *vraiment mal?*
- much?
- *très mal*
- when I touch it?
- *(mal) quand je touche?*
- when you move it?
- *(mal) quand vous / tu le / la bougez / bouge?*

Can you move your... (See parts of the body - pages 411-417)
Pouvez-vous / peux-tu bouger...?

ILLNESS cont.

MALADIES suite

THE DOCTOR'S INSTRUCTIONS	*LES CONSEILS (m) DU MEDECIN*
You should stay in bed.	*Vous devriez / tu devrais rester au lit.*
You should not go to work / school / travel.	*Vous ne devriez pas / tu ne devrais pas aller au travail / à l'école / en voyage.*
I would like to do further tests.	*J'aimerais faire d'autres analyses.*
You need an X-ray.	*Il faut vous / te faire une radio.*
You need a scan.	*Il faut faire un scanner.*
I will make an appointment at the hospital for you.	*Je vais vous prendre un rendez-vous à l'hôpital.*
I would like a second opinion.	*J'aimerais un double diagnostic.*
It is nothing serious.	*Ce n'est rien de grave.*
You will be better soon.	*Vous irez / tu iras mieux bientôt.*
Are you allergic to anything?	*Etes-vous / es-tu allergique à quelque chose?*

THE TREATMENT	*LE TRAITEMENT*
a prescription	*une prescription*
Take it to the chemists.	*Apportez-la / apporte-la à la pharmacie.*
to get the prescription made up	*se faire préparer sa prescription*
antibiotics / penicillin	*antibiotiques (m) / pénicilline (f)*
a tablet / a capsule	*un comprimé / une gélule*
medicine / linctus	*médicament (m) / sirop (m)*
a five millilitre spoon	*une cuillère de cinq millilitres*
the dosage	*le dosage*
to swallow / to take	*avaler / prendre*
Shake the bottle before use.	*Agiter la bouteille avant usage*

ILLNESS - THE TREATMENT cont.

MALADIES - LE TRAITEMENT suite

MEDICINE cont.

MEDICAMENT suite

three times a day	*trois fois par jour*
before / after meals	*avant / après les repas (m)*
Take with food.	*Prendre en milieu de repas.*
Take on an empty stomach.	*Prendre à jeun.*
Do not drink alcohol.	*Ne pas boire d'alcool.*
Do not mix with other tablets.	*Ne pas mélanger avec d'autres médicaments.*
Do not take if pregnant.	*Ne pas administrer aux femmes enceintes.*
a suppository	*un suppositoire*
an inhaler	*un inhaleur*
antihistamine cream	*une crème antihistaminique*
antiseptic cream	*une crème antiseptique*
ointment / to rub on	*une pommade / passer*
aspirin / paracetamol	*aspirine (f) / paracetamol (m)*

GOING TO HOSPITAL

ALLER A L'HOPITAL (m)

an ambulance	*une ambulance*
a stretcher	*une civière*
the outpatients' department	*le service de consultation externe*
casualty	*les urgences (f)*
the enquiry desk	*le bureau d'accueil*

ILLNESS - GOING TO HOSPITAL cont.

MALADIES - ALLER A L'HOPITAL suite

BEING ADMITTED	*L'ADMISSION (f)*
Can you fill in this form, please?	*Pouvez-vous remplir ce formulaire, s'il vous plaît?*
Can I take your details, please?	*Puis-je prendre des renseignements vous concernant?*
• Surname	• *Nom (m)*
• Christian Name	• *Prénom (m)*
• Age	• *Age (m)*
• Date of Birth	• *Date de naissance (f)*
• Place of Birth	• *Lieu (m) de naissance*
• Nationality	• *Nationalité (f)*
• Address / Telephone Number	• *Adresse (f) / numéro de téléphone (m)*
• Next of Kin	• *Nom et prénom de votre plus proche parent*
• Medical History	• *Antécédents médicaux (m.pl)*
• Details of previous operations	• *détails des précédentes opérations (f)*
• Serious illnesses.	• *maladies graves (f)*
• Allergies	• *allergies (f)*
• Have you ever had any of the following illnesses?	• *Avez-vous eu l'une des maladies suivantes?*

A FRACTURE	*UNE FRACTURE*
to be assessed / examined	*être examiné*
to have an X-ray	*être radiographié*
to have one's arm in a sling	*avoir le bras en écharpe (f)*
to be bandaged up	*être bandé*
to be given a plaster cast	*se faire un plâtre*
to have a splint / to hop	*avoir une attelle / boitiller*
to walk with crutches	*marcher avec des béquilles (f)*
to lean on someone	*s'appuyer sur quelqu'un*
to use a wheelchair	*utiliser une chaise roulante*
to push / to steer	*pousser / diriger*

ILLNESS - GOING TO HOSPITAL cont.

MALADIES - ALLER A L'HOPITAL suite

PHYSIOTHERAPY	*PHYSIOTHERAPIE (f)*
a physiotherapist	*une physiothérapeute*
to do exercises	*faire des exercices (m)*
to increase mobility	*accroître la mobilité*
to use an ice pack	*utiliser un sac de glaçons*
to use a bag of frozen peas	*utiliser un paquet de petits pois surgelés*
to wrap in a towel	*envelopper dans une serviette*
to reduce the swelling	*diminuer l'enflure (f)*
to reduce the inflammation	*diminuer l'inflammation (f)*
to use a heat compress	*utiliser une compresse d'eau chaude*
to have ultrasound treatment	*avoir un traitement ultrason*
to do exercises every hour	*faire des exercices toutes les heures*
three times a day	*trois fois par jour*
to push / to pull	*pousser / tirer*
to squeeze	*presser*
to lift / a weight	*soulever / un poids*
to raise / to lower	*lever / baisser*
to massage	*masser*

OPERATIONS	*LES OPERATIONS (f)*
to have nothing to eat or drink	*n'avoir rien à manger / boire*
to sign a consent form	*signer un formulaire d'acceptation*
to put on an operating gown	*mettre une peignoir d'opération*
to be given a pre-med	*se faire administrer une prémédication*
to feel drowsy	*se sentir somnolent(e)*
to have a local anaesthetic	*avoir une anesthésie locale*

ILLNESS - GOING TO HOSPITAL cont.

OPERATIONS cont.

MALADIES - ALLER A L'HOPITAL suite

LES OPERATIONS suite

to be numb	*être engourdi*
an injection	*une injection / une piqûre*
to be given gas and air	*se faire administrer de l'oxygène*
a mask	*un masque*
to dull the pain	*atténuer la douleur*
to cover your nose and mouth	*couvrir son nez et sa bouche*
to breathe in	*respirer*
to have a general anaesthetic	*avoir une anesthésie générale*
to come round	*reprendre connaissance*
to have a sip of water	*boire une gorgée d'eau*
to have your pulse checked	*se faire vérifier son pouls*
to have your temperature taken	*se faire prendre sa température*
to listen to your heart	*écouter son coeur*
to call the nurse	*appeler l'infirmière*
Can I get you anything?	*Avez-vous / as-tu besoin de quelque chose?*
Is anything wrong?	*Quelque chose ne va pas?*
to ask for a bed pan	*demander un bassin hygiénique*
to ask for a drink	*demander un boisson*
visiting hours	*heures de visite*
to have a visitor	*avoir un visiteur*
to be given flowers	*se faire offrir des fleurs*
to receive Get Well cards	*recevoir des cartes de bons rétablissement*

DENTAL TREATMENT   *TRAITEMENT DENTAIRE*

THE DENTIST	*LE DENTISTE*
to make an appointment	*prendre rendez-vous*
to sit in the waiting room	*attendre dans la salle d'attente*
to go into the surgery	*aller dans le cabinet*
the dentist's chair	*le fauteuil de dentiste*
My tooth hurts.	*Ma dent me fait mal.*
My filling has come out.	*Mon plomb est parti.*
My tooth was knocked out.	*Ma dent est tombée.*

DENTAL TREATMENT	*TRAITEMENT DENTAIRE*
to have a look	*regarder*
to put a bib on	*mettre une bavette*
Open your mouth wide.	*Ouvrez / ouvre grand la bouche*
Does that hurt?	*Ca fait mal?*
Which tooth hurts?	*Quelle dent fait mal?*
to be given a local anaesthetic	*Avoir une anesthésie locale.*
an injection	*une piqûre*
Is it numb now?	*Est-ce qu'elle est endormie, maintenant?*
to drill a tooth	*passer la roulette*
to extract a tooth	*arracher une dent*
a laser beam	*un rayon laser*
to put a filling in	*mettre un plomb*
to bite one's teeth together gently	*serrer doucement les mâchoires*
to polish the teeth	*polir les dents (f)*
to wash / rinse the mouth out	*laver / rincer la bouche*
to spit	*cracher*
a tissue / to dry one's mouth	*un mouchoir / se sécher la bouche*
to dribble	*baver*
to find it difficult to talk / to drink	*avoir des difficultés à parler / boire*
Don't eat anything for a couple of hours.	*Ne mangez / mange rien pendant deux heures.*

THE OPTICIANS   *LES OPTICIENS*

My glasses have broken.	*Mes lunettes se sont cassées.*
Could you mend them for me?	*Pouvez-vous me les réparer?*
I have lost a contact lens.	*J'ai perdu une lentille de contact.*
Could I try to get a replacement?	*Pourrais-je essayer d'en avoir une rechange?*
I can't see very clearly.	*Je ne vois pas très bien.*
I have double vision.	*Je vois double.*
I keep getting headaches.	*J'ai tout le temps des maux de tête.*
Could I get my eyes tested, please?	*Pourrais-je avoir un examen oculaire, s'il vous plaît?*
A screw has come out of my glasses.	*Une vis est partie de mes lunettes.*
Can you mend my glasses for me?	*Pouvez-vous me réparer mes lunettes?*
Will you have to send them away somewhere?	*Allez-vous les envoyer quelque part?*
How long will it take to repair them?	*Combien de temps cela prendre de les remplacer?*
I am going back to England in five days.	*Je retourne en Angleterre dans cinq jours.*
Will they be ready by then?	*Est-ce qu'elles seront prêtes à ce moment?*

EYE SIGHT TESTS   *LES EXAMENS OCULAIRES*

Do sit down.	*Asseyez-vous.*
Look over there.	*Regarder là-bas.*
Look at the writing.	*Regardez l'écriteau.*
Read as much as you can.	*Lisez tout ce que pouvez voir.*
Can you read the next row down?	*Pouvez-vous lire la ligne en dessous?*

EYE SIGHT TESTS cont.

LES EXAMENS OCULAIRES suite

Take your glasses off.	*Enlevez vos lunettes.*
I am going to try different lenses.	*Je vais essayer des lentilles différentes.*
Does it look clearer like this or like this?	*Vous voyez plus clair comme ceci ou comme cela?*
Clearer with this lens or without it?	*Plus clair avec, ou sans cette lentille?*
I am going to look in your eye with a torch.	*Je vais examiner votre œil avec une lampe.*
Look up / down / left / right / straight ahead.	*Regardez en haut / en bas / à gauche / à droite / tout droit.*
You can put your glasses on again now.	*Vous pouvez remettre vos lunettes maintenant.*

PREVENTIVE MEDICINE

LA MEDECINE PREVENTATIVE

RELAXATION	*LA RELAXION*
to avoid stress	*éviter le stress*
to practise relaxation	*pratiquer la relaxation*
to relieve tension	*soulager la tension*
to do breathing exercises	*faire des exercices respiratoires*
to meditate / practise meditation	*méditer / pratiquer la méditation*

EXERCISE	*EXERCICES DE GYMNASTIQUE*
to take enough exercise	*faire suffisamment d'exercices (m)*
to walk more	*marcher davantage*
to keep fit	*garder la forme*
to go to keep fit classes	*aller à des cours pour garder la forme*
to go jogging / swimming	*faire du jogging / de la natation*
aerobic / anaerobic	*aérobic / anaérobie*
to warm up / to stretch	*s'échauffer / s'étirer*
suppleness exercises	*des exercices d'assouplissement*

PREVENTIVE MEDICINE - EXERCISE cont.	*LA MEDECINE PREVENTATIVE - EXERCICES DE GYMNASTIQUE cont.*
weight lifting	*haltérophilie (f)*
to get breathless	*être essoufflé(e)*
to work up a sweat	*se mettre à suer*
to exercise three times a week	*faire de la gymnastique trois fois par semaine*
to exercise for at least twenty minutes	*faire des exercices pendant au moins vingt minutes*

SLEEP	*LE SOMMEIL*
to get a good night's sleep	*avoir une bonne nuit de sommeil*
to need eight hours' sleep	*avoir besoin de huit heures de sommeil*
to lie in	*faire la grasse matinée*
to get up early	*se lever tôt*
to go to bed late	*se coucher tard*
to dream	*rêver*
to have nightmares	*faire des cauchemars (m)*
to suffer from insomnia	*souffrir d'insomnie (f)*
to take sleeping tablets	*prendre des somnifères (m)*

DIET	*LE REGIME ALIMENTAIRE*
to eat a balanced diet	*avoir un régime équilibré*
to eat sensibly	*manger équilibré*
vitamins / minerals	*les vitamines (f) / minéraux (m.pl)*
carbohydrates / protein	*les féculents (m.pl) / protéine (f)*
fibre	*fibre (f)*
vegetarian / vegan	*végétarien / végétalien*
to drink too much caffeine	*prendre trop de caféine (f)*
to count calories	*compter les calories (f)*
to cut down	*réduire*
to have small portions	*prendre des petites parts (f)*
to have a little of everything	*prendre un peu de tout*
a calorie controlled diet	*un régime faible en calories*

PREVENTIVE MEDICINE

LA MEDECINE
PREVENTATIVE

DIET cont.

LE REGIME ALIMENTAIRE
suite

a strict diet	*un régime stricte*
a diabetic diet	*un régime diabétique*
to binge	*avoir des impulsions (f)*
anorexia nervosa	*anorexie mentale (f)*
bulimia	*boulimie (f)*
to lose / gain weight	*perdre / prendre des kilos*
to lower one's cholesterol level	*diminuer son taux de cholestérol*
to be a desirable weight	*avoir un poids idéal*
to be a little overweight	*avoir quelques kilos en trop*
to be underweight	*être trop maigre*
to be obese	*être obèse*

ALCOHOL CONSUMPTION

LA CONOMMATION
D'ALCOOL

to drink sensibly	*boire raisonnablement*
a unit of alcohol	*un taux d'alcool*
to be a social drinker	*être un alcoolique mondain*
to drink too much	*boire trop*
to get drunk	*se saouler*
to have a hangover	*avoir une gueule de bois*
to be dehydrated	*être déshydraté(e)*
to be an alcoholic	*être alcoolique*

SMOKING

FUMER

cigarettes / cigars / a pipe	*cigarettes (f) / cigares (m)/ une pipe*
tobacco / nicotine / tar content	*la tabac/ nicotine (f)/ goudron (m)*
How many do you smoke a day?	*Combien en fumez-vous / fumes-tu par jour?*
to try to cut down / to be addicted	*essayer de réduire / être dépendant*
to inhale / lung cancer	*inhaler / cancer (m) du poumon (m)*

DRUGS — *LES DROGUES*

soft / hard drugs	*drogues douces / dures (f)*
stimulants	*stimulants (m)*
cannabis	*cannabis (m)*
to smoke / to inject	*fumer / injecter*
ecstasy / an E	*ecstasy*
a tablet	*un comprimé*
a pusher	*un piston*
illegal	*illégal*
I think he / she has taken some drugs.	*Je crois qu'il / elle a pris de la drogue.*
Do you know what he took?	*Savez-vous / sais-tu ce qu'il a pris?*
to be unconscious	*être inconscient*
I think we should get help.	*Je crois qu'on devrait demander de l'aide.*
He / she is drinking a lot of water.	*Il / elle boit beaucoup d'eau.*

ALTERNATIVE THERAPIES — *LES THERAPIES PARALLELES (f)*

AROMATHERAPY — *L'AROMATHERAPIE*

essential oils	*les huiles essentielles (f)*
a drop	*une goutte*
to blend	*mélanger*
a carrier oil	*une huile de base*
to massage / a massage	*masser / un massage*
to inhale	*inhaler*
an essential oil burner	*un brûleur d'huile essentielle*
to put in the bath	*mettre dans le bain*
a compress	*une compresse*

HERBALISM — *LA PHYTOTHERAPIE*

a herbalist	*un / une herboriste*
a herb / to gather / to store	*une herbe / ramasser / conserver*
an infusion / a decoction	*une infusion / une décoction*
a tincture / a compress	*une teinture / une compresse*

ALTERNATIVE THERAPIES cont. *LES THERAPIES PARALLELES suite*

HOMOEOPATHY	*L'HOMEOPATHIE (f)*
a homoeopath	*un homéopathe*
a remedy	*un remède*
constitutional treatment	*un traitement constitutionnel*
the potency	*la puissance*
the dose	*la dose*

CHIROPRACTIC AND OSTEOPATHY	*CIROPRACTIE (f) ET OSTEOPATHIE (f)*
a chiropractor	*un chiropracteur*
an osteopath	*un ostéopathe*
to manipulate	*manipuler*
the joints	*les articulations (f)*

CRIME

LES INFRACTIONS

THEFT	*LE VOL*
I've been robbed.	*J'ai été volé!*
Someone has taken my..	*On m'a pris...*
• bag	• *mon sac*
• wallet	• *mon portefeuille*
• purse	• *mon porte-monnaie*
• money	• *mon argent (m)*
• credit card	• *ma carte de crédit*
• watch	• *ma montre*
• jewellery	• *mes bijoux (m.pl)*
a thief / a pickpocket	*un voleur / un pickpocket*
a car thief / a joyrider	*un voleur de voiture*
to break into	*entrer par effraction dans*
to steal / to snatch	*dérober / voler (à la tire)*
to mug	*agresser*
to rob a bank	*voler une banque*
to steal from the till	*voler la caisse*
to shoplift / a shoplifter	*voler (à l'étalage) / un voleur à l'étalage*
a hijacking / to hijack	*un détournement / détourner*
a kidnapping / to kidnap	*un enlèvement / enlever*
to demand a ransom	*demander une rançon*
to take a hostage	*prendre un otage*
to hold up / a hold-up	*faire un hold-up / un hold-up*
terrorism	*terrorisme (m)*
a murder / to murder	*un meurtre / assassiner*
to kick	*ruer de coups*
to stab	*poignarder*
to thump	*taper / donner un coup de poing*
to cosh	*cogner*
to knock someone out	*assommer quelqu'un*
to strangle	*étrangler*
to suffocate	*suffoquer*
rape / to rape / to be raped / a rapist	*viol (m) / violer / être violé(e) / un violeur*

CRIME cont.   *LES INFRACTIONS suite*

HELPING THE POLICE	*AIDER LA POLICE*
a witness / to witness	*un témoin / témoigner*
to say what happened	*dire ce qu'il s'est passé*
to recognize	*reconnaître*
to identify	*identifier*
a suspect	*un suspect*
to be cautioned	*être mis en garde*
to be taken into custody	*être placé en garde à vue*
to be arrested	*être arrêté*
to be let out on bail	*être libéré sous caution*
to be innocent	*être innocent*
to be guilty	*être coupable*

LOSING OR DAMAGING IMPORTANT POSSESSIONS

PERTE OU DOMMAGE D'IMPORTANTES POSSESSIONS

I'VE LOST MY...(abc)	***J'AI PERDU...***
bag	*mon sac*
briefcase	*mon porte-documents*
bus pass	*ma carte de bus*
camera	*mon appareil-photo (m)*
cheque book	*mon carnet de chèque*
cheque card	*ma carte bancaire*
contact lens	*ma lentille de contact*
credit cards	*mes cartes de crédit*
diary	*mon agenda (m)*
foreign currency	*ma monnaie étrangère*
glasses / spectacles	*mes lunettes*
handbag	*mon sac à main*
Identity card	*ma carte d'identité*
key / keyring	*ma clef / mon porte-clefs*
money	*mon argent (m)*
passport	*mon passeport*
purse	*mon porte-monnaie*
rail pass	*ma carte de train*
rucksack	*mon sac-à-dos*
shoulder bag	*mon sac*
suitcase	*ma valise*
ticket	*mon ticket*
travellers cheques	*mes traveller-chèques*
wallet	*mon portefeuille*
watch	*ma montre*

LOSING OR DAMAGING IMPORTANT POSSESSIONS cont.

PERTE OU DOMMAGE D'IMPORTANTES POSSESSIONS suite

I'VE BROKEN MY..

- camera
- contact lens
- glasses / spectacles
- watch

I'm sorry but I have broken your…
I will pay for it.
My parents will get you another.

J'AI CASSE…

- *mon appareil photo*
- *ma lentille de contact*
- *mes lunettes*
- *ma montre*

Je suis désolé(e), j'ai cassé votre…
Je vais vous le / la rembourser.
Mes parents vous en donneront un autre.

I'VE TORN MY..

trousers / skirt / coat / dress / shirt

Could you mend it for me, please?

I've lost a button.
My button has come off.
Could I sew it back on, please?

Have you a needle and thread I could use?
My zip has broken.
Do you have a safety pin?

J'AI DECHIRE…

mon pantalon / ma jupe / mon manteau / ma robe / ma chemise

Pouvez-vous / peux-tu me le réparer s'ilvous / te plaît?

J'ai perdu un bouton.
Mon bouton est tombé.
Je peux le recoudre, s'il vous plaît?

Avez-vous / as-tu une aiguille et du fil que je pourrais utiliser?
Ma fermeture éclair s'est cassée.
Avez-vous / as-tu une épingle à sûreté?

FORM FILLING / PERSONAL INFORMATION	*REMPLIR UN FORMULAIRE / RENSEINGNEMENTS PERSONNELS*
Could you fill in this form, please?	*Pouvez-vous remplir ce formulaire, s'il vous plaît?*
in block capitals	*en lettres majuscules (f)*
Please print clearly.	*Ecrivez lisiblement.*
Please use pen or biro.	*Utilisez un crayon à plumes ou un bic.*
Have you a pen I could borrow, please?	*Avez-vous / as-tu un crayon que je pourrais emprunter, s'il vous / te plaît?*
Please put one letter in each square.	*Mettez une lettre dans chaque case, s'il vous plaît..*
Please sign and date the form at the end.	*Signez et datez le bas de la page.*

Personal details	*Renseignements personnels (m)*
Title	*le titre*
Surname / Christian names	*le Nom / les prénoms*
Date / Place of Birth	*date (f) / lieu (m) de naissance (f)*
Age	*âge (m)*
Gender / Sex	*sexe (m)*
Marital Status	*statut marital (m)*

ADDRESS	*ADRESSE (f)*
House name / number	*le nom / le numéro de la maison*
Street	*rue (f)*
Town	*ville (f)*
City	*cité (f)*
County / Area	*département (m) / région (f)*
Country	*pays (m)*
Postal Code	*code postal (m)*
Where are you staying at the moment?	*Quel est votre actuel lieu de résidence?*
Where do you live?	*Où habitez-vous?*

FORM FILLING / PERSONAL INFORMATION

REMPLIR UN FORMULAIRE / RENSEINGNEMENTS PERSONNELS

TELEPHONE NUMBER	*NUMERO DE TELEPHONE*
Country code	*indicatif national (m)*
Area code	*indicatif départemental*
Work telephone number	*numéro de téléphone professionnel (m)*
Home telephone number	*numéro de téléphone personnel*
Mobile telephone number	*numéro de téléphone mobile*
FAX number	*numéro de fax*

GETTING THINGS TO WORK	*FAIRE MARCHER LES CHOSES*
How does this work?	*Comment ça marche?*
Can you show me how to use this?	*Pouvez-vous / peux-tu me montrer comment utiliser ceci?*
This isn't working properly.	*Ca ne marche pas bien.*
Is there something wrong with it?	*Il y a quelque chose que ne va pas?*
Am I doing something wrong with this?	*Je fais quelque chose de mal avec cela?*
Can I watch you use it?	*Je peux vous / te regarder faire?*
Can I try to use it now?	*Je peux essayer de l'utiliser maintenant?*
How did you do that?	*Comment avez-vous / as-tu fait cela?*

Your French Exchange
Index

Whilst every care has been taken to prevent errors in the text and to make this reference book easy to use, Yarker Publishing would be grateful to be notified of any mistakes you may have noticed for correction in future editions and would also welcome any suggestions for further improvements by way of topics which might be included or any ideas concerning ways in which you might find it quicker to locate the vocabulary and phrases you need. Please address any comments to:-

Yarker Publishing
Gordon House
276 Banbury Road
Summertown
Oxford
OX2 7ED